8.9.'04

W9-DGP-839

Vienna
Paradox

Other Books by Marjorie Perloff

The Vienna Paradox

A MEMOIR

by
Marjorie
Perloff

A NEW DIRECTIONS BOOK

Portions of this book first appeared in *Modernism/Modernity*, *PN Review*, *Common Knowledge*, and *Western Humanities Review*.

Book design by Sylvia Frezzolini Severance
Manufactured in the United States of America
New Directions Books are printed on acid-free paper.
First published as New Directions Paperbook 983 in 2004
Published simultaneously in Canada by Penguin Books Canada Limited

Library of Congress Cataloging-in-Publication Data

Perloff, Marjorie.
  The Vienna paradox : a memoir / by Marjorie Perloff.
      p. cm.
  Includes bibliographical references and index.
ISBN 0-8112-1571-7 (acid-free paper)
  1. Perloff, Marjorie. 2. English teachers—United States—Biography.
  3. Critics—United States—Biography. 4. Perloff, Marjorie—Homes and haunts—
Austria—Vienna. 5. Refugees, Jewish—United States—Biography.
  6. Perloff, Marjorie—Childhood and youth. 7. Jewish families—Austria—Vienna.
  8. Jewish families—United States. 9. Austrian Americans—Biography.
  10. Vienna (Austria)—Biography. 11. Perloff, Marjorie—Family.
  I. Title.
PS29.P47A3 2004
810.9—dc22

2003028141

New Directions Books are published for James Laughlin
by New Directions Publishing Corporation,
80 Eighth Avenue, New York, NY 10011

CONTENTS

ILLUSTRATIONS

Unless otherwise indicated, all illustrations are in the author's family collection.

Prologue

Figure 1, p. 7. Palais Fanto, Vienna. Courtesy, Arnold Schoenberg Center, Vienna.

Figure 2, p. 10. Lili Schüller, *Portrait of Ilse Schüller*, 1908.

Figure 3, p. 14. Otto Wagner, Villa 2, 1912–13. Details of entrance and wall decoration. Photograph by Gerald Zugmann, Vienna.

Figure 4, p. 14. Ludwig Wittengstein, Kundmanngasse. South perspective, present situation. Photograph by Marghareta Krichanitz. Courtesy, The Pepin Press, Amsterdam.

Figure 5, p. 15. Neue Galerie, grand staircase. Photograph by David Schlegel. Courtesy, Neue Galerie, New York, © 2003.

Figure 6, p. 17. Café Sabarsky, with grand staircase in background, Neue Galerie. Courtesy, Neue Galerie, New York, © 2003.

Figure 7, p. 18. Reinhold Völkel, *In the Griensteidl Café*, 1896. Watercolor. Museum der Stadt Wien.

Figure 8, p. 20. Café Herrenhof, Herrengasse 10, March 1938. Bildarchiv. d. ÖNB, Vienna.

Figure 9, p. 22. Raimund Abraham, Austrian Cultural Forum, East 52nd Street, New York, 2002. Photograph by Robert Polidori.

Chapter One

Chapter Two

Chapter Three

Chapter Four

Chapter Five

Epilogue

PREFACE

IN 1996, I PUBLISHED A BOOK CALLED *WITTGENSTEIN'S LADDER*, which suggested that Wittgenstein's writings have been as seminal for the poets and artists of the later twentieth century as they have been for philosophers. In the Preface, I talked a little bit about my own Viennese background and remarked that although my parents had not known the Wittgensteins directly, there was a slight connection through Wittgenstein's cousin, the great economist Friedrich von Hayek, who was my father's close friend and the founder of the intellectual "club" known as the Geistkreis, to which my father belonged. But this personal reference was a very minor note in a book that otherwise focuses directly on Wittgenstein's writings vis-à-vis those of Gertrude Stein and Samuel Beckett, Thomas Bernhard and Ingeborg Bachmann, as well as some contemporary American poets like Robert Creeley and Lyn Hejinian.

When the book appeared in 1996, my friend James Laughlin, the founder and publisher of New Directions, himself a committed poet, essayist, and critic, wrote to me, "Why don't you write a memoir about *your* Vienna and let us publish it?" It was a flattering and challenging suggestion, but at first I was quite hesitant. For one thing, I am a critic not a biographer or memoirist, and the notion of personal confession or family anecdote has never appealed to me. For another, I had left Vienna as a refugee from the Nazis in 1938 when I was six. Actual memories of the Vienna years were therefore limited. Moreover, unlike so many authors of refugee memoirs, I had no horrific tale to tell. My family's upheaval was psychological and cultural but not at all life-threatening. We were never in a concentration camp, no immediate relative was imprisoned, and when we came to the United States, sponsored by a cousin of my father's, we had sufficient funds to get by, even if quite meagerly.

I also hesitated because I was aware of the sheer number of refugee memoirs already in print. I have a whole shelf of books belonging to this genre, and even if I count only those written by Austrians, there are dozens, ranging, in recent years, from Leo Spitzer's charming *Hotel Bolivia: The Culture of Memory in a Refuge from Nazism* (1999) to Ruth Kluger's deeply painful *Still Alive: A Holocaust Girlhood Remembered* (2001). But reading these accounts, I realized that my situation was quite different from that of the typical Jewish refugee. For my family was wholly assimilated, with many of my relatives having been baptized as Catholics or Protestants early in the century. Anti-Semitism, especially for my mother's prominent family, the Schüllers, was something that concerned *other people*; indeed, they were not free of anti-Semitism themselves. Highly cultured, intellectual, and snobbish, they often regarded *Kultur* as their true religion. Long after the dissolution of the great Austro-Hungarian empire in 1918, long even after the Anschluss in 1938, they remained proud of being Viennese, proud of inheriting such a rich cultural and artistic heritage.

Indeed, reading the family correspondence and memoirs, I came to see that there was, after all, an important story to tell. A story not so much of the emigration itself as of what it all meant to the upper-class Viennese Jewish community, which regarded itself as Austrian rather than Jewish. As a critic, I wanted to reread certain texts crucial to the question, from Stefan George's poems to my favorite children's book *Die lustigen Neun* (*The Jolly Nine*). What does it mean, I have asked myself as an American, to place High Culture on such a pedestal? How does that culture relate to politics and ethnicity? And what happened to Viennese culture when it was forced to assimilate into the democracy of the United States—a democracy deeply suspicious of High Culture, indeed of all distinctions between "High" and "Low," except for the clear-cut distinctions in wealth that characterize our nation?

There are no easy answers to these questions, and I remain decidedly ambivalent about my own cultural roots. As a professor of literature, I long for a world where people actually care about the artistic and intellectual life, a world where art and poetry might be regarded as more than Sunday "enrichment" but, on the contrary, central to life itself. At the same time, I am aware of the price High Culture exacts and the dangers of nonengagement in the actual public life of one's nation.

This book, then, is less a straightforward narrative than a collage in which I juxtapose literary text, historical information, personal anecdote, family memoir, and critical speculation so as to capture the contradictions that have made my own sensibility what it is. Indeed, the loop that my own critical writings have made from the German and English classics to Frank O'Hara and John Cage and back to the Vienna of Wittgenstein, who also happened to be one of Cage's favorites, seems curious even to me. Writing about the unknown, one comes, bit by bit, to understand it better. And so writing this book has been a source of great pleasure—and also pain. The refugee situation that determined my fate continues to impress me with its poignancy.

Sadly, James Laughlin died a year or so after urging me to embark on this project. Earlier, he had made a visit to Vienna and took a photograph of my apartment house, newly refurbished, at Hörlgasse 6. How I would have loved to discuss my ideas and share anecdotes with "J"! How we would have chuckled about those new Viennese vending machines that dispense *Schlag* and debated the issue of stamp scrip in pre–World War II Wörgl, as it was understood (foolishly, I felt) by the poet to whose publication and dissemination J had devoted so much effort over the years—Ezra Pound. And the issue of Italian baroque versus its Austrian counterpart would surely have come up along with questions about Viennese "modernism" as insufficiently "modern," by the light of Imagist and Objectivist norms. J was not an "easy" person and he had known significant personal and professional disappointments throughout his life. But in all the years I knew him, he insisted on maintaining a stance of lightness and wit, a grace under pressure that is rare today—or any day. *The Vienna Paradox* is dedicated to the memory of this most charming of men. "They will come no more, / The old men with beautiful manners . . . ."

ACKNOWLEDGMENTS

THE VIENNA PARADOX DIFFERS FROM MY PREVIOUS BOOKS IN being the beneficiary—or victim?—of the Internet revolution. Electronic dissemination has made it possible to send drafts and manuscripts to one's friends and colleagues with the mere flick of a finger, and so feedback has become an entirely different proposition. More often that not, my recipients made suggestions and emendations, and thus I found myself writing and rewriting—and rewriting yet again. At a certain point, I felt as if the process could continue indefinitely, especially since my readers were by no means in agreement as to what to leave out, add, and so on. Then, too, I have, over the past few years, given a number of lectures derived from the book-in-progress, and my hosts and audiences at a variety of institutions also gave plentiful feedback. I have, in the process, incurred more debts than I can cite here, but let me single out those whose help and support was seminal: Barry Ahearn, David Antin, Luigi Ballerini, Mary Jo Bang, Charles Bernstein, Gerald Bruns, Matei Calinescu, Guy Davenport, Peter Gizzi, Peter Hare, Robert Harrison, Van Harvey, Priscilla Heim, Daniel Herwitz, Susan Howe, Thomas S. Hines, Lucille Kerr, Herbert Lindenberger, Walter and Sandra Mintz, Peter Nicholls, Jed and Suzy Rasula, Claude Rawson, Joan Retallack, Vincent Sherry, Sandra Stanley, and Susan Stewart. For help with the knotty problem of when and when not a given German word or phrase needed translation and for a thorough reading of the entire manuscript with a view to stylistic niceties, I owe special thanks to Michael Heim, whose own translations have long been an inspiration to me. Portions of the book have been published in periodicals: the "Prologue" in *Modernism/Modernity*, Chapter 1 and the "Epilogue" in *PN Review*, Chapter 2 in *Common Knowledge*, and Chapters 3 and 4 in *Western Humanities Review*. I thank the editors of these journals— Jeffrey Schnapp, Michael Schmidt, Jeffrey Perl, and Barry Weller—for their encouragement and enthusiasm.

The interest of my daughters, Nancy and Carey Perloff, was seminal to the project. And, as always, my husband, Joseph Perloff, read every word more than once and made very helpful suggestions. I am now looking forward to the day when my three grandchildren, Benjamin Lempert and Alexandra and Nicholas Perloff-Giles, can read about their Viennese roots.

My New Directions editor Peter Glassgold, whose own books on anarchy are in some ways antithetical versions of the same political phenomena and hence germane to my own meditations, has been everything an editor could possibly be. I also want to thank Griselda Ohannessian and Peggy Fox, who inherited the mandate for this book from James Laughlin and have been wonderfully encouraging and wise.

MARJORIE PERLOFF
PACIFIC PALISADES, CA
2003

Seductive Vienna

Liberal in its constitution, [Austria] was administered clerically. The government was clerical, but everyday life was liberal. All citizens were equal before the law, but not everyone was a citizen. There was a Parliament, which asserted its freedom so forcefully that it was usually kept shut; there was also an Emergency Powers Act that enabled the government to get along without Parliament, but then, when everyone had happily settled for absolutism, the Crown decreed that it was time to go back to parliamentary rule.

—Robert Musil, *The Man Without Qualities*, 1952[1]

—For a long time I thought my difficulty as a writer was that I write in German, for my relation to Germany is only one of language, formed as I was by a storehouse of experiences and feelings from a different place. I am from Austria, from a small country that, to say it euphemistically, has tried to step outside history but has an overpowering, monstrous past.

—Ingeborg Bachmann, Interview, 1969 [2]

It was really an absurd idea
to come back to Vienna

But of course the world consists only of absurd ideas.
—Professor Robert in Thomas Bernhard, *Heldenplatz* [3]

GABRIELE VON BÜLOW, FOR WHOM I WAS NAMED, WAS THE daughter of the great Prussian nineteenth-century language philosopher and humanist Wilhelm von Humboldt; her uncle was the equally renowned naturalist Alexander von

Humboldt. She herself, married to a diplomat and statesman, was a prolific writer, known today mostly for her
extensive correspondence. Not only is Humboldt
University in Berlin named for her father; there is also a
Gabriele-von-Bülow Oberschule in Berlin.

But what did I, the daughter of Maximilian Mintz,
whose Viennese Jewish family originally came from Galicia
(Poland) and Russia, and Ilse Schüller, both of whose Jewish
grandfathers (Sigmund Schüller and Emil Rosenthal) were
textile manufacturers, the former in Brünn (Brno), the latter in Hohenems near the Swiss border), have to do with the
Prussian aristocracy? Why, for that matter, was my father
named for the late fifteenth-century Hapsburg emperor,
Kaiser Maximilian I?

No doubt Gabriele von Bülow appealed to my parents—and especially to my mother—as an intellectual
woman, even as Gabriele's father was admired as a link to
Goethe, whose work von Humboldt disseminated, and
Goethe was, for my parents, the Great Writer and Thinker
of the Modern, as opposed to the Ancient, World. It is difficult for Americans to understand the thirst for culture
(*Kulturdrang*) of the Viennese-Jewish assimilated, if not
actually baptized, upper bourgeoisie—a *Kulturdrang* that
began with the "Emancipation" of 1867, when Kaiser Franz
Josef promulgated a new constitution that guaranteed freedom of religion and civil rights for all people of the Austro-
Hungarian empire, thus paving the way for the right of Jews
to own property, attend public schools, and enter most of
the professions. The Austrian Jews' extraordinary success
following Emancipation—a success always shadowed by the
widespread anti-Semitism of the empire—was to come to

an abrupt halt with the German Anschluss of Austria in March 1938. But even in their new homes in New York or Los Angeles, São Paulo or Sydney, those refugees that managed to escape the Nazis continued to be attracted to Viennese culture, with its ideals of *Bildung, Wissenschaft*, taste, and connoisseurship in the arts. My own parents and grandparents, settled in Riverdale—a name, they were pleased to note, much more respectable than the Bronx of which it is a part—continued to speak warmly of the Vienna Opera or the Kunsthistorisches Museum or the Burgtheater as cultural sites unrivaled in America, even as *Dobostorte* and *Palatschinken* (crepes)—those desserts of the Austro-Hungarian empire—were judged to be unarguably superior to such counterparts as Apple Brown Betty, custard, and—worst of all—Jell-O, a dessert judged by the Viennese refugees in New York to be, quite simply, not fit to eat!

The question of Viennese *Kultur* is still very much with us, even though the world of the Dual Monarchy, known affectionately as *k und k* (for *kaiserlich und königlich*, imperial and royal), collapsed almost a hundred years ago, a casualty of the Great War. In Los Angeles, where my husband and I have lived for the past twenty-five years, German and Austrian refugee culture played a decisive role in the late '30s and '40s. The composer Arnold Schoenberg had settled here by 1934; the writers Thomas Mann, Bertolt Brecht, Lion Feuchtwanger, and Theodor Adorno followed in the early '40s, all four settling in Pacific Palisades, not far, as it happens, from my own house on Amalfi Drive. Evidently, the German and Austrian émigrés were drawn to the Palisades because the hilly, wooded terrain, with vistas of the ocean, reminded them of their beloved Italian Riviera;

indeed the area is now called the Riviera, and the street names, like Amalfi Drive, are all Italian: Capri, Sorrento, San Remo, Napoli—even the improbable Ravoli (for *Ravioli*?), which is around the corner. The former Feuchtwanger home, the spectacular Villa Aurora close to the Pacific at the foot of the Palisades, is now the Foundation for European-American Relations, funded by the German government through the Goethe Institute and designed to foster understanding of new developments in literature and art as well as to commemorate the great achievements of exile culture. On the lovely Spanish patio of the Villa Aurora, one can observe—after the lecture or concert—an interesting mélange of aging émigrés and young German artists and writers nibbling on little finger sandwiches (*Brötchen*) and sipping white wine.

After the war, Mann, Brecht, and Adorno, among others, returned to Europe; they had, after all, never become acclimated to an America they had found, especially in its Hollywood incarnation, wholly inimical to a meaningful cultural and literary way of life. Schoenberg, like such Austrian film directors as Fritz Lang, remained; the composer wrote some of his major works, like *A Survivor of Warsaw*, here in his Brentwood home. But to what extent has his oeuvre been absorbed into American musical culture? And what does such absorption really signify? As someone whose "real" identity was once that of Gabriele Mintz, I cannot help but think about these questions.

Indeed, the reception of Schoenberg's work in America provides an interesting paradigm of the contradictions of cultural dissemination as I have come to know them. A baptized Austrian Jew (later reconverted to Judaism),

Schoenberg was teaching at the Prussian Academy in Berlin when Hitler assumed power in 1933.[4] He fled to the United States, taking up residence in Los Angeles, where he spent the last seventeen years of his life. "I still remember," the composer later wrote about his Vienna years, "a man saying with authority about me: 'And if he were Mozart himself he must get out.'"[5] In Los Angeles, he taught first at the University of Southern California (U.S.C.), then at U.C.L.A., and influenced a whole generation of American composers, including John Cage, whose Schoenberg stories are legendary. He never set foot in Europe again.

After his death, Schoenberg's family donated his extraordinary estate—an archive consisting of major scores and manuscripts, visual works, letters, and the composer's entire library—to U.S.C., where the Schoenberg Institute opened in a small modernist structure in 1975: the university paid around $500,000 for the building and $300,000 annually for maintenance and concert activities. When I accepted a chair in the U.S.C. English Department in 1977, the Institute was a major attraction for me. Under the directorship of Leonard Stein, one of Schoenberg's most accomplished pupils, it organized concerts, sponsored a journal, and had excellent small exhibitions of the composer's manuscripts, his Expressionist paintings, and his correspondence with various artists and writers. At the entrance, there was a charming replica of Schoenberg's study on Rockingham Road.

But although Schoenberg had developed a devoted following in the Los Angeles of the war years and had his orchestral works performed under the direction of Otto Klemperer and Leopold Stokowski, he remained, in the

eyes of the musical public, an "esoteric," largely incomprehensible composer. It is emblematic that when, after his
retirement in 1946 from U.C.L.A., Schoenberg applied for
a Guggenheim Fellowship so as to finish his great opera
Moses und Aaron, he was turned down. At the new U.S.C.
Schoenberg Institute, concert attendance was low, and the
university trustees evidently wanted "more bang for the
buck," as one administrator put it. Specifically, the university wanted the Institute to add classroom space and to broad-
en the repertoire away from Schoenberg so as to attract a
larger audience. The composer's sons, said to be "difficult"
in U.S.C. circles, finally became exasperated and decided to
take their archive elsewhere. But although various universities and institutions expressed at least some interest,
nowhere were sufficient funds or the appropriate facilities
forthcoming.

In 1998, accordingly, the Schoenbergs gave their
father's archive back to his birthplace. In Vienna, it was
offered strong government support—an unimaginable situation in the United States. The Austrian government spent
$4,000,000 to turn a 6,500-square-foot space in the Palais
Fanto into a state-of-the-art research center, exhibition
space, and concert hall. The government also agreed to
continue to support the Schoenberg Center "for the duration," with a budget of around $1,000,000 a year. The
Center's director, Christian Meyer, declared that
"Schoenberg was the most important Austrian composer of
the 20th century, and this is an invaluable opportunity for
Austrians to have direct access to an important aspect of
their culture which they might not know as well as they
should."

Perhaps this "aspect of their culture" has remained shadowy to the Austrians because of the amnesia of the Nazi years and their aftermath. Still, one can only marvel at the Austrian government's generosity and the taxpayers' willingness to support such a cause. The Center [Figure 1] is housed in the heart of Vienna's Old City, just across the Schwarzenbergplatz from the Musikverein, the home of the Vienna Philharmonic and a short walk from the famous Vienna Conservatory of Music. Such proximity means that

FIGURE 1. Palais Fanto, Vienna

conductors like Zubin Mehta and Claudio Abbado can drop in to look at manuscripts of works they plan to conduct. The Center immediately began a round of concerts, symposia, and special events, and now sponsors fellowships, internships, and courses, as well as a state-of-the-art website and computer projects whereby rare and precious manuscripts are being digitized. The composer's own house on the outskirts of Vienna in Mödling has also been reopened, with a permanent exhibition and lecture series.

After the difficulties the Schoenberg heirs experienced in Los Angeles, they are evidently delighted with the new facility. Their negotiations with the Austrian government, for example, included a private audience with the chancellor. Again, this would be almost unimaginable, not only in the United States, but in most other nations, even small ones like Austria. Nevertheless, I remain slightly skeptical. For however inspiring it is to witness government sponsorship of a facility like the Schoenberg Center, I can never quite forget that the Palais Fanto is just minutes from the Rathaus, at whose sessions of parliament Jörg Haider's neo-Fascist Freedom Party has had, in the course of the past decade, sizable representation. And I recall that Ingeborg Bachmann, who was born into a proto-Nazi family in Klagenfurt in 1926, remarked frequently on the euphemism "the seven years" (*die sieben Jahre*) as a designator for World War II—a war in whose aftermath Austria, as an "occupied" country, escaped both the de-Nazification campaign undergone by Germany and the Iron Curtain, which swallowed up all its eastern neighbors, including Czechoslovakia and Hungary.

Then, too, there is a personal irony for me in the idea

that the new Schoenberg Center should be housed in the Palais Fanto, to which I have family ties. The Center website has this to say about the Palais's original owner:

David Fanto began his career as an apprentice for a paper shop in Vienna. As a successful businessman he later bought oil fields in Galicia, Rumania, and Poland. He founded one of the first Austrian refineries in Pardubitz and participated in oil-drilling concerns in the Near East. During the war years there was a sharp recession for the mineral oil business. In 1916 David Fanto bought Pottenbrunn Castle near St. Pölten. In 1917 he built the city palace (named after him) at Schwarzenbergplatz 6. After the war he was active in Czechoslovakia on behalf of the restoration of the monarchy. David Fanto died in 1922. He left behind two daughters, and a son, Richard Fanto, who inherited Pottenbrunn Castle.

Richard Fanto may have been the heir to his father's oil millions, but his fate points to a very different side of Viennese *Kultur*. As a wealthy young man, Richard Fanto had one consuming desire: to become a professional cavalry officer in the most elite and exclusive of regiments: Kaiser Franz Josef's own Yellow Dragoons. As my cousin Herbert Schüller tells it in his unpublished memoir, written in English for his children and grandchildren in 1995, Yellow Dragoons "wore red trousers, blue tunics with yellow epaulettes . . . over which they had a shiny metal cuirass, or breastplate, and a strangely curved helmet." For a young man of Jewish descent, even a baptized and practicing Catholic as was Richard Fanto, to become a member of the Yellow Dragoons was all but impossible. But David Fanto brought it off by arranging a marriage between his son and the daughter of an impoverished field marshall, Baron Horsetski. After World War I, the Fanto fortune collapsed, as did Richard's marriage, and this once elegant dragoon, a brilliant horseman who had won countless trophies, spent his days trying to manage his meager funds and playing cards at the Jockey Club. His daughter Ina, who had been brought up in a convent, was to become an ardent Nazi—a high official in the Bund Deutscher Mädchen.

Meanwhile, David Fanto's younger daughter Lili, married to my grandfather Richard Schüller's brother Hugo, a physician, had a very different fate. A talented artist whose 1908 painting of my mother (at age 4) hangs in my dining room today [Figure 2], she spent the early years of her marriage shuttling back and forth between Vienna and her Paris

FIGURE 2.
Lili Schüller,
*Portrait of
Ilse Schüller*,
1908.

studio. Her sons Herbert and George were brought up almost entirely by governesses. The outbreak of the war changed everything: Paris was now out of bounds, and the forty-year-old Hugo was soon called to military service, physicians being in short supply. Alone in Vienna, Lili began an affair with a man named Herman Blau, who happened to be married to Grandmama Erna Schüller's sister Hedi, thus putting my grandmother between sister and sister-in-law. The double divorce that split both families was naturally a great scandal. I can still remember hearing, as a young girl, the story of the bitter 1918 court case, when Lili Fanto Schüller, asked why she wanted to divorce Hugo, replied that he was not very good in bed. Grandfather Schüller, by then a leading government official, was so angry at this "vulgar" comment that he evidently didn't speak to anyone for a whole day, and, given the circumstances, Uncle Hugo won custody of both of his sons. But the loss of the Fanto fortune and marriage to the much less elegant and more transparently Jewish Herman Blau (even though he changed his name to the more neutral Berndt upon marriage), led to a series of business disasters. When the two escaped Hitler in 1939, the fifty-six-year-old Lili became a seamstress in a garment factory in Elmhurst, Long Island. For the next fifteen years or so she sewed belts on the assembly line, while her husband Herman worked as a shipping clerk. She lived to be 101, maintained, in large part, by the two sons, Herbert and George, she had treated so cavalierly in their childhood. I remember meeting her once at George's house in Washington in the 1960s: she was very much the grande dame in black dress and pearls, even as her brother Richard continued till he died to play the

cavalry officer and boast of his one-time acquaintance with
the Hapsburgs.

So it seems strange to me to think that the Palais Fanto
is now a center for avant-garde music and home to the
estate of one of the greatest composers of the century,
whose own later years were spent in difficult exile in Los
Angeles. And yet Vienna's acquisition and promotion of
the Schoenberg oeuvre, now known around the world, has
oddly spurred the Angeleno musical establishment to take
a new look at the composer's work. A decade after U.S.C.
gave up the Schoenberg archive and U.C.L.A. crassly sold
the naming rights for Schoenberg Hall to a pop music
executive, Los Angeles concert groups organized an elaborate "Schoenberg Prism" (2001–2)—a six-month festival of
concerts, lectures, and symposia—that succeeded in bring-
ing the composer full circle to his adopted home, even as
the composer's name, in response to a wave of protests
from the U.C.L.A. faculty, was restored to Schoenberg
Hall.[6] As is so often the case in American cultural and
artistic life, it was the "foreign" imprimatur that made the
difference.

The current absorption in the Viennese arts is hardly
limited to music. In the summer of 2002, for example, as
unlikely a spot as the Berkshires in western Massachusetts
featured a five-museum event called the "Vienna Project":
"Gustav Klimt Landscapes" (with side exhibits on the architecture of Joseph Hoffmann and Otto Wagner, and one on
the "Homes of Wittgenstein") at the Clark Institute in
Williamstown; "Prelude to a Nightmare: Art, Politics and
Hitler's Early Years in Vienna, 1906–13," at the Williams
College Museum of Art; "Uncommon Denominator: New

Art from Vienna," at Massachusetts Museum of Contemporary Art in North Adams; "Secession Graphic Art," at the Berkshire Museum in Pittsfield; and an exhibition of Lisbeth Zwerger's illustrations for *The Wizard Of Oz* at the Norman Rockwell Museum in Stockbridge.

Why Vienna in Williamstown? In Pittsfield, Stockbridge, and North Adams? *The New York Times* speculated that it is precisely the paradox of Vienna that once again fascinates us.[7] On the one hand, there is Vienna, the great imperial city, with its opulent, gorgeous, erotic painting and design; on the other is Hitler's Vienna (the title of Brigitte Hamman's book, on which the Williams College Museum show is based),[8] whose housing was so substandard that young men arriving to seek their fortune in the capital often ended up, as did Hitler, in bedbug-ridden shelters that were breeding grounds for violence and political upheaval. A second—more specifically artistic—tension is that between the curves, spirals, and heavy ornamentation of the Secession [Figure 3] versus the austere modernism of the "Kundmanngasse" [Figure 4], the house Wittgenstein designed for his sister Margarete, in keeping with the verbal "purity" of the *Tractatus Logico-Philosophitus.* How does the second emerge from the first? Is it a case of continuity or reaction?

I wondered about these relationships on a recent trip to New York, when I had a chance to visit two new institutions that represent the tension between fin-de-siècle and high-tech Vienna. The former, the Neue Galerie is located on the corner of Fifth Avenue and 86th Street, just three blocks below Frank Lloyd Wright's Guggenheim Museum and four above the Metropolitan Museum. Its home is a lavishly

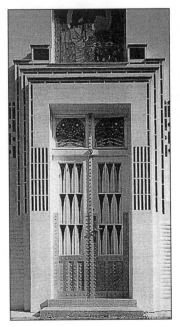

FIGURE 3. Left, Otto Wagner Villa 2, 1912–13.

FIGURE 4. Above, Ludwig Wittgenstein, Kundmanngasse.

restored Beaux-Arts mansion (1912–14; see Figure 5), designed by Carrere & Hastings, the architects of the New York Public Library. Mrs. Cornelius Vanderbilt III once lived here, but ironically the building more recently belonged to YIVO, an organization devoted to the study of Yiddish culture. The Neue Galerie itself was the brainchild of the art dealer Serge Sabarsky, a refugee from the Nazis who had settled in New York and opened a gallery on Madison Avenue, and the collector Ronald S. Lauder, an heir to the Estée Lauder cosmetic fortune. In 1957, Lauder had evidently used his bar mitzvah money to buy his first drawing by Egon Schiele. A decade later, he met Sabarsky, and together the two gradually assembled a superb collection of Schieles, Gustav Klimts, and Oskar Kokoschkas, as well as exquisite Viennese furniture and decorative art by Joseph Hoffmann, Otto Wagner, and Adolf Loos, along with a fine—but less unusual—collection of German Expressionist art. In 1986, after a stint at the Pentagon, Lauder was named U.S. ambassador to Austria and during his stay in Vienna, where he was joined by Sabarsky, the collection took its final shape.[9]

Ascending the Grand Staircase and wandering through the beautiful high-ceilinged rooms with their arresting Klimt portraits and the erotic drawings of Schiele, I experienced a strange sensory overload. My parents' generation had felt nothing but contempt for these artworks, dismissing them as "decadent," not yet truly modern. But today, this self-consciously decorative and opulent painting—

FIGURE 5.
Neue
Galerie,
grand
staircase

especially the Klimt landscapes, apparently composed with
the help of the telescope and hence flattened out to look
oddly like Japanese screens, seem nothing if not up-to-date;
indeed, many of the new works at the Massachusetts
Museum of Contemporary Art can be traced to the work of
the pre–World War I era, produced, as that work was, in a
moment when Jewish culture played a major role in the
Austrian arts, as did the Czech, Hungarian, Rumanian,
Bulgarian, and Slavic cultures that animated the capital.
The interdisciplinary connections of the artworks in the
Neue Galerie are also striking: the same ornament that
defines Secession furniture, china, and glassware is found in
posters and calling cards, opera programs and book covers.

On the lobby floor of the Neue Galerie, to the right of
the entrance, is the elegant Café Sabarsky. This brilliantly
designed restaurant [see Figure 6] alludes slyly and subtly to
fin-de-siecle Vienna without pretending to replicate the real
thing. Here is a description by a restaurant reviewer named
Janet Forman:

Run by Kurt Gutenbrunner, chef at New York's sophisticated
Austrian restaurant Wallsé, the café is rife with sumptuous details
such as marble tables and reproductions of Adolph Loos's 1899
black-bent-wood chairs—on sale in the design shop for $900 each.

The menu reinvents such Viennese classics as open-face
Trzesniewksi-style sandwiches, *matjes* herring with egg and apple,
chestnut soup and cod strudel with Riesling *sauerkraut*. . . . Slide
across a banquette covered in extravagant 1912 floral textile over-
looking the most fashionable part of Fifth Avenue, place a volup-
tuous $6 Sacher torte to your lips, and for an hour you can be the
vamp Sally Bowles or an enigmatic expressionist painter in liber-
tine Berlin of the Golden Twenties.[10]

FIGURE 6. Café Sabarsky, Neue Galerie

Note the slippage in which early modernist Vienna is equated with Weimar Germany as seen through the lens of
Christopher Isherwood. But it doesn't really matter in the
case of this elegant stage set, which has, of course, little to
do with the historic cafés of Vienna—the Griensteidl
[Figure 7], the Landtmann, the Herrenhof, the Central—
frequented daily by such important persons as Sigmund
Freud and Alfred Adler, Hugo von Hoffmannsthal and
Robert Musil, Karl Kraus and Leon Trotsky. Note that, as
the painting of the Griensteidl makes clear, the turn-of-the-
century Vienna café was a male enclave. For its patrons, it
was primarily a refuge from the unheated, hopelessly dingy
flats and furnished rooms where many of them lived due to
Vienna's acute housing shortage. One drank coffee (always

FIGURE 7. Reinhold Völkel, *In the Griensteidl Café, 1896*.
Watercolor.

served with a glass of water), read the papers, played cards
and chess, and chatted with friends. The Café Sabarsky is
thus largely simulation. Ours is not the world of Arthur
Schnitzler's *Der Weg ins Freie* (*The Road into the Open*), that
troubling saga of an anti-Semitic society in which the aristocratic hero Georg von Wergethin repairs night after night
to his favorite café, where he engages his Jewish alter ego
Heinrich Bermann in discussions about art, philosophy, and
culture. The Café Sabarsky caters not to regulars whom the
waiters know by name, but to tourists, art professionals, and
a good number of Ladies Who Lunch—a clientele that
must often wait on line for the better part of an hour to gain
entrance. Authentic? When I once asked my mother and

her sister Susi whether they used to frequent the *Kaffeehaus*, they became quite indignant. "Never," they insisted, did they set foot in a café! They had better things to do with their time. What they really meant is that the few women who did frequent the cafés were not the right sort. Ladies from *einer guten Familie* ("a good family") were not seen there. They preferred the *Konditorei*, or pastry shop—for example, Demel's or Sluka's—which, unlike the café, was designed for ladies as well as gentlemen and served gorgeous finger sandwiches and cakes. But the fact is that my mother and aunts barely went to the *Konditorei* either: they were too busy with their studies or household routine.

And there are other anomalies. Around the time that I was reading in the papers about the elegant Adolf Loos chairs in the Café Sabarsky, I came across Tina Walzer and Stephan Templ's *Unser Wien: "Ariesierung auf Oester-reichisch"* (*Our Vienna: Arianization Austrian Style*), a minutely documented study of the appropriation of Viennese Jewish property—whether businesses, hotels, art galleries, cinemas, architectural monuments, museums, bookshops, or cafés—by the Nazis in the spring and summer of 1938.[11] As their catalog "Topography of Theft" makes clear, the bulk of this property has remained in the hands of the appropriators (or their clients), and there has never been a true restitution to the dispossessed and their heirs. For each important café, for example, the authors list the original owner(s), the appropriator(s), and the café's later fate. Thus Bela Waldmann and Marcus Klug, the owners of the Café Herrenhof (frequented by writers like Max Brod and Franz Werfel), were imprisoned the day of the Anschluss and the café became state property [Figure 8].

FIGURE 8. Café Herrenhof, Herrengasse 10, March 1938.

The Graben-Café, designed by Josef Hoffmann in 1928 and owned by Hugo Fürst, was torn down. And the Café Raimund, across the street from the Volkstheater and hence a rendezvous for directors and actors, lost its most illustrious clientele when the Nazis pursued such directors as Rudolf Beer and Egon Friedell, both of whom committed suicide within weeks of the Anschluss.

Reading Walzer and Templ's grim catalogue of theft, I found myself, perversely, all the more curious about the romantic café culture of imperial Vienna. Nostalgia, the longing for a past that has never quite existed, with its concomitant feelings of loss and displacement, is, as Svetlana Boym has argued so tellingly in her book on the subject,[12] the inevitable by-product of exile. On a sunny Saturday, when my husband and I finally dined at the Café Sabarsky, the experience surpassed all expectations. One taste of the pea soup, bright green and sweet, with little bits of lobster floating on top, triggered a Proustian recollection: just such pea soup had been served at Hörlgasse 6 where I lived for the first six and a half years of my life. Again, the *Matjes* herring topped with thin slices of apple and red onion struck me as delicious beyond words, recalling summer vacations in the mountains of Seefeld. And the *Sachertorte* and *Dobostorte* which we sampled tasted precisely like the one our cook Kati had made in Vienna. Seated at a little marble-top table on the Adolf Loos reproduction-chair and sipping first Schlumberger Cuvée Klimt and then a mélange, I was totally happy. Yet—and here is another irony—I have been back to Vienna four times during my adulthood and have never had a meal nearly as good in Vienna itself. But then service in Vienna today is a far cry from that of Schnitzler's Vienna. It tends to be brusque and rude, the dishes served by surly waiters (one immediately wonders if they are anti-Semitic), whereas the Café Sabarsky is all smiles, all around.

A visit to the Neue Galerie is thus a classic nostalgia trip. But the Austrian government itself is aware of the need to go beyond the image of early modernist Vienna, however beautiful and opulent its artwork and design. Indeed, in April 2002 a very different institution opened its doors—this time on East 52st Street between Fifth and Madison Avenues—namely the Austrian Cultural Forum. This astonishing structure of concrete, glass, and steel [see Figure 9] was designed by the Austrian architect Raimund Abraham, who has lived in New York since the early 1970s. The Forum's brochure describes the building this way:

FIGURE 9.
Raimund Abraham,
Austrian Cultural
Forum,
East 52 Street,
New York, 2002.
Photograph by Robert Polidori

The body of the Forum tower tapers as it rises, complying with zoning laws levels that alternately step and slope. Glazed with dramatic glass panels that seem to be in a state of constant suspension, the forceful but mysterious image of the building has elicited comparisons to dagger blades and guillotines, thermometers and metronomes, Easter Island totems and pyramids of a future not yet imagined. The structure consists of what Abraham has dubbed "three elementary towers" defined by the extreme conditions of a site only 25 feet wide and 81 feet deep: the Vertebra is the stair tower at the back of the site; the Core is the central structural tower containing the Forum's functioning spaces within a meticulously constructed, interrelated arrangement, and the mask is the glass articulation of the street façade, punctuated by a protruding, box-like volume that in fact accommodates an interior program area with spectacular views.[13]

The website for the Forum is itself a work of art: flash-art images of the towers and their skylights, seen from both inside and outside, in shades of white, gray, and black, are intersected by aphorisms taken from the writings of Freud or the avant-garde poet Ernst Jandl, and abstract geometric forms—primarily black squares and rectangles—traverse the field vertically while John Cagean sounds are played continuously. On the left, a series of tiny parallel lines (evidently modeled on the compressed floors) move vertically toward the top of the screen where they intersect. When clicked, these lines give way to words, providing information about the Forum's activities—its calendar of avant-garde concerts, performances of digital art and music, lectures, poetry readings—as well as a display of the different floors and their role in the building.

It is a state-of-the-art digital performance that provides a feast for the eye and ear—the dream, perhaps, of a new Vienna for the New Artist. But again, it isn't that simple. For Abraham, born in the small Tyrolean town of Lienz in 1933 and growing up to the sight and sound of the "iron sky" covered with airplanes dropping bombs, the notion of death is never far away. In a November 2001 interview reproduced on the website, he cites Adolf Loos's aphorism, "When you walk through the woods and come upon a hole

two feet wide, six feet long, and six feet deep, you know that
is architecture." "Death," he remarks, "has to work, it must
express itself and its meaning somehow just as do hope or
desire. Maybe it's a problem of a technocized, urban society that death becomes very much removed from our lives. I
grew up in a small town in Austria where there were funer-
als all the time. It was part of life." For that very reason,
monuments, Abraham believes, don't work. "Think about
the fact that no Holocaust memorial ever succeeds in the
end because no monument can ever be more monumental
than a concentration camp. . . . No building can match the
terrifying empty spaces of these original sites."

Not long after Abraham gave this interview, he
renounced his Austrian citizenship to protest Jörg Haider's
participation in the coalition government. Here again, an
image carefully created and polished to remind the international world, and especially the United States, of the great
cultural heritage and relevance of tiny Austria and its capital, is shadowed by the specter of a dark politics that never
seems to quite go away. By a curious coincidence, we
remember, 52nd Street, now graced by Abraham's brilliant
façade, was also—this time, west of Fifth Avenue— the site
of W. H. Auden's famous war dirge, "September 1, 1939":

> I sit in one of the dives
> On Fifty-second Street
> Uncertain and afraid
> As the clever hopes expire
> Of a low dishonest decade. . . . [14]

Perhaps we can read the Forum's "masked" tower structure
as a kind of unmasking of those "low dishonest decades" of

mid-century. The soaring glass façade prompts the viewer to pay homage to an Austria-in-Manhattan that might mark a new turn.

Or at least I would like to see it that way. But in 1944, when I changed my name from *Gabriele* (already Anglicized—or more accurately modeled on the French form—by the addition of an *l*) to *Marjorie*, as part of the process of becoming a U.S. citizen, I was wholly unaware of such cultural niceties. I was a thirteen-year-old eighth grader who yearned only to be as American as possible. In my class at the Fieldston School, which I had just entered on a full scholarship after seven years of public school in the Bronx, the most popular girl was named Margie; she also happened to be assigned to be my Big Sister in the new school. I so much wanted to be like this Margie that I still make my capital **M**'s oversize and round like her "progressive-school" script. I disliked *Gabrielle* because classmates and campmates always called me Gabby, a name, I'm afraid, all too appropriate as those who know me can attest. Then, too, a *gaby* is defined in the dictionary as meaning "fool" or "idiot": the word is now obsolete, but one can find it in Victorian novels in locutions like, "Don't be such a gaby!" As for the name Gabrielle, the children at my Bronx elementary school had been given to shouting, "*Gayyy-briel,* blow your horn!"

Accordingly, when we took out our citizenship papers, I asked to become Marjorie, Margie for short. I am surprised that my parents consented, since they were quite strict and quite insistent on my retaining the German language and reading German literature, but they did. And so I took on the name then linked to Herman Wouk's Marjorie

Morningstar and to sitcom characters named Marge. After I turned forty, I found it inappropriate to be called Margie, as in *My Little Margie*, and so, around the time when we moved from Washington to Philadelphia in 1972, I became Marjorie once and for all. I can now divide my friends into those I've known long enough to be Margie and those for whom I am Marjorie. But when I see the name in print together with the name Perloff, which is not my name but my husband's, there is always a moment when I wonder who Marjorie Perloff is. It just doesn't look or sound like me.

When my friend Charles Bernstein found out about my "real" name he wrote the following poem:

Gertrude and Ludwig's Bogus Adventure
for Gabriele Mintz

As Billy goes higher all the balloons
Get marooned on the other side of the
Lunar landscape. The module's broke—
It seems like for an eternity, but who's
Counting—and Sally's joined the Moonies
So we don't see so much of her anyhow,
Notorious novelty—I'd settle for a good
Cup of Chase & Sand-borne—though when
The strings are broken on the guitar
You can always use it as a coffee table.
Vienna was cold at that time of year.
The sachertorte tasted sweet but the memory
burned in the colon. Get a grip, get a grip, before
The Grippe gets you. Glad to see the picture
Of ink—the pitcher that pours before
Throwing the Ball, with never a catcher in sight.

> Never a catcher but sometimes a catch, or
> A clinch or a clutch or a spoon—never a
> Catcher but plenty o' flack, 'till we meet
> On this side of the tune.[15]

What does it all mean? Ludwig (Wittgenstein) and Gertrude (Stein) make a seemingly odd couple, but, as I suggest in *Wittgenstein's Ladder* and as Charles has noted in *Content's Dream* and *My Way*, they share a concern for the strangeness of ordinary language, an awareness that the slightest syntactic shift or the replacement of a single word in a sentence can change meaning radically.[16] Then too, both Ludwig and Gertrude were nonpracticing, secularized Jews (although Wittgenstein was baptized a Catholic at birth), assimilated enough to call into question particular Jewish practices. Both were homosexual and chose exile—he in Cambridge, she in Paris—at least in part so as to avoid scrutiny of their private lives. Both, moreover, received in their lifetime "plenty o' flack" (line 19) for their radical ideas and seemingly "nonsensical" writings. Theirs, like Schoenberg's, was a "Notorious novelty" (line 7), one that took decades to understand and assimilate.

It thus makes sense for Gertrude and Ludwig to share an "adventure." But the "bogus adventure" to which the poem alludes in the first few lines was obscure to me until Charles himself explained that he had in mind a Pete Hewitt film called *Bill & Ted's Bogus Journey* (1991), in which the two boy heroes have to battle with cyborg versions of themselves, created by an evil spirit who wants to destroy their heavy metal band. In the course of their adventure, Bill and Ted undergo terrible ordeals, but because, as the film's predecessor, *Bill & Ted's Excellent Adventure*, details, the two boys know the secret of the universe ("Be excellent to each other"), they are rewarded in the end by being turned into "good" Bill and Ted robots who conquer their evil twins and win the Battle of the Bands. [17]

I confess that I wouldn't have known these plots had I not looked them up with my favorite internet search engine, Google, and then watched a rerun or two on the cable channels. Science-fiction film adventure stories that deal with Martians, cyborgs, and heavy metal are not exactly part of my discourse radius. And that, of course, probably gave Charles his rationale. Billy's "bogus adventure," in which the "balloons / Get marooned on the other side of the / Lunar landscape," immediately introduces the idea of borders to cross—and in a "module" that's "broke" to boot. Everything in this landscape seems out of kilter: "Sally's joined the Moonies," "The strings are broken on the guitar," and although "The sachertorte tasted sweet," "the memory / burned in the colon"—an allusion to the lines in John Ashbery's "'They Dream Only of America'": "This honey is delicious / though it burns the throat."[18] The poem moves from the American pop culture of the sci-fi opening and the well-known 1950s ad for Chase & Sanborn coffee ("The morning cup will keep that grippe away!") to Vienna, "cold at that time of year" (an allusion to the early March weather at the time of the Anschluss), and then into a kind of sinister dreamscape, in which coffee dissolves in waves of "sand" and the preventable grippe modulates into "Get a grip, get a grip, before / The Grippe gets you." And then the transformation of "picture" into "pitcher" and the "pitcher that pours" into the baseball pitcher, "Throwing the Ball, with never a catcher in sight," gives us a premonition of a dark future. Even the nursery-rhyme rhythms of the conclusion—"Never a catcher but sometimes a catch, or / A clinch or a clutch or a spoon"—are jarring, leading up, as they do, not to the cow jumping over the moon, as one might anticipate, but to what will be "plenty o' flack, till we meet / On this side of the tune."

Which side is that? "Gertrude and Ludwig's Bogus Adventure" was prompted in part by a conversation I had with Charles about my escape, with my family, from Vienna on March 13, 1938, the day after the Anschluss. The adventure of Gabriele Mintz, his poem suggests obliquely—an adventure that takes Gabriele from the Vienna of Wittgenstein to the America of Gertrude Stein—had its own "bogus" dimensions with respect to the pretensions and impersonations of the cultural milieu in which it was rooted. Indeed, Charles's poem captures the curious tension that has characterized my own "adventure," which took me as a small child from the Vienna of *Sachertorte* and *Kaffee mit Schlag* to an America of Chase & Sanborn coffee, Pete Hewitt adventure films, Moonies, and baseball—all those trappings of Americana that my family dismissed as so much lowbrow entertainment for the untutored masses.

But, in a further twist, the poem undercuts this image as well. Is the perception of America as the land of pop and schlock accurate? In that case, why does the "Bogus Adventure" also encompass the very different America of a poet strongly influenced by Stein—namely, Frank O'Hara, to whose "Memorial Day 1950" (written when O'Hara was only twenty-four) Charles alludes obliquely in lines 8–10. In this elegiac poem, which pays homage to Stein and Picasso, Apollinaire and Rimbaud, "collages or sprechstimme," O'Hara recalls his alienation from his parents in the following surreal sequence:

> Wasted child! I'll club you on the shins. I
> wasn't surprised when the older people entered
> my cheap hotel room and broke my guitar and my can
> of blue paint.[19]

Then, in a later turn toward artistic vocation, the poet says, "Look at my room / Guitar strings hold up pictures. I don't need / a piano to sing." Just so, we read in Charles's poem, "when / The strings are broken on the guitar / You can always use it as a coffee table."

The pragmatism of this "solution" is very congenial to me. "Love," we read in "Memorial Day 1950," "is first of all / a lesson in utility." But becoming Marjorie was a complicated process, given that, for my family, the new American world was indeed "the other side of the / Lunar landscape." And the "adventure" I shall relate here is in one sense "bogus," in that memory has transformed so much of what "happened" that there is no way to recover the "real" past. But, like many émigrés, I remain fascinated by the cultural, social, and artistic legacy of that modernist Vienna, so much of whose energy seems to have been expended on the desire to downplay the Jewish presence that had, ironically, done so much to make Viennese culture the richly textured, complicated, and supersubtle culture it was. Indeed, the *Kulturdrang*, especially of the interwar years, seems to have gone hand in hand with a collective desire for *passing*—passing as someone or something one could never quite be—a desire that tragically ended only with the acknowledgment of the Holocaust.

Or has it in fact ended? Even now, as we learn in the Neue Galerie, nostalgia can be powerful. The *Sachertorte* was sweet. . . .

CHAPTER ONE
Anschluss: March 1938

A frontier is a division between countries. A history of a country is not a history of the changing of frontiers although many think so particularly those near the frontier the history of a country is why they like things which they have and which they do not exchange for other things for which they do not care.

—Gertrude Stein, *History or Messages from History* (1930)[1]

If we think of the world's future, we always mean where it will be if it keeps going as we see it going now and it doesn't occur to us that it is not going in a straight line but in a curve, constantly changing direction.

—Wittgenstein, *Culture and Value* (1929)[2]

WHENEVER I FIND MYSELF IN THE 30TH STREET STATION in Philadelphia or Euston Station in London or the Gare du Nord in Paris, I feel unaccountably sad. The lighting seems too dim, the air too heavy, and, down on the platform, the hum of the engines starting up especially melancholy. For years I thought I felt this way simply because most railroad stations are old, dark, and dingy, but when, once in Tokyo, I was waiting for the elegant bullet train on a sparkling clean and new platform and got the same familiar twinge of anxiety, I knew it must be something else. Like Wittgenstein in his critique of Freud, I tend to shy away from psychological explanation or linear narrative, but in this case, I think it's fair to say that my train phobia has to do with the night of

March 13, 1938, the night I left Vienna for Zurich on the train. I was six and a half.

That night is commemorated for me in two written accounts. The first comprises two very short chapters of a narrative I produced at age seven in a lined black-and-white school notebook—the kind of notebook standard in the New York City public schools in 1939. My story was called *Eine Reise nach Amerika* (*A Voyage to America*) and in the Table of Contents, Chapter One is called "Die Abreise" ("The Departure"). But in the text, where the German words, already a bit unfamiliar to a child who was feverishly turning herself into an American, are often misspelled, the title reads "Die Areise." To a student of poetic language, the slip is not insignificant, meaning as it does, "The 'A' Journey." A journey, no doubt to a happier world but hardly perceived as such at the time!

Here is my translation of my first two chapters, "Die Areise" and "Im Zug":

"THE DEPARTURE"

It was on the twelfth of March in the morning when my mother came into our room and said now we are no longer Austrians. Hitler has taken Austria. I cried hard but there was nothing to be done. Then when I went into my parents' room, I saw that our suitcases were packed and when my brother Walter and I asked why, my parents said maybe we will go away. Then the next day my grandmother, grandfather, and great-grandmother came for the last time. At 10 o'clock in the evening, we went to the train station where we met our cousins Hedy and Greta Strauss. As soon as we met, Greta said to my brother Walter, "Walter, why are you wearing your cap that way?" But since the train came, my brother couldn't answer.

"ON THE TRAIN"

On the train, we went to sleep right away. But my cousins, as is typical of them, complained they didn't sleep all night. In Innsbruck, we had to get out and go to the police station where they unpacked all our luggage and my poor Mommy had to repack everything. There was such a mob and we had to wait so long that Mommy said she would unpack a book and I sat down on our hat-box and read. When we finished, we went to the station restaurant where we had ham rolls that tasted very good. And as I was sitting in this restaurant, I didn't yet have any idea that later in America I would write a book. Well, I hadn't experienced much yet but, just wait, there will be much more!

Now compare this account, written by a second grader at P. S. 7, the Bronx, to the following letter sent by my mother, Ilse Schüller Mintz, to her sister Hilde, who had emigrated to London with her husband Otto Kurz the year before.

City Hotel, Zurich
15 III 1938

Dearest Hilde:

Where shall I begin? We have been through so much and I am so tired and confused that I only noticed now that I've been in the house for 1/2 hour and still have my hat on. And then there are so terribly many crucial decisions to make! But I will try to relate to you the events one by one.

When on Friday afternoon we heard the terrible news, our first thought was "Away!" We wanted to go to Budapest Saturday morning. I packed half the night, then lay awake in bed for a few miserable hours. In the morning, I learned that one couldn't cross the border. My first reaction was one of relief that at least we could still see our parents. Saturday was taken up with visits, while outside there were incessant shouts of "*Sieg Heil!*," bombers flew by overhead, and army vehicles drove down the street. The Ungers [friends] tried to go to Hungary by car but were turned back. Bommi [another friend] visited us, was practically in tears. Karl Schlesinger has killed himself. Hugo [Ilse's uncle] and Ritti [his wife] naturally in despair. I didn't get to see the Aunts. Papa [her father, Richard Schüller] calm, looks well, says he slept well.

Sunday at noon we heard by coincidence that one could still cross the border, but not to Hungary and Czechoslovakia. We inquired at the train station, the police, etc. and had this verified. So we finished packing and left in the evening: my father-in-law [Alexander Mintz], Stella, Otto, Hedy and Greta [Stella Strauss, my father's sister, her husband Otto and their twin daughters], and Aunt Gerti [Gertrude Schüller, the widow of Ludwig Schüller, Richard's brother]. Those who didn't have the same last name had to pretend not to know one another. This applied to the children as well: they were not allowed to speak and in fact didn't speak. We traveled comfortably second-class as far as Innsbruck. The children slept. In Innsbruck, there was passport control: for Jews, the order was, "Get off the train with your luggage." Aunt Gerti was allowed to continue. Evidently, they took her for Aryan although no one asked. We were taken by the S.A. to the police office, across from the railway station. There, we were held in a narrow corridor, heavily guarded. One after another, we were called into a room where our passports were examined, our money mostly confiscated (since the rules had been changed overnight). They took 850 marks and the equivalent in schillings. We didn't care in the slightest. Our thought was only: will they let us travel further? Will we be arrested? Then all of our luggage was unpacked piece by piece. Finally, we were allowed to leave.

We sat till 2 A.M. in the station restaurant, then we continued. In Feldkirch, everyone had to get out again and we were again searched, the children and I body-searched as well. Not a handkerchief was left unfolded. The tone: "Aha, from Vienna?

Surely from the Leopoldstadt!" Max [Maximilian Mintz, my father] had his war medal with him. "If you really served at the Front, you wouldn't be leaving." One had to force oneself to keep quiet. Back on the train, we passed one military convoy after another going the other way.

At 10 in the evening, we arrived [in Zurich]. Why they let us go we still don't know. The children were fabulous. When, after we had crossed the border, they were reunited with Hedy and Greta, they were immediately cheerful, despite everything that had happened.

Here we are deciding what to do next. Erwin [my mother's first cousin, son of Aunt Gerti] is naturally a great support; he is charm and graciousness itself. He thinks our parents will be able to enter Italy legally.

Enough for today. Can you imagine that the whole passage through snowy mountains under gorgeous blue skies didn't induce the slightest feeling of regret in me? From this you can surmise what the last days have been like. In Vienna, no one without a swastika, the Wasa Gymnasium [across the street from our apartment] a barracks for the Hitler Youth, etc. I'll write soon again and I hope better. Write: Zurich / main post office. To Vienna write very cautiously: about us only, "I have very good news from Ilse."

My first reaction today to the juxtaposition of my own account to my mother's is one of enormous gratitude and admiration for a mother who could make what must have been a nightmare trip so relatively benign for us children that my immediate memory, a year or so later, was of the delicious ham sandwiches we ate at what I euphemistically refer to as the station restaurant. And indeed, in the next chapter of *Eine Reise nach Amerika* I am already writing about the games we played at the Pension Schmelzberg in Zurich, where we spent the next two months and where the

only war on our horizon was the "war" my brother Walter
and I declared on our cousins and their new friend,
Winnetou. The latter was a slightly older girl, who was
staying with her Jewish mother (her father was evidently
"Aryan"[3]), at our *pension*: they too were trying to obtain a
visa. Winnetou, ironically enough, was named for the
Apache chief who is the protagonist of the exotic adventure
tales of Karl May, the popular author on whose fiction
Winnetou's dramatist father had evidently based one of his
plays. Ironically, Karl May also happened to be the favorite
boyhood author of Hitler. "I read him," Hitler was to recall,
"by candlelight and with a large magnifying glass by moon-
light." And when, some time later, May was exposed as having invented many of his historical and geographical "facts"
about American Indians, Hitler—who borrowed dress
clothes so as to attend a lecture May gave in Vienna in 1912,
a lecture calling for a future world in which there would
only be a single race—was thrilled by May's words and
remained a staunch Winnetou defender.[4] "At Easter," I
wrote in my third chapter, "Winnetou's mother told us we
should stop fighting. But suddenly the word came that we
were going to America and we had to learn English quickly." Mother, who had studied English at school, gave us
daily lessons. Within a few weeks we had learned enough to
perform *Little Red Riding Hood*. Walter, of course, was the
wolf and I Red Riding Hood. But since Mother and Daddy's
English had the standard British speech inflections that
German speakers in those days learned as a matter of
course, it did not quite prepare us for the actual language we
would soon be hearing in New York.

To begin one's exile from Nazi Austria with a performance of a Grimm fairy tale in which one of the actors was a refugee girl named Winnetou: this is the sort of paradox that haunted the Viennese-Jewish culture of my childhood. It is significant, for example, that my mother's words of explanation to us children were, "Now we are no longer Austrians. Hitler has taken Austria." There is no mention of our having to leave as *Jews*, no doubt because despite our nominal Jewishness, we had been brought up as *Austrians*. In the photographs taken on summer vacations in the Salzkammergut or the Tyrol, we children—and here even my mother (but not Great-grandmother Rosenthal)—are dressed in dirndls or lederhosen [Figure 1].

FIGURE 1.
Clockwise:
Gabriele and
Walter Mintz,
Ilse Schüller
Mintz,
Malwine
Rosenthal,
Seefeld, 1934

Indeed, the wearing of the traditional costume (*Volkstracht*), with its emphasis on *Heimat* and the *Land*, stems back to fin-de-siècle Vienna. In 1907, my mother Ilse is depicted on vacation in Igls, wearing a particularly elegant dirndl [Figure 2]: And in a 1913 photograph [Figure 3], posed in the studio as a scene in front of a little Alpine hut, Ilse and her sisters wear "simple" dirndls, while their two boy cousins Stephan and Friedl Berndt, the sons of Hedi and Herman Blau, sport lederhosen and peasant jackets. Against the backdrop of this "Alpine Hut," my mother is holding a butter churn, and the caption above the window reads "Da gibs koa Sünd!"—Austrian dialect for "Here there's no evil!"

FIGURE 2.
Ilse Schüller,
Igls, 1907.

FIGURE 3. Ilse Schüller, Igls, 1907. Clockwise: Stephan Berndt, Ilse Schüller, Friedl Berndt, Hilde Schüller, Malwine Rosenthal, and Susi Schüller, Igls, 1913.

As late as 1937 in Selva [Figure 4], my father, holding my hand, is wearing the familiar costume—loden jacket, lederhosen, embroidered suspenders, and high white socks and mountain boots—whereby the most sophisticated of Viennese urbanites might play at being so many authentic Germanic peasants. What my father did not know is that, within the year, there would be a new Nazi government that would pass a law forbidding Jews to wear dirndls and loden suits.

FIGURE 4.
Maximilian
and Gabriele
Mintz, Selva,
1937.

In pre–World War II Vienna, national identity regularly
trumped ethnicity, not to mention religion. So "assimilated"
were the Austrian upper-middle-class Jewish families like my
own, many of whose members had been baptized decades earlier, that the Nazi takeover of Austria and immediate expul-
sion and torture of the Jews came, as my mother notes, as a
terrible—and unanticipated—shock. Indeed, the Nazi police
taunt—"Aha, from Vienna? Surely from the Leopoldstadt"—
must have been perceived by my parents as the ultimate
insult: the Leopoldstadt was the enclave of the unassimilated

Eastern Jews—men and women in strange garb who spoke Yiddish and went to the synagogue—men and women who were entirely "foreign" to us and counted as vulgar (*ordinär*) and uneducated (*ungebildet*). Years later in New York, when someone once asked my father what he thought of a certain Austrian refugee who had become a professor of economics at a local university, he shrugged and said, "*Ein mieser Jud'* [an unattractive Jew, a poor slob] *von der Leopoldstadt.*"

Such class consciousness was exacerbated, in the case of my own family, by a particular circumstance. My mother's special sense of shock at the "terrible news" of the Anschluss —a coup with hindsight largely predictable for months before it occurred, if not as early as July 1934, when Nazi thugs openly murdered the devoutly Catholic and conservative but staunchly anti-Nazi Austrian Chancellor Engelbert Dollfuss—had to do with the position of my maternal grandfather, Richard Schüller. At sixty-eight, after a long and distinguished career as diplomat and statesman, Grandfather was a close advisor to Kurt Schuschnigg, who had succeeded Dollfuss and was to be the last chancellor of an independent Austria.

Richard Schüller was born in 1870 in Brünn (Brno) in what is now the Czech Republic. The son of a well-off wool manufacturer whose business failed in the late 1880s, he went to Vienna to study law and then economics with the famous Professor Karl Menger, supporting himself in part as a tutor (*Hauslehrer*) to the children of rich families. His dream was to become a professor, but in 1898 he was invited to enter the government, first in the Department of Commerce, then, after World War I, in the Foreign Office [see Figure 5]. In his memoir, published in Austria in 1990

FIGURE 5. Hofrat
Richard Schüller,
Vienna, 1898.

under the title *Unterhändler des Vertrauens* (*Negotiator of Trust*), Grandfather recalls that as the only Jew in the division, he was regularly begged by his superiors to "allow" himself to be baptized. He refused, not because he had any allegiance to the Jewish religion or even to Jewish culture, but because he disliked the idea of what was known as career baptism (*die Karrieretaufe*).[5]

Both his brothers, by contrast, were baptized Lutherans. The youngest, Hugo, we recall, was first married to the fabulously wealthy and Jewish Lili Fanto; later, he married a beautiful Catholic woman named Ritti Schiff, who, as it happened, refused to leave Vienna, supposedly because she knew no English and was terrified at the thought of emigration. So Hugo fled alone, first to London, where he was sent to a internment camp for enemy aliens on the Isle of Man, and then in 1939 to New York. The middle brother, Ludwig, studied law in Vienna and was also a *Hauslehrer*, primarily to one or the other of the twelve children of Theodor von Taussig, the director of the Boden-Kreditanstalt, which was the emperor's own bank. This "Jewish Lohengrin," as Ludwig was evidently known in Vienna society (UV, 106), married one of his charges, Gertrude—the Aunt Gerti mentioned in my mother's letter—who had no trouble at the Austrian border because, having been raised in a family that had converted to Christianity decades earlier, she was taken to be Aryan. The Ludwig Schüllers were the most elegant, rich, and snobbish members of the family. Their sons Erwin and Teddy had an English nanny and their perfect posture was said to be the result of sleeping on a board as young children. It was Uncle Erwin who was so "fabulously helpful" in obtaining our visa in Zurich. Ludwig himself had committed suicide in 1931, just a few months before I was born, when his own bank, Auspritz & Lieben, was the first to go under in the 1929 crash. His tragic death by drowning in the Danube resonated through my childhood years. Erwin himself was also to commit suicide some forty years later in New York, jumping from the window of a Madison Avenue skyscraper, perhaps because his own brilliant career had faltered, perhaps for private reasons.

And there were other Taussig / Schüller casualties. One of Gerti's many siblings was the well-established painter Helene von Taussig (born 1879), who studied with Maurice

Dennis in Paris and later lived and worked in Salzburg.
After the Anschluss, her house was appropriated and she
was no longer allowed to exhibit, but although Helene evidently had many opportunities to leave Austria, she stayed
on. With the outbreak of war in 1940, she moved to Vienna
and took refuge in a convent. But in 1942, the convent was
raided and, despite her age, Helene was deported to the
Izbica Lubelska concentration camp in Poland, where she
was killed. Many of her canvases were unfortunately lost,
but in the 1990s, her paintings [see Figure 6] were redis-

FIGURE 6.
Helene von
Taussig,
*Exotic
Dancer*,
c. 1926.

covered, and they have been the subject of numerous exhibitions, the most recent of which—ironically enough—was the 2002 *Juden in Salzburg.*"[6]

But there are more sinister stories. A recent collection of essays and memoirs on the Jews of the Tirol and Vorarlberg (an oxymoron of sorts, since very few Jews gravitated to the Austrian mountains) contains the story of "Ing. [Ingenieur] Robert Schüller."[7] Robert's father, a successful trial attorney in Vienna, was my grandfather's first cousin. One of four sons, Robert served in World War I; he won a Bronze Medal and Iron Cross for taking a munitions transport through heavy fire in the Dolomites. After the war he studied law and engineering briefly at the University of Vienna, then broke completely with his family and threw himself into political work for the D.N.S.A.P. (Deutsche Nationalsozialistische Arbeiterpartei), which was to become the Nazi party. Robert was a devoted Nazi *apparatchik* [see Figure 7] throughout his life: at one time he worked directly for Göring and his wife, who were posted in Innsbruck.

Ironically, Robert Schüller was undone after the longed-for Anschluss when the Nazis began their detailed background checks and discovered that he had, in fact, three Jewish grandparents. What was worse: he had had sexual relations with numerous Aryan women, including a Viennese prostitute who testified against him. Schüller was convinced Hitler would intervene; his widowed mother, Anna Röder, moreover, went so far as to claim that her own mother had had an affair with an Aryan the year she was born so that Anna's real father would have been one Johann Limbach rather than the Jewish Heinrich Röder. But none

FIGURE 7. Robert Schüller (second from the right) with
Gauleiter Cristoph (fourth from the right) March–April 1938.

of these protests helped: the one-time Gauleiter was con-
victed and sent to his death at Auschwitz. At his trial in
Innsbruck, his last words were, "I was, have been, and
remain a National Socialist."

The sordid saga of Robert Schüller suggests what terrible consequences *passing* could have in a society governed
by such racial hatred. But in the 1920s, when the Nazis were
still treated as political thugs, in and out of jail for various
crimes (Robert Schüller was frequently jailed), and
Socialism was powerful in "Red Vienna," things appeared to
be very different. These were, in any case, Grandfather
Schüller's years of diplomatic renown. Handsome, charming, socially adept, a great ladies' man, Grandfather held

one high post after another—for example, he was chief
negotiator for Austria of the Peace Treaty of Brest-Litovsk
with the Russians in 1917 and, later, Austrian ambassador to
the League of Nations in Geneva. At the same time, he
managed to produce important scholarly works on mone-
tary theory and trade policy.

In the immediate aftermath of World War I, when, in
Grandfather's words, "the Austrian Monarchy, more than
600 years old, fell to pieces silently in a few days" (UV, 216),
Grandfather's first priority was to save his country, no matter what the effort. In "Finis Austriae," he described in
moving detail the autumn of 1918, when the former multi-
national, multiethnic empire was broken into seven parts—
Austria, Czechoslovakia, Hungary, Poland, Yugoslavia,
Rumania—and the territories ceded to Italy. The new
Austrian republic, now consisting only of the city of Vienna
and the Alpine territories, had lost three quarters of its former food supply and ninety percent of its coal, precipitating
a series of crises for the newly elected Social Democratic
government led by Karl Renner, with Viktor Adler as secre-
tary of state. So desperate was the situation in the winter of
1919 that the people of Vienna looted shops and stole wood
for fuel from the Wienerwald. Grandfather, now serving
Renner in the Foreign Office, sought in vain to get the necessary foreign loans from the Allied Powers. When these
failed to help, he turned to Italy, which, as one of the victo-
rious powers of World War I, now saw Austria as a useful
buffer between itself and Germany. In 1923, Grandfather
made the first of many major trade agreements with the rep-
resentative of the new Italian premier, Mussolini, whom he
began to visit regularly. Mussolini, as the memoir tells it,

seems to have placed great trust in Grandfather's judgment on issues of trade, and their fruitful association evidently helped to quell the terrible inflation then plaguing Austria.

The idea that Mussolini's Fascist regime was the self-declared enemy of all democratic process, and that *Il Duce*, who advocated the necessity of continuous imperialist conquest as a way to keep the empire alive, was not to be trusted, does not seem to have been an issue. Grandfather's allegiance was never to "party," much less to ideology, but to the Austria he had been serving so successfully since the turn of the century. If, in the immediate postwar years, he had been happy to work with the Socialist leaders Otto Bauer and Viktor Adler, later he was equally content to serve the conservative Christian Socialist Ignaz Seipel. Grandfather seems to have been a genuine patriot: if he was at home in aristocratic circles, he also loved to sit in a Grinzing *Heuriger* (as the Austrian wine bar is called), drinking schnapps or beer with the locals, with whom he swapped jokes and stories in the Viennese dialect of the *Volk*, with its soft vowels and dropped consonants. Not surprisingly, then, although he knew precisely how precarious the financial and economic situation of Austria had become, Grandfather was blind to the insidiously growing Nazi presence that was to culminate in the Anschluss.

I surmise this from a story my cousin Herbert Schüller, born in 1905, tells in his memoir. In the winter of 1938, Herbert, whose business and family were based in Budapest, decided to take a ski vacation with his younger brother George in the Arlberg. Passing through Vienna at the beginning of March, he saw "in the streets and many other places hordes of yelling and shouting young men . . . milling around with swastika bands around their arms. They seemed entirely uncontrolled by the police and were a nuisance to everybody who did not cry with them, 'Heil Hitler.'" Even Herbert, who describes himself and his wife Lorle (then pregnant) as living "the sybaritic life of the Hungarian upper middle class," became nervous and wondered whether it would be prudent to go on a ski vacation. On March 3, he visited Grandfather at his office in the Ballhausplatz and asked whether it would be safe to travel. "Let the rabble yell," was Grandfather's response. "They will soon get hoarse." So Herbert and George went on their ski vacation. On the night of the Anschluss they had no choice but to ski cross-country for hours before they could catch a train that would bring them back to Vienna and Budapest respectively—and soon thereafter into exile.

How could Grandfather have been so wrong at this fateful moment? In his memoir, recounting Schuschnigg's last speech to Parliament (a speech whose section on economic affairs Grandfather himself had written), he recounts Schuschnigg's plans for the plebiscite of March 13, in which seventy percent or so of the voters were projected to vote for an independent Austria, but which was suddenly canceled when Hitler brazenly declared the plebiscite null and void and ordered his troops to cross the border the night of March 11. "I went home," writes Grandfather, "and knew it was over." As for the next day, when his resignation was accepted by his former close colleagues and friends, without the proffer of his pension (after forty years of service), he admits dryly (UV, 176), "Despite everything, I had not had the right conception."

But what was the right conception, and who had it?

Egon Schwarz, a professor of German literature at Washington University in St. Louis, who was fifteen at the time and who came from a very different Jewish milieu—a lower-middle-class family living in very modest circumstances and observing the High Holy Days—recalls in his memoir that his mother had gone to Pressburg (Bratislava) for a few days to visit her family and had planned to come back in time for the plebiscite. When it was canceled and the Anschluss announced on the radio on the evening of March 11, he and his father were stunned. Hadn't Schuschnigg promised just a few days earlier that if the plebiscite succeeded, he would include Social Democrats in his government?[8]

Why was what seems with hindsight an inevitable outcome so hard to predict? I will come back to this difficult question later. On the 13th, in any case, the Mintz and Strauss families fled. A day or two later, Grandmother Schüller and her mother, Great-grandmother Rosenthal took a night train to Rome, where my Aunt Susi (my mother's middle sister who had married an Italian, Giorgio Piroli, two years earlier) lived. The two grandmothers then found asylum in England and later in the U.S. Grandfather stayed behind, partly because he was reluctant to leave without having settled the question of his pension, partly, I suppose, out of pride: he felt his colleagues might still need his counsel and he might still make a contribution. But within days, it became doubtful that he would be so much as *permitted* to leave. In response to his application to the Gestapo to emigrate to Rome, a letter came from the SS-Standartenführer Dr. Wächter that read as follows:

It is well known that Schüller functioned as a typical traitor of a Capitalist and freemasonly persuasion and that he was undoubtedly connected to the international plot to reduce Austria to slavery to the Western powers.

This letter, dated 20 June 1938, is signed "Heil Hitler!" A second letter, written a week later, explains that because of his advanced age, there is no point putting Schüller in a concentration camp, but that the permission to leave Austria would not be granted.

As for Grandfather's putative pension, not only did the Nazis consider his request laughable, but they now went after his other assets, including the securities he held in his Swiss bank account. According to the new law of April 27, 1938, Grandfather had to sign these over immediately: his list includes such items as thirty shares of Bendix Aviation at $12.00 a share and another thirty of American Metal at $25.00 a share. It is signed and dated "Wien, 11 Juli." By the time the government tried to obtain these stocks from Geneva, "the Jew Dr. Richard Schüller" had disappeared. But as late as January 2, 1939, the Reichsbank notified the Ministry for Commerce that these funds must be appropriated and delivered immediately [Figure 8]. The document has the handwritten codicil "Investigate!" (*Ausforschen!*), and the follow-up letters all refer to "the Jew Richard Schüller" or "Richard Schüller Israel."

I have typescripts of these documents, and whenever I see the "Heil Hitler!" above the official signature, my stomach churns. Grandfather himself, however, seems to have taken things calmly: in June 1938, Susi came from Rome and stayed with him in the beautiful old apartment on the

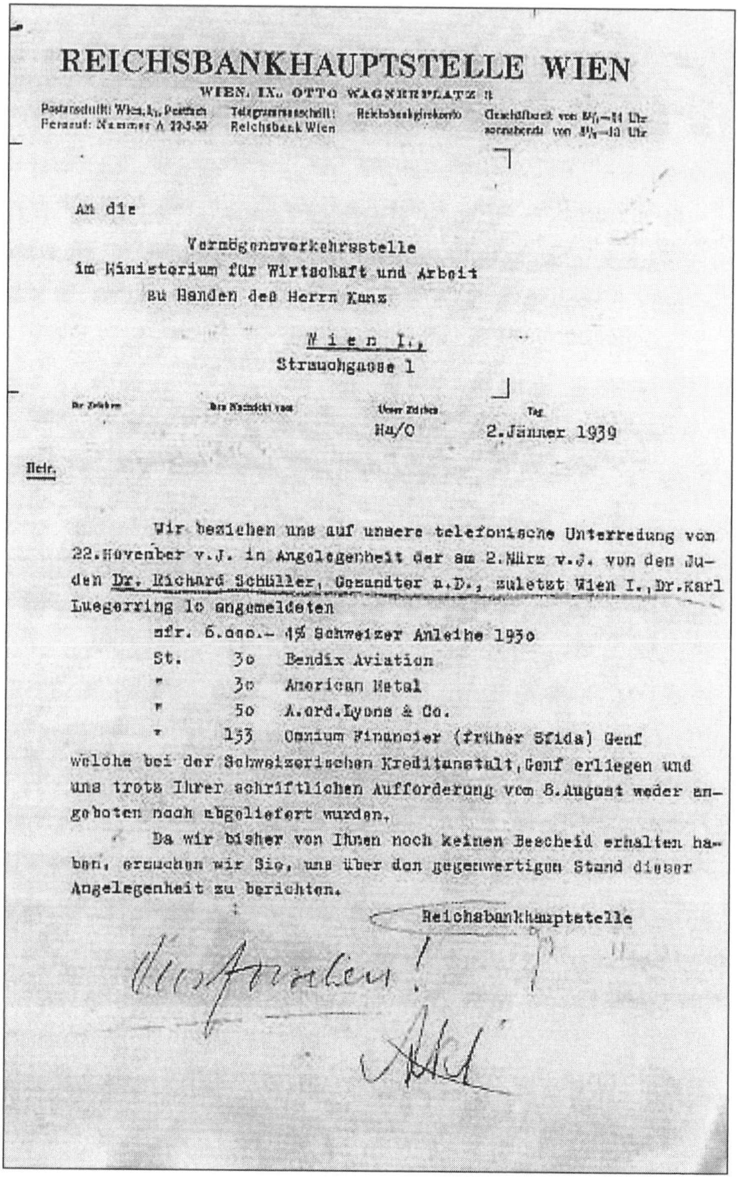

REICHSBANKHAUPTSTELLE WIEN

WIEN, IX., OTTO WAGNERPLATZ 3

An die

Vermögensverkehrsstelle
im Ministerium für Wirtschaft und Arbeit
zu Handen des Herrn Kunz

Wien I.,
Strauchgasse 1

Ha/O 2.Jänner 1939

Betr.

Wir beziehen uns auf unsere telefonische Unterredung vom 22.November v.J. in Angelegenheit der am 2.März v.J. von dem Juden Dr. Richard Schüller, Gesandter a.D., zuletzt Wien I.,Dr.Karl Luegerring 1o angemeldeten

sfr. 6.ooo.- 4% Schweizer Anleihe 193o
St. 3o Bendix Aviation
" 3o American Metal
" 5o A.ord.Lyons & Co.
" 153 Omnium Financier (früher Sfida) Genf

welche bei der Schweizerischen Kreditanstalt,Genf erliegen und uns trotz Ihrer schriftlichen Aufforderung vom 8.August weder angeboten noch abgeliefert wurden.

Da wir bisher von Ihnen noch keinen Bescheid erhalten haben, ersuchen wir Sie, uns über den gegenwärtigen Stand dieser Angelegenheit zu berichten.

Reichsbankhauptstelle

FIGURE 8. Notification from the Reichsbank, January 1939.

Ringstrasse, they played bridge with Aunt Ritti and her friends and went to such parks and cafés as still permitted Jews to be on the premises. He recalls the day in June when his tailor Wesely said, "Business is better. But if I were you, Excellency, I wouldn't stay in this city" (UV, 180). And indeed in July, Grandfather's escape took place. He took the night train and then bus to Gurgl, high in the Austrian Alps on the Italian border, where Susi and Giorgio were waiting for him. All three took a mountain trail up the Ferwalljoch [Figure 9]. Here is Grandfather's later account:

FIGURE 9. Giorgio Piroli, Ferwalljoch, near Gurgl, July 1938.

It was a beautiful day, the ascent easy. We lunched, met no one, no Austrian border guards. After about three hours, when we had reached the top, Susi gave me a little shove and said, "Now you're in Italy." She and Giorgio turned around and went back. From the frontier on, the trail was bad: a steep ridge that was supposed to have a rope rail but the rope was broken and hung down. Then a snowfield where two Italian border guards with a police dog came toward me. They said passage on this path was forbidden and I must immediately go back. I said, "I am fleeing." They: "Yes but you cannot proceed without permission." I: "I'm tired, may I rest in your barracks and then explain." They: "But afterwards you will have to go back." They left me, since they knew I couldn't go forward or back. It had become foggy and I had to climb along steep ridges and couldn't see the ground.

In the barracks, I found a dozen soldiers and the lieutenant and sergeant that I had met in the snow. . . . An old Tyrolean woman was waiting on them. I had tea with rum, went outside with the lieutenant, told him who I was without mentioning Mussolini, and suggested that he ask his commander what should happen to me. Evidently he regarded this as an interesting distraction from the boredom of border patrol. He let me sign a protocol that I had been taken a prisoner for forbidden border crossing. I was thrilled. Slept in a room with the sergeant and his dog after I had eaten a schnitzel. In the morning we made our way to Merano, walking rapidly for four hours; I felt it in my legs. The Italians were nice, carried my rucksack, gave me food and drink, photographed our group. [Figure 10.] Down in the valley, we took a car . . . and in Merano they took me to a hotel and requested only that I not go too far away. I went for a walk, ate some onion roast and drank two pitchers of beer. The commander said that the lieutenant should have sent me back. But since my passage was a fait accompli, he would ask the prefect in Bolzano what to do. The prefect, in turn, said he would make inquiries in Rome. At night, he came to me with a friendly smile and said I was free and the guest of the Italian government. A telegram had come from Rome: "L'amico Schüller è benvenuto—Mussolini." A police detective accompanied me to Florence, took care of all my needs, and put me on a bus to Vallombrosa [where Grandmama and Great-Grandmama, Giorgio and Susi, Mother, Walter, and I were on hand to welcome him].

Wonderful days in Vallombrosa, reunited and freed from the worst pressure, despite the uncertainty of the future. (UV, 180–81)

FIGURE 10. Richard Schüller with Italian Military Border Guard, Alpine Pass, en route to Merano, Italy, July 1938.

The photograph of Grandfather with the Italian soldiers [Figure 10] hangs in my study. What intrigues me is that, whereas the soldiers are wearing the appropriate alpine uniform, Grandfather is wearing a tweed suit with knickers, a vest, a shirt and tie, a hat, and he is carrying an umbrella. Everyone is smiling, but again, consider the ironies of the whole situation. At a time of hysterical nationalist frenzy, the Austrian Jewish diplomat is saved by *Il Duce*, the Italian Fascist dictator, because of their longstanding diplomatic friendship. Richard Schüller can converse with the soldiers who arrest him in fluent Italian. Again, had he not been trained all his life as an Austrian sportsman, had he not known these mountains intimately from countless summer vacations and winter ski trips, he probably wouldn't have made it. Discipline—the discipline that allowed a man close to seventy to do without any of the amenities we now take for granted—stood him in good stead. He must, after all, have slept in those clothes: I doubt he carried a clean shirt or even a toothbrush in his rucksack. And he knew he had lost all his material belongings.

At the same time, I find Grandfather's actions between March and July 1938 somewhat troubling. He might easily have been imprisoned, interred, or killed by the Gestapo, as were many of his friends. He let his wife and family leave without him because he was determined to get his pension—which he never got, although many years later there were some war reparations. He thought that his old friends and colleagues would remain loyal to him; of course they did not. It is not clear that, even after his *Sound of Music* mountain-style escape, he fully understood what had happened—and what would happen to other Austrian Jews less fortunate than himself. On the contrary, after the Vallombrosa idyll, when our immediate family had left for America and he remained in Rome for another three months before going on to London, where he hoped to obtain some work and a visa to the United States, he talks of "once again enjoying Rome" and spending charmed hours in his beloved Vatican Museum and with former diplomatic friends. Felice Guarneri, the president of the Bank of Rome, reports Mussolini having asked him, "*Che crede è venuto tra le monte?*" ("Guess who's come over the mountains?"). *L'amico Schüller.*" (UV, 181). Grandfather makes no criticism, here or anywhere in the correspondence I have seen, of the Italian Fascist government and its new alliance with Nazi Germany.

Grandfather's values were, in this regard, the values of his time and place. Equal rights were deemed to be less important than individual integrity and heroism, grace under pressure, the ability to win over others by the force of one's own personality, and, above all, *action* rather than introspection as to what might have been, especially since the fledgling Austrian Republic was increasingly threatened by dire food shortages, financial collapse, and possible dissolution. As for *Amerika*, although Grandfather had spent happy days there on a lengthy diplomatic mission in 1928, it was too strange and too remote a place to figure largely in one's consciousness. In 1928 America, Grandfather recalls, when he was taken for a drive up the Hudson by an embassy official, he was amazed to see limousines equipped with machine guns to ward off "gangsters," and he was shocked by the extremes of wealth and poverty on exhibit in New York. The skyscrapers, beautiful as they were at night, were

spoiled in daylight by the ugly fire escapes that Theodor
Adorno would later complain about in *Minima Moralia*. In
Chicago, when Grandfather was met at the train by a
Colonel Causey and a Colonel Smith, who had been sta-
tioned in Vienna, the two Americans immediately produced
bottles of bootlegged whiskey, much to Grandfather's
bemusement.

My own view of *Amerika*, if I could claim to have a view
at age seven, would have been similar. My favorite children's
book at the time of emigration was called *Die lustigen Neun*
(*The Jolly Nine*) by one Beate Jacoby, published in Stuttgart
in 1930. It was this book that my mother unpacked so that
I might read it while sitting on the hatbox in the Innsbruck
police station on the night of March 13. Just nine months
earlier, Mother had read it to me when I broke my left arm
on summer vacation in Selva. In those days, a fracture was a
major event, and the country doctor in the Italian border
village couldn't see me till the following morning, when he
made a huge plaster cast which remained on my arm for
months. But the night of the fall (the boy whose family was
renting the upper floor of our *pensione* was carrying me
around on his shoulders and dropped me), I was in great
pain, alleviated by Mother's reading of my favorite chapters
of *Die lustigen Neun*.

What made this book so special? Jacoby tells the story
of the Overbeck family—a Herr Professor Overbeck who
teaches music at the Leipzig Conservatory, his wife Helene,
depicted as the ultimate charming, tactful, good-humored,
and kind Mother, and their eight children (five girls, three
boys). Into this household comes ten-year-old Brigitte, a
cousin from Dresden and only child, whose ailing mother

has to spend some months in the sanatorium. How Brigittchen is assimilated into the noisy, rowdy Overbeck family constitutes the plot of *Die lustigen Neun*. Overprotected and somewhat spoiled, she learns how to hold her own in family fights (there is even a mock trial where she is accused of various "crimes" by the "big ones"), goes to school for the first time (she had been educated at home), and participates in naughty games, like taking little bites from the sausages Mother Helene has prepared for a buffet dinner for the Professor's colleagues.

On the surface, the world of *Die lustigen Neun* could hardly be less political, but in retrospect, its motivation is both conservative and staunchly nationalist. Large families represent the good—Brigitte is always pitied for being an only child—and mothers know their place and devote themselves to their children. Pauline, the trusted maid, serves fine meals, but everything is simple and wholesome, with no frills. The girls share one room, the boys the other. The Herr Professor, whose privacy is always respected, rules this household with unquestioned authority. Christmas preparations are endless, and a whole chapter details Brigitte's initiation into the specific rituals of her first Christmas in Leipzig. Visits to the fair are enlivened by exotic snake charmers who speak "Turkish" charms, like "Toni, millijoni, makkaroni, maledoni, schima, schima, schima"—charms that make the Frau Professor laugh when the children repeat them at home, since she knows very well just how "Turkish" these snake charmers really are. And so on.

But the episode relevant to my own story begins in the chapter "A Visit from Amerika." One morning at breakfast, the Herr Professor receives a letter that surprises him exceedingly. Who is it from? None other than his old schoolfriend Waldemar Stiefel, who emigrated to America "many years ago." Stiefel has a sixteen-year-old son who wants to study music at the Conservatory with Professor Overbeck, and Waldemar wishes him to come for a trial visit to see if he has sufficient talent, so he proposes that the professor take the son into his home for the duration. "*Echt amerikanisch*," remarks Helene. "Clear and straightforward and as practical as possible." When Father protests that it's an imposition to expect the Overbecks to take in a total stranger, Mother declares herself ready to do so. After all, there *is* the guest room! The children are excited: "A strange sixteen-year-old boy, and an American to boot." How amazing! The invitation is issued and accepted but without divulging anything, not even young Stiefel's surname. True, Waldemar Stiefel refers to his son as "My Benjamin," but, as Mother explains to the nine children, that might just mean "my youngest," as it does in the Bible story. Joseph, the oldest Overbeck boy, holds this as probable, since "Benjamin Stiefel can't be the name of any sensible person."

Is this a veiled anti-Semitic slur? I would guess so, and if Waldemar Stiefel is Jewish, it makes better sense that he emigrated to Amerika. What normal bourgeois of the Overbeck circle would have done so? Soon, in any case, a telegram arrives, announcing Benny's impending arrival. The Overbecks are stunned: one should write a letter giving the hosts plenty of time to prepare, not a telegram saying the Stiefels have already arrived in Hamburg! Again, this mode of behavior is designated as *echt amerikanisch*. And, sure enough, Benny's visit turns out to be a disaster.

He is rude, insults the older children, owns too many expensive clothes and shoes, and even has his own alarm clock! He refuses the Professor's invitation to have a glass of beer, saying he prefers soda water, much to the disgust of the older Overbeck boys, who say that soda water tastes like feet that have gone to sleep! So much for Prohibition America! When the time comes for the entrance exam to the Conservatory, Benny, who has been too lazy to practice properly, fails. Waldemar arrives and seems pleased, because now Benny will be happy to go into his father's business—a business never specified but evidently highly lucrative. On Benny's last night in Leipzig, he goes to a student party and drinks too much of the unaccustomed beer. Back home, he locks himself out after putting on his nightshirt, and the good Pauline mistakes him for a ghost. Thus ends Benny's absurd adventure at the Overbecks. The rich, "pushy," *echt amerikanisch*, and probably Jewish visitor is no match for the good traditional family of the Herr Professor. For however different from one another the eight Overbeck children and their cousin are, theirs is a life of order and rule, of custom and ceremony.

This was, in any case, the book that I was reading in Innsbruck while our suitcases were being searched and our money taken away. The spring of 1938 was an odd sort of idyll. Fortunately, both my grandfathers had good-size bank deposits in Switzerland: Grandfather Mintz, who was an eminent *Justitzrat*, had had the foresight to deposit his legal fees from foreign clients in Swiss banks; Grandfather Schüller had deposited much or all of his League of Nations salary in Geneva. These funds, itemized in the notorious document described above, tided us over. I learned only much later from my cousin Hedy, who is four years older than I and thus overheard some of the late-night family conversations at the Pension Schmelzberg in Zurich, that the decision to apply for visas to the United States was by no means an automatic one. Otto Strauss evidently thought the Nazi Anschluss might blow over and perhaps we could go back to Vienna. My parents considered emigrating to a familiar Italy, where they would be reunited with Susi and the Schüller grandparents. It was only Grandfather Mintz who had the foresight to know that these were simply not viable alternatives for Jews, that indeed we *must* go to America.

In his youth, Alexander Mintz had aspired to become a writer: he was a member of the literary coterie of Arthur Schnitzler, Hermann Bahr, and Peter Altenberg that met at the Café Griensteidl. Later in New York, he came back to the love of his youth and wrote a novel about the social life of Vienna in the interwar years. Unfortunately, it was unfinished when he died quite suddenly of a heart attack in 1941. In her journal, his daughter Stella reports that once having settled down as a lawyer and married Amélie Schur, the heiress of a wealthy and prominent Russian Jewish family, whom he met in Baden-Baden, he became a more observant Jew, in keeping with norms of the Schurs. Accordingly, he understood, as the wholly assimilated Schüller side of the family evidently did not, that as Jews we must leave not only Austria but Europe itself.

But when, in late May, the longed-for visas actually came through, the thought of leaving became very painful, especially for my mother, deeply attached as she was to her own mother and grandmother. The old ladies were, for the moment, safe in Rome with Susi, and despite the great expense, Mother decided to take Walter and me to Italy for a farewell visit before our August sailing. Daddy remained behind to take care of our affairs. We spent the first weeks in Ostia, where, with the help of a large rubber tube, I learned how to swim in the beautiful Mediterranean. Then we went to Vallombrosa in the mountains near Florence, where we were reunited with Grandfather Schüller as well as the two grandmammas. Here, in translation, is a letter I wrote Daddy from Vallombrosa, one of the last I wrote in German:

Dear Daddy:

I can't say that it was nice of me not to write you for such a long time. But in Ostia there was really no time. In the morning: get dressed, go to the beach, in the afternoon, go to the beach again and then go to sleep. But here I promise to write often. Here there are huge strawberries [a not very convincing drawing follows]. Are there already strawberries in Zurich? Every day we go for a walk. I got a beautiful new dress. It has blue flowers.

Best wishes,
your Gabriele

Was I really this unaware of the larger situation that necessitated all these movements? Or was it just good form to convey only good news? In *Eine Reise nach Amerika*, I record, like the good little Austrian girl I was, how nice it was that our summer vacation (*Sommerfrische*) involved both the ocean and the mountains—the perfect combination.

In mid-July, Mother, Walter, and I took the cross-continental train trip that would culminate in Rotterdam, from where we were sailing for America. This particular journey

sounds somewhat fraught, even in my matter-of-fact and
cheerful childhood account. First, we had to make a stop in
Berne for our Belgian visa, since Belgium now required a
visa merely for passage through its territory. We arrived at
dawn in a terrible rainstorm and had to wait for hours for the
consulate to open. "Mutti bought us something to eat and
we sat in a little churchyard and ate. Luckily it stopped rain-
ing and was quite nice." Finally, the visas secured, we got
back on the train for Basel, where we met my father, and the
next day we proceeded on to Holland. On the train ride
through Belgium, "a friend of my father's who didn't have a
Belgian visa was immediately thrown off the train." I can still
see this incident because my father looked so upset. The
train stopped at a little station, and the man was forced to get
off. There was also talk of a girl who had been "fine" when
she got on in Switzerland but had developed polio en route
to Belgium and had to be carried off the train at a local stop
because she was wholly paralyzed. I don't know if this story
was true, but for years I had an irrational fear of polio.

When we arrived in Rotterdam there was universal
relief. Aunt Hilde and Uncle Otto came from London to
see us off. As for our ship, the *Veendam*, three chapters of my
little book are devoted to its pleasures, as compared to a single one for the escape from Vienna. I describe at great
length the cabins, the stationary bicycles in the sports room
that even had speedometers, and the hopscotch contest at
which I won a Dutch doll. The banquet table on the final
evening was especially impressive: "The New Amsterdam
was there, with three stories made out of sugar, also a glass
swan and a wheelbarrow with ourdouver (*sic*) inside." Time
stood still: I had no thought for the next day or week or

year, I don't recall wondering what New York and our new house would be like, where I would go to school, and so on.

Once in the United States and settled in Riverdale in a small garden apartment with two bedrooms (my parents slept in the living room), I seemed to become an American overnight. My chapter "*Schule*" ("School") begins in German, detailing what grades Walter and I and the twins were in, and suddenly switches into the not quite grammatical English of "After three days I and George [a new refugee friend, formerly Hansi Kaufmann, the son of the philosopher Felix Kaufmann] skipped to 2A." And then comes a list of my friends: Josephine Adair, Mary Philip, Jeanne Kohlhep, Nina Trachtenberg, Cynthia Bakermann, Rose Leved, and Beverly Kipnis. "We were the smartest 2A class. In 2A we did 2B work and in 2B we did 3A work. I got a 100 and AAs all term." It seems Gabriele had indeed arrived. And so patriotic was I in those prewar years that a whole chapter is devoted to "The Statue of Liberty" and contains the familiar song:

> My country 'tis of thee
> Sweet land of liberty
>   Of thee I sing.
> Land where my fathers died
> Land of the pilgrim's pride
> From every mountain side
>   Let freedom ring.

It wasn't, of course, exactly the land where *my* fathers had died and the "pilgrim's pride" meant little to me. But I knew somehow, without being at all able to articulate it, that

I was very lucky to be in America, now newly spelled with a
c. And whatever has happened in the years that followed,
that special feeling for America has never disappeared.
However critical I have often been of our schools and universities, our politics and popular culture, our materialism
and Benny Stiefelesque lack of manners, however I long for
that Viennese *Kultur* that was so deeply ingrained in me,
however much I want to visit the museums and galleries of
Berlin and Rome, lecture at French or German universities,
and sit in the cafes and gardens of Prague or Vienna, when
my plane touches down in the United States and it's time to
go through Passport Control and Customs, I always feel
enormously relieved. Even after the attack of 9/11, I know
that I am home and nowhere near a threatening or threatened national border.

Americans who were born here take this openness very
much for granted. When they drive up the Merritt Parkway
and pass the sign that says "Welcome to Connecticut!" they
barely take note. That's just a state line, after all, not a border! And even the Canadian or Mexican borders, more
closely patrolled though they have now become, don't con-
found them. But when I visit Austria or Germany, I continue to be fearful of those signs that read *Die Grenze*. Indeed,
in the early '80s, when the reunification of Germany was
still wholly unanticipated, and my husband Joseph and I
were crossing from West to East Berlin on the S-Bahn, I
became acutely anxious. The eastward leg was quite
uneventful, but on the return trip, when huge crowds
pushed and shoved their way through the lines at the border control, and the East German officials were glaring at
us and shouting directions, I panicked and clutched my

passport as if "they" would force me to stay, indeed, as my life depended on it. My husband, born and raised in New Orleans, couldn't understand my fear. After all, nothing had happened.

Such stress reactions are, of course, wholly trivial in the context of the Nazi atrocities of the Hitler years, and despite my fear of frontiers, by the 1980s I knew that, although America had become, ironically enough, the "land where my father died," and my mother as well—in 1973 and 1978 respectively—I was not quite the all-American girl I had long tried to be. A part of me would always look to Europe, and specifically to Vienna, as home. And so, in 1994, when a young feminist historian named Doris Ingrisch invited me to Vienna to speak about my mother's career as an economist, at a conference called "Women Intellectuals & Exile," I accepted with pleasure.[9] But the early December week I spent in Austria contained all the familiar tensions. I walked down the snowy Kärntner Strasse from the Hotel Astoria to the Opera, knowing that I would be perfectly safe, even at midnight, in the well-patrolled metropolis. I bought beautiful table linens in a shop on the Graben called Zur schwäbischen Jungfrau, founded in 1720. Doris and her husband took me to a wonderful production of *Die Zauberflöte* at the Opera. And on December 8, the Feast of the Immaculate Conception, I wandered into the Michaeler Kirche and heard Bach and Mozart played magnificently on the organ during mass in the gorgeous Baroque interior.

The conference itself was more problematic. One of my fellow speakers was the historian Erika Weinzierl, who has written widely on modern Austrian history and even on such "problems" as Austrian anti-Semitism. But to me, who had just flown in from California and was seated right next to her, she did not address a single word the entire evening. Was it that she was anti-Semitic? Anti-American? Anti-feminist? Or just not interested in strangers? I never found out. But in the discussion period, when a young woman asked the panel what her career chances in Vienna might be, given her status as a citizen of Carinthia, close to the then Yugoslav border, Professor Weinzierl and her colleagues merely shrugged as if to say, well, yes, if that's your background, it can hardly be surprising that you don't find a job!

In Vienna, as a few days later in Salzburg, where I had been invited to lecture by Dorothea Steiner, a charming professor of American Studies, I was often asked how it was that I, primarily a scholar of modern Anglo-American poetry, knew German. I would explain that I was originally Austrian and had left the country as a small child. Again and again, I would be asked why. When I said that I had been a refugee, there was invariably dead silence and the subject was quickly changed.

In his great memoir *Die Befreite Zunge (The Tongue Set Free)*, Elias Canetti, the son of Sephardic Jewish parents, describes his odyssey from the small polyglot city of Ruschuk in Bulgaria, where he was born in 1905, to Manchester, England, where he had a proper Victorian nanny and his father was a successful businessman until his sudden death in 1913, to Vienna, chosen by his very young and stage-struck widowed mother as the place she wished, for the time being, to settle. The following anecdote describes a school incident that took place during Canetti's first year in the imperial capital:

Paul Kornfeld was the boy I walked home with . . . . He was tall and thin and a bit awkward, his legs seemed to want to go in different directions, there was always a friendly grin on his long face. "You walk with him? Herr Tegel [the teacher] asked me upon seeing us together in front of the school. "You're offending your teacher." Paul Kornfeld was a very bad pupil, he answered every question wrong if he answered at all; and since he always grinned at such times—he couldn't help it—the teacher was hostile to him. On the way home, a boy once scornfully shouted at us: "Yids!" I didn't know what that meant. "You don't know?" said Kornfeld; he heard it all the time, perhaps because of his conspicuous way of walking. I had never been yelled at as a Jew—either in Bulgaria or in England. I told Mother about it, and she waved it off in her arrogant way: "That was meant for Kornfeld. Not for you." It wasn't that she wanted to comfort me. She simply didn't accept the insult. For her, we were something better, namely Sephardim. Unlike the teacher, she didn't want to keep me away from Kornfeld, on the contrary: "You must always walk with him," she said, "so that no one hits him." It was inconceivable to her that anyone would dare to hit *me*.[10]

The drawing of such fine and subtle distinctions—cultural, social, ethnic—in the face of a Vienna that was gearing up to eliminate the very possibility of distinctions among Jews: this was the modus operandi of the world of my parents, a world so self-contradictory one can never quite describe it.

CHAPTER TWO

"German by the Grace of Goethe"

Kennst du das Land, wo die Zitronen blühn,
Im dunkeln Laub die Gold-Orangen glühn,
Ein sanfter Wind vom blauen Himmel weht,
Die Myrte still und hoch der Lorbeer steht—
Kennst du es wohl? Dahin! Dahin
Möcht ich mit dir, o mein Geliebter, ziehn!

[Do you know the land where the lemons grow,
Where, in the dark trees the gold oranges glow,
A soft wind blows in the blue sky,
The myrtle silent and the laurel high—
Do you know it well? Down there! Down there
I would with you, oh my lover, repair!
                        —Goethe, *Wilhelm Meisters Lehrjahre*[1]

Paul [Wittgenstein] spent years traveling round the world from one opera house to another, only to announce in the end that the Vienna Opera was the greatest of them all. *The Met's no good, Covent Garden's no good, La Scala's no good.* None of them was any good compared with Vienna. *But of course,* he said, *The Vienna Opera is really good once a year.* Once only a year—but all the same! He could afford to visit all the famous opera houses of the world in the course of a *crazy* three-year trip, getting to know all the moderately great, really great, and positively outstanding conductors and the singers whom they courted or chastised. His head was full of opera, and as his life became progressively more dreadful—with increasing rapidity during his latter years—it too became an opera, a grand opera of course, which naturally had a tragic ending.
                    Thomas Bernhard, *Wittgenstein's Nephew* (1982)[2]

LISTENING TO THE MYSTERIOUS CHILD MIGNON SING THE
song about the land where the lemons grow, Goethe's
Wilhelm Meister observes that the longing expressed in the
refrain "*Dahin! Dahin*" ("Down there! Down there!"),
repeated with variation in the next two stanzas, is as urgent
as it is irresistible in its promise. My father, who was given
to dramatic recitations of "Kennst du das Land," explained
to us children that Mignon's song was the touchstone of
poetry, that here Genius with a capital *G* was to be found.
And Goethe's genius was, of course, emblematic of the great
Germanic tradition—a tradition that would be called into
question, in the post-Nazi era, in such devastating fictions
as Thomas Bernhard's *Wittgenstein's Nephew*. In this mem-
oir/novel, the narrator renews acquaintance with his old
friend Paul (a mathematician who happens to be the great
philosopher's nephew), who is confined in the Vienna mental hospital ironically called the Ludwig Pavilion, next door
to the Hermann Pavilion, where the narrator himself is
being treated for lung disease. The twin disorders of the
two friends become emblematic of Bernhard's own love-
hate for a seductive High Culture that went hand in hand
with the mendacity of the war years, especially as they
played out in a Vienna that, as early as the 1920s, had put up
so little resistance to the Nazi ethos.

Take the case of my art historian uncle, Otto Kurz,
married to my mother's sister Hilde. Kurz, as his lifelong
colleague Ernst Gombrich relates in a moving memoir,[3] was
born in 1908, the only child of a physician originally from a
small Jewish community in Moravia. Unlike my immediate
family, Uncle Otto remained openly Jewish, if largely secularized. While still a student at the Humanistisches

Gymnasium, he worked part-time in the library of the Museum of Art and Industry, where he began his own research, gathering data for his first articles, published before he was twenty, on such arcane topics as the popularity of Dürer's prints in early 16th century Portugal, as evidenced in Johannes Cochläus's 1512 edition of Pomponius Mela's *Cosmographia*. Gombrich, Kurz, and Hilde Schüller all met in 1929 in the seminar (the Zweites Kunsthistorisches Institut) of Julius von Schlosser at the University of Vienna. Schlosser was considered the leading Austrian art historian of his time. Gombrich recalls that the first seminar paper he heard Kurz read was on a board game designed by the German Renaissance carver Hans Kels. His erudition, Gombrich recalls, was legendary even in this very scholarly circle.

But this zeal for *Wissenschaft* was offset by what were, to say the least, troubling circumstances. "These were tense and unhappy times in Austria," writes Gombrich, "and the chances of employment for a young scholar were exiguous in the best of cases, and non-existent for students of Jewish extraction." But not only were there zero job prospects for Jews earning doctorates in art history; there was, even before Hitler came to power in 1932, persistent physical harassment:

The University enjoyed 'extraterritorial' immunity from police interference, which led to a reign of terror by Nazi thugs. Kurz was among the victims of their brutal violence when he was assailed in the University Library and hit over the head with a steel truncheon. After his recuperation he was welcomed back by Schlosser to his seminar with a line from Schiller: "*Monument von unserer Zeiten Schande*" ["Reminder of the disgrace of our time"], but

Schlosser had no more power or determination to put an end to
this disgrace than had the other members of the professorial body.

Kurz's story, as other accounts of the period confirm, was
entirely typical: in *Vienna and Its Jews*, George Berkley
describes a particularly nasty conflict in the medical school's
Anatomical Institute in 1930 and observes, "The entire
University was becoming a battleground, for it was becoming increasingly common for Nazis to beat up Jewish students, then toss them down the ramp to the sidewalk where
the waiting police would then charge the victims with dis-
turbing the peace."[4]

   From the perspective of the American university today,
the notion of, so to speak, legalized physical assault seems
almost unimaginable, and Gombrich's account, grim as it is,
doesn't really explain the situation. Why couldn't the
prominent Professor von Schlosser, himself an Aryan, "put
an end to this disgrace"? Why couldn't he go to the university authorities and complain about the treatment of his
own students? Were university officials so anti-Semitic that
they would have shrugged it off? More important: why, ten
years before the Anschluss, did the university students
themselves, many of them Socialists, accept the status quo?
Furthermore: why did students want to study arcane topics
of art history if indeed there was not the slightest possibility of obtaining any sort of suitable position? Gombrich
reports wryly that precisely because they had no prospects,
students like Kurz and himself continued to study beyond
their graduation (provided they could live cheaply at home),
and that he and Otto used their postgraduate years to learn
Chinese from a kind missionary at the Ethnological

Museum. Otto, he reports, also studied Arabic. The question is why.

An interview Gombrich gave to Deutschland Radio on the occasion of his ninetieth birthday in 1999 (he was to die two years later) provides a starting point.[5] For all his international renown, Gombrich declares himself to be at home neither in Vienna (where he evidently had few contacts), nor in Germany (where he had received, one after another, the Goethe, Hegel, and Erasmus prizes), nor in the England where he had resided for over sixty years, holding, at various times, not only the Directorship of the Warburg Institute, but also the most prestigious chairs at both Oxford and Cambridge, as well as having been knighted in 1972. "*Ich bin,*" Sir Ernst insists emphatically, "*kein Engländer*" ("I am *not* an Englishman"). In response to a question about the highly educated class (*Bildungsbürgertum*) of his parents' intellectual circle, which evidently counted Schoenberg, Freud, and Mahler as acquaintances, Gombrich replies, "*Bildung* is actually the legacy that comes to us from Goethe." This tradition, he admits "also has its dark side . . . the so-called comprehensive *Bildung* in the German-speaking world was not so comprehensive. Shakespeare belonged to it but not Jane Austen, the great Russians counted, but no Bulgarian." *Bildung*, it seems, was thus quite exclusionary. Nonetheless, Gombrich's own allegiance is firmly to the great Germanic tradition. Asked what role Jewish culture played in his childhood, he replied:

Actually none. My parents had converted. I went to Protestant religious school and can still recite the articles of the Lutheran Creed that we had to memorize. How does one define a Jew? I have been forced to think about this question longer than I have cared to. Jewishness is either a religion, and I don't belong to it, or, according to Nazi teaching, a so-called race, but I don't believe in race.

When the interviewer presses him a bit, asking whether he might at least consider the Jewish tradition as a cultural force, Gombrich gave this answer:

I don't believe that there is a separate Jewish cultural tradition. I think the German Jews were largely assimilated. Many didn't even know that they had Jewish roots. The tradition of *Bildung*, which also played a large part among the Jews, was something quite different . . . . But when one is asked today, one naturally says Yes, I'm Jewish. The right answer would be, I am what Hitler called a Jew. That's what I am.

Candid as these answers are—and Gombrich explains that his lack of Jewish self-identification precludes any interest in, say, the plans for the new Jewish Museum designed by Daniel Libeskind for Berlin[6]—they also testify to a curious blindness on Gombrich's part. The difference—whether religious, ethnic, cultural, or mere quirk of fate—between himself and those German-speaking people who were *not* Jews was, after all, what determined the trajectory of his life, beginning with his and Otto Kurz's move in 1936 to the London-based Warburg Institute. If homelessness was, as Gombrich thought, his particular condition, if, as is implied, the community to which he belonged was one neither of nation nor of ethnicity but the international community of art historians or, more broadly, of scholars and intellectuals, the fact remains that the actual community in question was defined by very particular historical cir-

cumstances, including his years of internment as enemy
alien in England and his financial struggle to support his
wife—a pianist who had studied with Rudolf Serkin in
Vienna—and son.

Yet Gombrich's insistence that his tradition, far from
being in any way Jewish, is the tradition of Goethe was
entirely characteristic of his milieu. In an important study
called *German Jews: A Dual Identity* (1988), Paul Mendes-
Flohr begins by reminding us that Germany was a "belated
nation," becoming a nation-state only after 1870 under
Bismarck. Before 1870, proponents of a unified German
identity were obliged to appeal either to ethnic or to cultural criteria. The former gave us what was called the
Volksnation—the concept of "a given people, which, onto-
logically prior to the state, is bound less by an original
accord than by a common relation of its members to some
combination of historical memory, geography, kinship, tradition, mores, religion, and language."[7] To be *German*, in
this scheme of things, was a question of shared myth, ethnicity, and history. The alternative to this construction of
nationality was the *Kulturnation* of German Enlightenment
culture—the liberal cosmopolitan ethos of *Bildung*, which
had its roots in the classical Greek notion of *paideia*. *Bildung*
was more than "civilization," since, as Wilhelm von
Humboldt pointed out (now it may be clearer why my parents named me after his daughter Gabriele), it was con-
ceived as having a distinct spiritual dimension. Thus the
cult of *Kultur* was gradually transformed into a kind of religion (PMF, 27).

The German (and Austrian) Jews obviously chose the
second alternative. Even if they had wanted to, they could

hardly have been assimilated into the *Volksnation*, whose ethnicity, history, and foundational myths they did not share. But their assimilation into the *Kulturnation* was not without its own problems. In the words of the liberal rabbi Benno Jacob in 1927, the Jews were assimilated "in the accusative" but never fully in the "dative," which is to say that "they assimilated the cultural values of Germany" but "were not assimilated *into* German society. They remained by and large socially apart" (PMF, 3). The Jews were Germans, the historian Wolfgang Benz quips, "by the grace of Goethe" ("*Deutsche von Goethes Gnaden*," see PMF, 5). In pre–World War I Germany, Mendes-Flohr notes wryly, "A set of [Goethe's] writings was the standard bar mitzvah and confirmation present. Many a rabbi wove citations from Goethe into his sermons" (PMF, 27).

Walter Benjamin is a case in point. On the eve of World War I (in which the German Jews fought patriotically for their "nation"), Benjamin, studying in Freiburg, writes a friend that when he "picks up a volume of Goethe" and comes upon a phrase like "*Gross ist die Diana der Epheser*" ("Great is the Diana of Ephesus"), which he takes to be "the most beautiful title of any German poem," he is moved to the point of "los[ing] control." And a few years later, he writes his friend Gershom Sholem, "I am . . . becoming convinced that Goethe—at least in his later years—was an extremely pure person who let no lie cross his lips and into whose pen no lie flowed."[8] Benjamin was to write two of the finest Modernist essays on Goethe: the now classic 1923 interpretation of *Die Wahlverwandschaften* (*Elective Affinities*) and the biographical essay "Goethe" of 1928. Benjamin knew Goethe's work inside out the way a devout Christian might know the Bible, so that even in his later years, when his interests encompass much more contemporary—and offbeat—literature, art, film and the material culture of the Arcades Project, his writings are full of references to his early master.

If Goethe was the literary hero of the youthful Benjamin circle, Kant was its philosophical patron saint. In 1915, the Jewish philosopher Hermann Cohen argued that Kant's ethical idealism bore a fundamental affinity to the ethical monotheism of the Hebrew Bible. The link was considered so close that one Salomo Friedländer produced a catechistic text called *Kant für Kinder* (1922), full of questions like, "Who is our truest guide [*Führer*] on the road to truth?" Answer: "Immanuel Kant!" (PMF, 29–30). And again, Benjamin's essays—indeed of the Frankfurt School as a whole—often begin by positioning themselves in relation to Kantian metaphysics, ethics, or aesthetics. "This is my conviction," writes Benjamin to Scholem in 1917. "Anyone who does not sense in Kant the struggle to *conceive doctrine itself* and who therefore does not comprehend him with the utmost *reverence* . . . knows nothing of philosophy. Thus all adverse criticism of his philosophical style is also pure philistinism and *profane* gibberish" (CWB, 98, my emphasis). Conviction, doctrine, reverence, the profane: this is the vocabulary of devotional writing.

In thus regarding themselves so squarely inside the Kantian-Goethean tradition, the German Jews chose to ignore the serpent in their Garden of Eden: their self-image as keepers of the cultural flame was not necessarily shared by the Aryan intellectuals and artists who were their counterparts. In 1894, for example, the beloved writer Theodor

Fontane produced a poem responding to the many letters of congratulation he had received on the occasion of his seventy-fifth birthday:

> A hundred letters arrived.
> I was dazed with joy,
> Puzzled only by the names
> And by the places from which they came. (See PMF, 6)

Fontane, himself an ardent proponent of the *Volksnation*, expresses malicious surprise that his fan letters bear "names with 'berg' and 'heim' . . . . Meyers come in battalions, / also Pollacks and those who reside even further East, / Abram, Isaac, Israel" (PMF, 6–7). In a similar vein, the poet Stefan George confessed to a friend in 1902 that the Jews "are very gifted in the distribution and transformation of values. To be sure, they do not experience [erleben] things as elementally as we do. *They are altogether different people*. I will never allow them to become the majority in my Society or Year Book."[9]

In this climate, Gombrich's disclaimer, "I am what Hitler called a Jew," should more accurately read, "I am what most 'native' German writers and intellectuals called a Jew." In the interwar years, the *Literatenjuden*, as the Jewish literati were called by Benjamin and his circle, had great successes, but there was always a cloud hanging over them. Think of Martin Heidegger, considered by many the great German philosopher of the 20th century, who repudiated his own (part Jewish) mentor Edmund Husserl and, as a member of the Nazi Party in 1933–45, participated in the university's purge of the Jews. So much for the "special relationship"

Jewish intellectuals had with Kant, Schopenhauer, and Nietzsche, the last-named being, of course, the philosopher the Nazis claimed as their forebear. "The very *Bildung*," writes Mendes-Flohr, "that promised to integrate the Jews into the common fabric of humanity left them in the end virtually isolated within a German society overtaken by nationalism and its invidious myths and symbols" (PMF, 41).

In Vienna, the astonishing success of the Jews, both financial and professional, contributed even more markedly to their undoing. In post-Emancipation Austria, with its conservative Catholic base, the Jews encountered a good deal less overt competition from their Aryan counterparts than was the case in Germany. In the Hapsburg empire, the "absence of a dynamic, indigenous middle class animated by the Protestant ethic of capitalism" facilitated Jewish entrepreneurship.[10] Indeed, Berkley posits, "the country's aristocrats were more interested in breeding and racing horses than in building factories, while its tradesmen were more devoted to playing cards than scrounging for business. Such habits left a vacuum that the newly emancipated Jews hastened to fill" (GBE, 70). They built the country's steel mills and railroads, developed its textile and meat-packing industries, established most of Vienna's leading banks, discovered (like David Fanto) oil deposits in Galicia, and opened many of the fashionable shops along the Ringstrasse. There were even Jews in Parliament (in 1890, fifteen elected Jews sat in the Reichstag), and there was active participation of Jews in the Social Democratic Party, whose founder Viktor Adler was a baptized Jew.

The statistics tell an astonishing story.[11] In 1910, the empire's Jewish population stood at almost 5%, more than that of any other European nation. But in the urban centers, the numbers were much larger: Vienna was 8.7% Jewish, Prague 10%, and Budapest 25% (and hence nicknamed *Judapest*), as compared to only 4–5% in Berlin and 1% in Germany as a whole. By 1910, 60% of the physicians in Vienna were Jews, and Jews controlled the majority of clinical chairs at the University's Medical School. The majority of Vienna's attorneys were Jewish, as were its journalists; 48% of the secondary school population in Vienna was Jewish, as was one out of every three gymnasium and university students. For women, the figures were even higher: 42% of Jewish women attended a gymnasium as compared to 4% of other women.

The overrepresentation of the Viennese Jews in business and the professions came to a boiling point after World War I, when a full third of the shrunken and impoverished Austrian population lived in Vienna and the Eastern Jews, or *Ostjuden*, were pouring into the city from the distant provinces of the former empire, mainly the poor shtetls of Galicia. *Ostjuden* soon became as much a term of opprobrium among assimilated Jews as among non-Jews. By 1923, the Jewish population of Vienna had reached 10% (3% in the country as a whole). The number may seem insignificant, but it was double that of Berlin, and it occurred in a country that was in economic and financial crisis. Moreover, despite the success of Jews in the professions, business, and the intellectual/art world, there were almost no Jews (my Grandfather was a signal exception) in the civil service, the ministry, the diplomatic corps, or the armed forces. And of course the Church played a major role in the political life of the nation: for the better part of the 1920s, the Austrian chancellor was the Christian Social leader Ignaz Seipel—a conservative priest who remained a monarchist and regarded the Socialists as the enemy. In his memoir, Grandfather describes him as follows: "Iron will, strong character. His mind worked like a precision machine. He had no knowledge of economics. But when I explained an issue to him for ten minutes, he understood it perfectly, although he often came to a different conclusion than I and was sometimes precisely right" (UV, 133).

Grandfather prided himself on getting along well with Monsignor Seipel, but how long could the latter's rule have lasted, even under more favorable circumstances? The end of the Seipel era (he stepped down without warning in April 1929, unable to cope with the turmoil of the impending crash and the Socialist attack on the Church) set the stage for the virulent anti-Semitism of the Nazis. In 1931, the year of my birth, the Nazi vote rose 36% in the local elections in Upper Austria, and in the capital of Carinthia, Klagenfurt—today the stronghold of Jörg Haider's Freedom Party—the Nazis emerged as the city's second strongest party. They also did well with student groups, winning, for example, two thirds of the seats in the student senate of the Agricultural Institute of Vienna (GEB, 201–2). In these circumstances, a professor like Julius von Schlosser evidently lacked the nerve or the will to do something about the random beatings of his own students.

As for Gombrich and Kurz themselves, perhaps they were able to keep their equanimity in an increasingly unsavory political milieu because they took such pride in their scholarly and critical abilities. Such intellectual self-confidence is almost unimaginable today. Gombrich and Kurz knew that they were, after all, graduates of the finest schools of Vienna (Gombrich attended the Theresianum—"that select school," as Musil puts it, "for the sons of the aristocracy and gentry that supplied the noblest pillars of the state"),[12]—and that they were studying art history at one of its leading centers. To be beaten, even in the University library, by anonymous Nazi thugs was thus regarded as the kind of bad luck one doesn't take too personally. As for politics, if one had any sense, one stayed, so to speak, *above it*— "above" unfortunately turning quickly into "below."

This was the world I was born into on September 28, 1931, just three months after the Kreditanstalt, the last of the old established banks to have survived the monarchy, collapsed with huge debts. The financial crisis was matched by a diplomatic one, when Austria's plan for a customs union with Germany was blocked, primarily through French pressure, as contravening Austria's Geneva pledges of independence.[13] In May 1932, Engelbert Dollfuss became chancellor. Another devout Catholic, this time of peasant stock, Dollfuss had studied theology in Vienna and was preparing for the priesthood when World War I broke out, and he became a decorated officer. Shifting from the military to the civil service and then the ministry, he earned distinction for his work in agriculture. As chancellor, he ruled autocratically, soon dissolving Parliament (when it made trouble for him), outlawing both the Nazi Party and the SPD (Social Democratic Party), and relying heavily on a paramilitary police force known as the Heimwehr. The saving grace of what was in essence a Fascist government was its firm opposition to Hitler—an opposition that rallied cabinet ministers like Grandfather. [See Figure 1.]

FIGURE 1. Richard Schüller (fourth from left), with Engelbert Dollfuss (fifth from left) and, seated next to Dollfuss, Cardinal Innitzer, Rome, June 1933.

Dollfuss's reign was as short-lived as it was shaky. In March 1934, the Rome protocols between Italy, Austria, and Hungary were signed, allying Dollfuss with another proto-Fascist leader, Admiral Horthy of Hungary as well as with Mussolini. The Rome protocols gave Mussolini a foothold in the Danube basin, Hungary acquired backing against the French-sponsored "Little Entente" (Czechslovakia, Romania, and Yugoslavia), and Austria got a guarantee for protection against German aggression. A triumphant Dollfuss came back to Vienna and in May had his new constitution promulgated. The Dollfuss constitution allowed for only "advisory" powers on the part of Parliament.

Grandfather's account of the Rome protocols, as well as the other trade and tariff treaties between Austria and Italy that he negotiated, makes me more than a little uneasy. True, Mussolini was still the enemy of Hitler—a situation that did not change until his disastrous Abyssinian campaign in 1936—but *Il Duce* openly issued manifestos like the 1932 statement "What is Fascism?" which not only made the case for war as a permanent necessity for the nation wishing to achieve "nobility," but also stated unequivocally that "Fascism combats the whole complex system of democratic ideology and repudiates it," "affirms the immutable, beneficial, and fruitful inequality of mankind," and "denies, in democracy, the absurd conventional untruth of political equality dressed out in the garb of collective irresponsibility."[14] Of course, I tell myself, government officials like Grandfather didn't have much choice. If he wanted to save his country—and it was touch and go—he had to do business with other nations, and England, France, and the United States were not forthcoming. What other nation could be a trading partner? And so, I suppose, Grandfather swallowed his reservations, although he never so much as mentions reservations in his memoir.

Two months after the signing of the Rome protocols, in any case, Dollfuss was dead, assassinated on July 25 in a dramatic Nazi putsch that became the subject of some of the most biting scenes in Brecht's *The Resistable Rise of Arturo Ui* (1941), especially the scene where Ui seduces Mrs. "Dullfeet," in a sequence based on the great seduction of the Lady Anne in *Richard III*. But the event itself was hardly comic: Dollfuss, whatever his errors, was the last holdout against Hitler; Kurt Schuschnigg, the moderate and conciliatory chancellor who succeeded him, was doomed from the start. The news of Dollfuss's murder, writes my Grandfather, "was like an iron fist that pressed down on my heart" (UV, 171). For what hope could there be once the Nazis had dared to kill an Austrian chancellor right in his presidential office? Inexorably, the nation moved toward *Finis Austriae.*

GEORGE KREIS / GEISTKREIS

Just a year before Dollfuss was assassinated, another important figure born in a peasant village died—the great German symbolist poet Stefan George. George was born in Rüdesheim on the Rhine in 1868. In the years when my father was a student at the Akademisches Gymnasium (he graduated in 1917), George was a cult figure—a kind of perfect *fin-de-siècle* aesthete turned Nietzschean prophet of doom. A great formalist whose aim was to purify the German language, ridding it of all solecisms, foreign terms, and portmanteau words, George is little known in the United States, perhaps because his verse is so difficult to translate and because his post–World War I advocacy of a "secret Germany"—a new youthful elite that would uphold proper German spiritual values against the onslaught of an oppressive technological modernity—seemed to look ahead to a Fascism that, in all fairness, George vigorously resisted. Indeed, in 1933, when the Nazis enlisted his support, he fled to Switzerland, where he died.

In a penetrating essay written shortly before the poet's death, Walter Benjamin expresses his love for the early George—the poet of "beautiful and perfect" love songs like

"Die Entführung" ("The Abduction")— but is critical of the later poetry:

George failed to extricate his poetry from the enchanted circle of symbols that—unlike those of Hölderlin—did not come to the surface like springs emerging from the rich soil of a great tradition . . . . At its core, [his symbology] is not really different from the array of symbolic ideas and images derived from the church and the nation that were being proclaimed in France by Barrès at the same time that the "circle" [an adoring band that included Hugo von Hofmannsthal, Max Kommerell, and Friedrich Gundolf] was being formed around the Master. . . . This is why the treasure of secret signs in his poetry already has the appearance of being the impoverished, anxiously preserved property of "style."[15]

Style, Benjamin posits, came to overwhelm and eclipse meaning: "The style is that of *Jugendstil*—in other words, the style in which the old bourgeoisie disguises the premonition of its own impotence by indulging in poetic flights of fancy on a cosmic scale and abusing the word 'youth' as a magic incantation with which to conjure up intoxicated visions of the future" (WB 707).

Adorno was even more critical. In the famous "Lyric Poetry and Society" (1957), one of George's songs to "Maximin" in *Der siebente Ring* (*The Seventh Ring*, 1907) is used as an example of the limitations of bourgeois individualism.

Im windes-weben	[In the weaving wind
War meine frage	My question was
Nur träumerei.	Only daydream.
Nur lächeln war	Only a smile was

Was du gegeben.	What you gave.
Aus nasser nacht	From the wet night
Ein glanz entfacht—	A spark was kindled—
Nun drängt der Mai:	Now May presses on:
Nun muss ich gar	Now must I live
Um dein aug und haar	Day after day
Alle tage	In endless longing
Im sehnen leben.	For your eye and hair.][16]

The last four lines, Adorno admits, "count among the most irresistible in German poetry," but they "seem to be . . . from some corpus neglected by the language, irretrievably lost. The *Minnesänger* could have created such lines if they . . . one would almost say, if the German language itself had succeeded." The reference is to the exquisite sound structure of these breathless two-stress lines, with their internal chiming ("gar" / "haar" / "tage") within the tight formal network of the twelve-line stanza, rhyming *abcdaeecddba*. So tight is the poem's formal texture and structure that it lends an air of universality, of medieval popular song, to what is the expression of the poet's grief at the loss of the beloved— the boy "Maximin" who died when he was only sixteen.

But the homoerotic lyrics to "Maximin" (George had met the "beautiful boy" in question by accident on the street a year before his death) are, according to Adorno, open to criticism in that they presuppose "as a condition of [their] very possibility an individualistic, bourgeois society, and the individual who exists for himself alone." True, the ironic detachment of *"Im windes-weben"* "bans the commonly accepted form, no less than the themes, of bourgeois poetry," but a poem like this one "can speak from no other standpoint . . . than precisely those bourgeois frames of

mind which it rejects . . .and so it feigns a feudal condition."
It contains, in short, no dialectical analysis of the speaking
subject, thus relying on neo-Romantic "stylization" to "save
it from conformism."[17]

Nevertheless for the war generation, to which my
father, born in 1899, belonged, George was, as Benjamin
notes, "the great poet [of modernity], the perfecter of the
decadence whose playfulness he rejected in order to create
for death the space it was to claim for itself at this crucial
turning point. He stands at the end of an intellectual line
that began with Baudelaire" (WB, 711). Coming back from
the war to the impoverished and insignificant little republic
that was now Austria, my father and his friends evidently
found a resonant chord in George's disenchanted vision.
They read Schopenhauer and Nietzsche and became ardent
aesthetes. The beautiful *Jugendstil* editions of *Das Jahr der
Seele* and *Der siebente Ring*, published by Georg Bondi in
Berlin in the late '20s, which I inherited from Daddy, are
considered museum exemplars of book art, with cream-col-
ored linen cover, gold lettering, and elaborate geometric
design [Figure 2].

My father's gymnasium friends were products of the
then classical humanistic education of the German secondary school: eight years of Latin, five of Greek, eight years of
German literature, and three or four of French and English,
as well as a year of philosophy. When I began Greek as a
sophomore at the Fieldston School in New York, Daddy
proudly recited the first few pages of the *Iliad* to me in the
original. But because these young men were inherently
bourgeois, they were soon attending the University and
preparing for practical careers—in my father's case, the law.

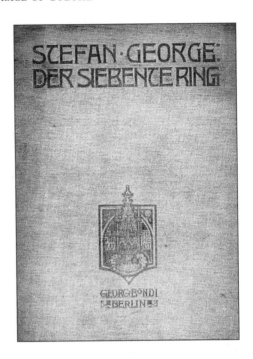

FIGURE 2. Stefan George, *Der siebente Ring* (Berlin: Georg Bondi, 1922).

By 1926, when he married my mother, who was completing her doctorate in economics (Vienna, 1927), Daddy was in private law practice with his father, Alexander Mintz, and his passion for poetry and the other arts had been incorporated into the separate world of the circle known as the Geistkreis. This circle was founded in the fall of 1921 by Friedrich Hayek, the soon to be famous economist, best known for *The Road to Serfdom*, and the legal scholar Herbert Fürth, who was Grandfather Mintz's and Daddy's law partner. Members included such other economists as Gottfried von Haberler, Oscar Morgenstern, and Fritz Machlup, all to become well-known academics in the United States, the art historians Otto Benesch and Johannes Wilde; the musicologist Emanuel Winternitz; the political

philosopher Erich Voegelin; the phenomenologists Felix
Kaufmann and Alfred Schütz; the historian Friedrich
Engel-Janosi; and the mathematician Karl Menger.[18] Many
of these (mostly Jewish) intellectuals held what we now call
day jobs: Winternitz, for example, was a lawyer like my
father, Schütz a banker. Fortunately for them, their work
was not excessively demanding and they could devote
evenings to the theater, opera, concerts, and their own areas
of reading. My father was a devoted member of the
Geistkreis, absorbed in the writing of presentation papers
on such topics as Proust's *Albertine disparue*, then still a
largely esoteric text.

The combination of money-making career and serious
intellectual stimulation after hours was possible in part
because professional men in Vienna, right until the
Anschluss, had virtually no household responsibilities. The
bourgeois home was the wife's domain, and even she was
relieved from most routine housework and much of the
childcare by the servants, who lived in and were paid very
low wages. In his memoir, Grandfather recalls that as a
young husband and father in the pre–World War I years,
he never gave orders to the maids (this was Grandmama's
job) and had never set foot in a shop except when he had to
be fitted for a new suit by his tailor. The next generation
was less extreme, but it remains true that even middle-class
families almost invariably had a *Kinderfräulein* so that the
gnädige Frau could devote herself to more "elevated" activities. My mother actually disliked this state of affairs and
took care of us herself as much as possible, but it is true
that, cynical though it sounds, one reason the Jewish wives
of Vienna were so fearful of emigration, even in the face of

the Nazi threat, is that they were so dependent on their household help.

My father was a distant figure in my early childhood—an elegant presence in dark suits or evening clothes, sporting a pince-nez, a perfectly folded handkerchief in his breast pocket, and a cigarette between his fingers [Figure 3]. Daddy's beloved Geistkreis, as the list above indicates, did not admit women. This was evidently a source of resentment: years later Mother told me that her role, when the Kreis met at our Hörlgasse apartment, was to serve coffee and cake and leave the room discreetly when the actual discussion began. Such

FIGURE 3.
Maximilian
Mintz,
Vienna,
1934

self-effacement was the rule even though a related intellectual circle, this one at the University and primarily for economists, called the Mises Seminar (for its leader, Ludwig von
Mises), did accept women and included my mother and other
women economists like Marianne Herzfeld and Steffi
Braun. Indeed, Mother was a proud intellectual like
Daddy: both she and her two sisters had doctorates, she in
economics, Susi in history, and Hilde in art history. The
stage had been set by their mother Erna Rosenthal
Schüller, who had herself attended, in 1902, the Women's
Academic Lecture Circle (Verein zur Abhaltung akade-
mischer Vorträge für Damen), known in the trade as the
Damenakademie, because only women with sufficient
means—that is, *ladies*—could attend. It was at the
Damenakademie that Erna Rosenthal heard a lecture by
Richard Schüller that led to their marriage in 1903.

Grandmama Schüller, born in 1880, was in many ways
as remarkable as her husband. In a memoir written in
English for her grandchildren, she recalls a rather lonely
childhood, since she was taught at home by governesses
until she was ten and saw very little of her parents. A book-
ish child, unlike her more frivolous younger sisters, Hedy
and Ida, Erna's great moment came when she was ten: it was
finally noticed that she couldn't see so much as the clock on
the wall, and she was taken to an oculist. "I very well
remember," she writes, "how exalted I felt when, with my
new glasses, I saw everything in quite a different way." But,
in keeping with the custom of the day, she was not allowed
to use her glasses except for short periods so as not to strain
her eyes. And of course a young girl could not be photographed wearing glasses! [See Figure 4]

FIGURE 4.
Erna
Rosenthal,
Vienna,
1889.

When Erna was fourteen, her father, Emil Rosenthal, fell ill with what she refers to as a "diseased brain" and spent the rest of his life—four years—in a mental hospital where "Mother devoted her whole time to looking after him." The mysterious illness, I learned only when I was grown up, was syphilis, a disease, so his young daughters were told, one contracted from spending too much time in the *Kaffeehaus*. One would think that Erna was terribly traumatized, but although she remarks in her memoir, "I very well remember the exciting day before Father was taken away," she was, she quickly adds, much more absorbed in her relationship with her new governess, an Englishwoman named Gertrude Arundel White, than in a father who, at best, had spent precious little time with his children and who, on their rare and dreaded visits to the sanatorium, "hardly recognized us."

After Great-grandfather Rosenthal's death in 1898, Malwine Rosenthal, herself only forty, dressed in black for the rest of her life. A misogynist of sorts—though a witty and bemused one—she chose never to remarry and devoted herself to the strict upbringing of her three daughters. She was an avid reader and letter-writer: in 1939–41, when we were already in New York and she and Grandmama still in England, she wrote Walter and me vivid and elaborate stories about London life during the Blitz in her crystal-clear handwriting. Throughout her life, she spent long hours embroidering beautiful tapestries [Figure 5]. She lived to be one hundred and three.

Her daughter, Erna Rosenthal Schüller was more outgoing, more social, and practiced Culture with a vengeance. I don't mean this sarcastically, for her love of art and literature was as infectious as it was sincere. She spoke and wrote fluent French, English, Italian, and Spanish; she played the piano every day and read fiction, drama, biography, and belles-lettres in her various languages. She knew the Kunsthistorisches Museum and the Vatican Museum in Rome inside out and especially loved Raphael and Titian, Tintoretto and Rubens. I still see her poring over the *Times Literary Supplement*, checking off those books she thought she might order. The Rosenthals, originally from

FIGURE 5. Malwine Rosenthal, Vienna, 1905.

Hohenems in western Austria, were not social snobs like the Schüllers, but Grandmama was certainly an intellectual snob in that she wanted contact with "the best that is known and thought in the world." It was fortunate that she had this consuming interest in books and ideas, for in her younger married years she must have been very much alone. Grandfather was invited to nightly social events—balls, soirées, dinners, banquets—from which Grandmama, as the

Jewish wife, was excluded. It was the protocol that resulted from his refusal to undergo baptism for the sake of his career, the *Karrieretaufe*. Like "*le petit Swann*" in Proust's *Le côté de Guermantes*, Grandfather was a pet Jew in the high diplomatic circles of Vienna: he socialized with many aristocrats and had dozens of beautiful medals bestowed by foreign governments.

Grandmama insisted she did not want to go to these "frivolous" affairs anyway, and perhaps she really didn't. For many years, she worked almost full-time, though as a volunteer, for a settlement house for indigent women. The rest of her time was devoted to family and culture. She could walk from her beautiful apartment on the Schottenring to the Opera House, the Burgtheater, and various concert halls. She adored Vienna, where she lived for the first fifty-eight years of her life, not only for its art, but for its natural beauty:

Its wooded hills were not, as Wilhelm von Humboldt said of North Germany, "only trees, grass and plants thrown together without order and grace," but gracefully curved, the forests well tended, charming views everywhere, the meadows a carpet of many colored wild flowers. No fences, no signs of "No Trespassing," but pretty foot-paths, the wood full of primroses and violets in spring, sparkling brooks, and all this reached by tram in one-half hour from the city's center!

Even this description of the landscape of the Wienerwald is seen through the prism of von Humboldt's observation. *Cultivation* was all. As for religion, Grandmama's reading had convinced her that Christianity was a decided advance over Judaism, which in keeping with her time and class, she thoroughly disliked. The Jewish religion, she believed, was "primitive" and "violent"; it was based on the doctrine of an eye for an eye, whereas Christianity was closely linked to Greek thought and was hence necessarily less "crude." I don't know if Grandmama had read Matthew Arnold, but she believed in his distinction between Hebraism and Hellenism, between the narrow moral imperative of the former and the latter's "sweetness and light." As for the irony that, despite that sweetness and light, she could not attend social events with Grandfather because she was the Jewish wife, Grandmama merely shrugged it off as inevitable.

Grandmama's conversation was peppered with comments that such and such novel or play was really *Kitsch* and that so and so was uncultured (*ungebildet*). Everything and everyone was exposed to her razor-sharp judgment. She considered her own daughters vastly superior to her sisters' children, whether Ida's daughters, Anni and Lotte—the former extremely pretty but said to be shockingly *ungebildet*, the latter, who was to become a psychoanalyst, not quite socially adept (*salonfähig*)—or Hedi's sons Stephan and Friedl [see Chapter 1, Figure 3, p. 41], genial little rascals (*Laußbübe*) who were to emigrate to Chile and become quite successful businessmen. The cousins on the paternal side— Ludwig's sons Erwin and Teddy and Hugo's Herbert and George—were more acceptable because better educated than the Rosenthal cousins, but no more than the Rosenthals were they immune to criticism. The "bad boy" in this regard was Teddy Schüller, a mediocre student whose Gymnasium performance was too weak for university entrance and hence was sent to Frankfurt to learn the publishing business. My grandfather then helped him to obtain a good position in a British publishing house, and by the early '40s he had found his niche at Oxford University Press, where he was to remain for the rest of his career. During the war, when Grandmama and Great-grandmother Rosenthal had to spend some months in Oxford while waiting for their U.S. visas to come through, Teddy would evidently cross the street rather than have to greet these elderly Austrian ladies, who might have compromised his new "English" identity. Grandmama was indignant: to think that this ordinary young man, who owed his entire career to her husband, the Sektionschef and Herr Minister, should pretend not to know her was too much! But after the war, our families were gradually reconciled; indeed, one of Teddy's two sons, Andrew Schüller, who is himself an editor at Oxford, is one of my favorite relatives.

Meanwhile, Herbert Schüller, who did have the requisite Gymnasium education with its eight years of Latin and five of Greek and who, like my father, had studied law at the University of Vienna, matriculating in 1926, decided that he did not want to practice law. In his memoir, he explains:

Although getting employment in 1926 was not easy, it was no great problem for me. My uncle Richard Schüller was at that time the highest ranking civil servant in Austria. I went to him and explained my situation, and he promised me his help. After only about one week, he told me to make an appointment with the president of a large textile concern. I doubt that the president actually needed another employee, but whether he did or not, it was quite impossible for him to refuse a request from my very powerful uncle, especially if it concerned his own nephew. Thus, I became an employee of the Hemp Jute and Textile Industry

Corporation and remained in different capacities with it until we left Europe for the United States.

My father [Hugo] was not pleased by my step, but was mostly angry at my uncle because he had placed me in a textile industry and not with a more prestigious industry such as steel, electric equipment, or automobiles.

Here Herbert unwittingly pinpoints the motives that drove his particular social caste: a reliance on preferment, a sense of class, and a strain of anti-Semitism. He is not at all embarrassed about getting his position through my grandfather; that, after all, was how it was done. As for the textile industry, no doubt it was less "prestigious" than the steel industry because, like the New York garment industry, textiles was a business dominated by Jews. Indeed, so anxious were men like Herbert Schüller to escape classification as Jewish that the ultimate compliment in our family was that X or Y didn't "look Jewish." "All the Rosenthals," Grandmama Schüller declares in her memoir, "were fair. None of them looked in the least Jewish, none kept any of the Jewish traditions. They were wholly liberal, optimistic, and good-tempered." Were Jews, then, illiberal, pessimistic, and ill-tempered? Erna's three daughters—Ilse, Susi, and Hilde—were similarly pronounced not to look Jewish. Hilde, the youngest, was a very pretty blonde. Gombrich, in his 1981 obituary, recalls her at nineteen, having the "head of a princess," with "her golden hair, her striking eyes with their dark lashes, her fair complexion and her radiant smile." All the more disappointing, the Schüllers evidently felt, that this lovely girl had chosen to marry the deeply learned but impecunious Otto Kurz, a man, moreover, whose looks were almost stereotypically "Jewish."

My father, whose family was more traditionally Jewish than my mother's, with cousins from Riga and various Russian provinces, had made his bar mitzvah and never, to my knowledge, tried to pass as Aryan. But the Mintzes had more money than the Schüllers and were considered extremely distinguished (*vornehm*). They lived in a large, dim apartment on the Doblhoffgasse near the Rathaus and gave very formal dinners. Justitzrat Alexander Mintz, whose wife Amélie had brought him a large dowry, had his share of aristocratic clients. Then, too, Daddy had been a brilliant student, both at the Akademisches Gymnasium and at the University and was extremely well connected socially, so he was considered a highly appropriate match (*eine gute Partie*) for Ilse Schüller. As a child, I loved to hear the stories about my parents' first meeting at a ball or about the time when Daddy, in tails, arrived at a party and whisked my mother off in a fiacre. In family photographs, she was a beautiful young girl [Figure 6] and then, holding chubby little Gabriele, a smiling lovely mother [Figure 7]. But by the time my own memories of her come into focus—namely in New York—Mother seemed to take life rather seriously. She rarely laughed. The shock of emigration, I realized only many years later, had made her lose her mirth, her natural *joie de vivre*. I remember being quite surprised when Susi or Hilde told me what a great ringleader Mother had been at school, where her constant laughter and animated chatter prompted her friends to make up a jingle in which Ilse Schüller was compared to a millwheel no miller could control—"*ein Mühlrad ohne Müller.*"

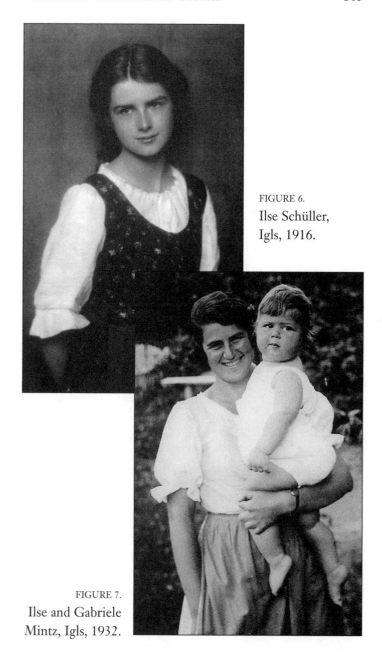

FIGURE 6.
Ilse Schüller,
Igls, 1916.

FIGURE 7.
Ilse and Gabriele
Mintz, Igls, 1932.

The most difficult—and in some ways the most interesting—of the three Schüller sisters was Susi. In a rare
moment of irritation, Grandfather describes Susi as having
been a "capricious and egotistical" child (UV, 104). She was
also very attractive, charming, and apparently had male
admirers from the time that she was eight. In her university days and after, she had many romances but had not yet
met the "right" man when in 1932, Grandmama took Susi,
then twenty-six, and Hilde, twenty-two, on a vacation to the
Lido in Venice. One day, the story goes, Susi went for a
swim and cut her foot. A handsome young Italian came to
her rescue, and they fell in love [Figure 8].

FIGURE 8. Giorgio Piroli and Susi Schüller, Abbazzia, Italy,
1932

Back in Vienna, Susi had a hard time corresponding with Giorgio, who didn't know a word of German and supposedly had a dictionary whose pages were torn out after the letter "M." "But when you're in love," Susi once told me, "you don't need words." That sounds wonderfully romantic, and Giorgio was indeed handsome [Figure 9]:

FIGURE 9.
Giorgio Piroli,
Capri, 1935.

But there were difficulties. Giorgio Piroli was a medical student training to be a gynecologist. He had no money, and he and Susi could not marry for years. His family owned a farm near Perugia. They had probably never known anyone Jewish before and seem to have been quite sympathetic to Mussolini. Giorgio had done his military service in the now-Fascist army, and one of his sisters, Mimi, married an army officer, who was later introduced to me as *Il Generale*, having fought in the Abyssinian campaign. In the 1970s and '80s, when I would sometimes stay with Susi in Rome, Mimi and the general were frequent guests at her bridge games or larger parties. Such was the family Susi married into in 1935, three years before the Anschluss.

I have never quite understood the attitude of my grandparents to Susi's marriage. They seem not to have been disturbed by the thought of their daughter marrying an Italian who, no matter how handsome, charming, and probably quite apolitical, came from a petty-bourgeois Catholic family in Fascist Italy. Grandfather, whose connections in Italy were extensive, bought Susi the elegant apartment on the Viale Mazzini (not far from St. Peter's), in which she was to live the rest of her life. After Giorgio's death in 1982, Susi sold it to a TV executive (the media had moved into the neighborhood) for a handsome sum, retaining the right to live there till her own death. The apartment had a separate wing used by Giorgio for his consultation and waiting rooms. I believe that Grandmama was especially pleased about the marriage because her plan was to winter regularly in Rome, with its milder climate, incredible beauty, and of course its art treasures. In the winter of 1937, she succeeded in making the first visit, which turned out, sadly enough, be her last one as well—at least until after the war.

But of course I am speaking from hindsight. At the time, given the tense situation in Austria, my grandparents may have thought that Italy was actually a safer place to live than Vienna. Anti-Semitism was not nearly as widespread in Italy as in Austria and Germany. Besides, Grandfather spent weeks and months in Italy every year and was close to Italian officials in high places. Susi moved to Rome, was baptized a Catholic, and in 1939 gave birth to her only child, Riccardo. During the war, the Pirolis suffered great hardships, and in its aftermath, when the Italians could not pay their medical bills, Giorgio's practice never quite recovered. Susi was not on speaking terms with some of the Piroli relatives, but she knew how to make the best of things and no doubt comforted herself with the notion that she was living in one of the greatest cities in the world—a city whose art and history she soon knew inside and out—in the most fascinating of countries. "*Kennst du das Land, wo die Zitronen blühn?*" That was Goethe's Italy, and his *Italienische Reise* (*Italian Journey*) was one of Susi's and Grandmama's favorite books. On weekends, Susi and Giorgio made excursions to Ostia Antica and the new Etruscan sites; on holidays they went to Pompeii and Paestum, Taormina and Rimini. By the time I met Susi, they knew the stones not only of Venice, but of every archeological site and Romanesque church in the region. *Kulturdrang* was again the driving force, although it seems to have been more surface than substance.

Whenever I visited Rome, I had the sense that Susi was oddly isolated. True, she became an independent scholar of distinction, producing two very large and well regarded historical studies under the name Schüller Piroli. The first, *2000 Jahre St. Peter* (*Two Thousand Years of St. Peter's*), is an elaborate, beautifully illustrated and documented study of the architectural development of the great Roman church from early Christian basilica to the present. The second and more original book, *Borgia*, reconsiders the complex motives and relations of the notorious Renaissance family, whose members were accused of everything from murder and incest to witchcraft and cannibalism. *Borgia* was translated into Spanish and French, and shortly before her death in 1994, Susi was invited to a conference on historiography in Germany—her first conference!—that dealt with some of the problems she had raised.

At the same time, Susi never belonged to any academic or scholarly community. Most Italian academics of the postwar era were firmly on the Left, whereas Susi was so afraid of Communism that if the municipal government planted tulips in the Campo di Fiori, she was convinced it must be some sort of Communist plot. She did not, in any case, have the credentials to become a professor in Italy. In all the years I visited, the only fellow scholars I ever met or heard about were various prelates from the Vatican Library and a single Austrian professor who taught history both at the University of Innsbruck and at the University of Rome. Susi's social circle consisted primarily of Giorgio's medical friends and their wives. She once told me somewhat ruefully that these friends had no idea she had ever written a line, much less a whole book. Under these circumstances, it is remarkable she was so productive. But Susi was not paid for her work, and it often struck me that her own particular version of *Kulturdrang* did not quite carry through to the next generation.

Riccardo Piroli, my cousin, was educated in Jesuit schools; indeed, he learned that he was half-Jewish only when he was twenty-one. He studied finance and statistics

at the University of Rome and then worked as an actuary
for an insurance company. Like his parents, he was an art
and archeology buff and loved to squire guests from the
United States around the Etruscan Museum in the Villa
Giulia. Mostly, however, Riccardo liked to have a good
time. He and his wife, Giuliana Segnalini, who worked for
the telephone company, loved restaurants, night clubs, and
parties. Guiliana came from a large, closely knit, traditional Italian family: her father, Susi once told me proudly, was
"an official of the Quirinale," which meant, in fact, that he
worked in security at the Quirinale Palace, which is the
official residence of the president of the republic. The
young Pirolis had no children. Their apartment, which
Giorgio had bought years earlier as a real estate investment, was in a distant and ugly outlying set of apartment
blocks. Its streamlined glitzy furniture included a circular
bed, but I don't recall seeing books anywhere, and when
my husband and I once went to lunch there, we watched
the soccer game on a TV mounted from the ceiling, rather
like those in American hospital rooms. Riccardo had certainly succeeded in the game his forebears had played so
hard: he *passed* as just another Italian. But at what price?
And where was *Bildung* now?

Giorgio died of heart disease in 1982, and poor
Riccardo, dangerously obese, died a few years later of heart
failure. Susi, by now very much alone, presided over her
household (she always retained her housekeeper, Ginetta,
who was a superb cook), took care of her fifty-odd canaries,
whose morning feeding and bath was an elaborate ritual,
and remained as charming and manipulative as ever. She
would put on one of her many fur coats, don hat and gloves,

and parade down the street to obtain the best bargains in
gourmet food or clothing. When I attended a conference on
William Carlos Williams at the American Studies Center in
Rome in 1986, Susi came with me to the U.S. consulate
reception in a palazzo near the Botteghe Oscure and
charmed all my American and Italian friends. She was
pleased by the attention but highly critical of the young
people's clothes, the buffet table, the décor. At moments like
this, Susi lapsed into the sense of class she had acquired as a
young girl in Vienna. As for her Jewish heritage, if and
when the word *Jewish* came up, Susi's eyes would glaze over
as if she didn't quite know what was being talked about.
Then she would change the subject. Her Oxford cousin,
Teddy, responded to the word *Jewish* in exactly the same
way, reminding me of Proust's closeted Marquis de Saint-
Loup, whose eyes glazed over when someone mentioned
that an acquaintance might be homosexual.

   I cannot recall whether I attended either Susi's or
Hilde's wedding; I am not even sure where these weddings
took place. Indeed, however well I came to know my aunts
later in life, I have no Vienna memories of them at all. This
is curious. For much as I remember all that happened on the
day of the Anschluss and thereafter in Zurich and Ostia,
Vallombrosa, and New York, much as I can describe my sec-
ond-grade teacher at P.S. 7—one Miss Donnelly—when I
try to remember my first-grade schoolroom in Vienna, I
draw a total blank. I have no image of teachers, children, or
particular activities. The only reason I know I attended first
grade is that by the time we got to Zurich, I certainly knew
how to read and write *Kurrentschrift*, as the Austrian call the
German script. I was also told that I had been a first grader.

Perhaps the memories in question were too traumatic, too close to the moment of departure. For I do have memories, plenty of them, of an earlier time and especially of the apartment at Hörlgasse 6 [Figure 10]. Our apartment was on the fourth floor of a "good" but not fashionable building in the quiet Ninth District, near the University and the Votifkirche. I can still see the nursery, a large room with high ceilings, in which everything was painted white. On the left wall as one entered, there was a large porcelain stove, which was the only source of heat. I remember Kathi,

FIGURE 10.
Hörlgasse 6,
1998

our maid, stoking the fire every morning and again in the evening in winter. Walter's bed was against the far wall, mine across from it. In the center was a little white table and chairs and a number of "grown-up" chairs we used when we played our favorite game, which was, ironically enough, train. We lined up the chairs, and Walter was the conductor, I, the passenger, or sometimes the other way around. The nursery had two large windows facing the street, as seen above—the street where we were to see the "Heil Hitler" activity on March 12, 1938. The floor was linoleum, and I can picture Walter playing for hours with his Abyssinian soldiers—a gift, no doubt, from Susi and Giorgio. I also see us at the little white table having our supper—often *Papperl*, as the white gritslike cereal, which I hated with a passion, was called. To induce me to eat it, Kathi had to place a little piece of chocolate in the center of the white mass, where it melted and formed dark brown streaks.

The dining room was usually out of bounds, but sometimes we had *Gabel-Frühstuck* (second breakfast) at the smaller table by the window, and on special occasions we were allowed to have dinner with the grownups—a very formal occasion, made worthwhile by the promise of cake for dessert: *Rosatorte* (orange filling, pink icing), *Dobostorte* (caramel icing, layers of chocolate cream), *Linzertorte* (round almond cake layered with marmelade), *Nusstorte* (nut cake), and of course the rich chocolate *Sachertorte*. And adjacent to the dining room was the *Salon*, or living room, which we were rarely allowed to enter. It had floor-to-ceiling bookcases on two sides, and I still cringe at the thought that on March 13, 1938, when a new decree ruled that the

Jewish refugees could not leave the country with more than a few suitcases, my parents' elaborate library, which had taken years to build, was entirely lost. But my main memory of the *Salon* was the annual gift-offering ritual (*Die Bescherung*) at Christmas. It was rather like the one in *Die lustigen Neun*: we had to wait in the dark little anteroom next door until Mother rang the bell and we were allowed to enter and see the tree with its candles (electric lights were considered beneath contempt) and find our presents underneath in the semidark.

The Christmas *Bescherung*, Easter egg hunts—these remained part of our well organized lives until we left Vienna—and indeed for years afterward in New York. Every morning we were taken to the Rathauspark, either by the *Kinderfräulein* (Kathi) or Mother. As the pictures on page 116 demonstrate, we were "properly" dressed even for the park: at two, Walter sports an elegant double-breasted coat with velvet collar, leggings with straps, and a little cap [Figure 11]. At four, I wear a pretty little dress [Figure 12], at five, a red skirt with suspenders monogrammed *GM* and red knit sweater. I had just gotten my first permanent wave, then quite a novelty, especially for children. In memory, the avenues, flowerbeds, and fountains of the Rathauspark loomed large, but when I returned to Vienna for the first time in 1955 and visited my childhood playground, I was surprised to find it no more than two or three square city blocks and, like Marcel recalling the Champs Elysées in *A l'ombre des jeunes filles en fleur*, I now found the little park utterly unremarkable. I had a park friend named Dundi whom I loved and with whom I played ball, hopscotch, and jump rope. We went to the park every day but Sunday, when

FIGURE 11. Walter
Mintz, Rathauspark,
Vienna, 1931

FIGURES 12 AND 13.
Gabriele Mintz in
the Rathauspark,
1935, 1936

we often went on "excursions," this time with Daddy, Mother, and various relatives or friends, frequently up the Kahlenberg, much to my disgust, since, Austrian or not, I never regarded hiking with much pleasure. Only the promise of the *Jausenstation* on top, where we were allowed to have ice cream, made the uphill climb palatable.

It was in many ways an idyllic childhood. Mother spent a great deal of time with us, reading to us from *Die Oberheudörfer* (*The People from Oberheudorf*) and *Pickerl: Ein lustiges Wiener Märchen* (*Pickerl: A Merry Viennese Fairytale*), whose tiny, Lilliputian hero has endless comic-pathetic adventures. A little later, we were exposed to the plays of Ferdinand Raimund: my favorite was *Der Verschwender* (*The Spendthrift*), that magic fairy tale in which the rich entrepreneur, in love with the peasant girl he meets in the forest (the *Giselle* theme), has to lose all his worldly goods so as to realize what really matters. German and especially Austrian children's books were more magical, less realistic than, say, *The Secret Garden*; theirs was a world still close to the Grimm and Andersen fairy tales.

Meanwhile, outside the protective domain of nursery and park, one political crisis followed another. Did we have any inkling of the "march of events"? Walter, two-and-a-half years older, was perhaps more aware of the situation than I, for I had only the vaguest of notions of why we could "no longer be Austrians," as my mother had put it. In the Rathauspark, there were children we were told not to play with: I did not know why. On summer vacations in the Salzkammergut and Tyrol, landladies and shopkeepers sometimes looked askance at us and there would be whispering among the adults as to why. And the concierge at

Hörlgasse 6 gave us insolent stares whenever we passed her door. Later, she was to appropriate all our furniture, household goods, china, silver, and artworks. But the situation remained hazy since, when there was something "serious" to be discussed, the grownups usually spoke French so that we couldn't understand. And there was such a network of relatives and friends, so many aunts and uncles (some real, some just called by those names) and cousins, that life seemed totally *normal*.

Not just seemed, but *was*. It is difficult for Americans at the turn of the 21st century to understand the disconnect between the personal and the political that characterized the bourgeois world of the interwar years in Austria. Unlike today, when adults speak freely (perhaps too freely?) in front of children, my parents made a rigid distinction between child talk and grown-up talk. Children had to be protected at all costs. Was this a good thing or not? I feel on balance that it was the right thing to do, it saves us from a great deal of fear and trauma. But it could also be argued that we were curiously unprepared for the future.

Until I was six and a half, I had no notion, at least not consciously, that anything might be wrong in my city or my country and that I was in any way different from others of my place and class, much less the target of anyone's discrimination. My main worry, as I remember it, was that I would be forced by an adult to do something *dull*. Here I no doubt took after Grandmama Schüller. It was *dull*, I thought, to go for walks (*spazieren*) with a group of adults, who were talking to each other about incomprehensible things. It was *dull* to "play" in the Rathauspark on days when Dundi wasn't there. And at night in the nursery, I pleaded with Walter not to go to sleep so we could play another round of Twenty Questions or have a pillow fight. To go to sleep as soon the lights went out: how *dull*! At the same time, I seem to have had a healthy share of what is now called "self-esteem." Accordingly, when things went wrong, I concluded that it must have been someone else's fault. When I was two, the story goes, I was playing at the edge of the water by the lake at St. Anton in the mountains and tumbled in. When I was fished out by my frightened mother, I apparently said quite calmly, "The water fell on me." It certainly was about to.

CHAPTER THREE

Losing Everything But One's Accent: The Refugee Years

Amerika, du hast es besser
Als unser Kontinent, das alte,
Hast keine verfallene Schlösser
Und keine Basalte. . . .

[America, you have it better
Than our continent, the old one.
You have no crumbling castles
And no basalt. . . .]
—Goethe, *Zahme Xenien* (1826)[1]

ARRIVAL IN HOBOKEN AND PASSPORT CONTROL—THAT RITE of passage for so many generations of immigrants—was, I recall in my *Reise nach Amerika*, a somewhat frightening experience. The officials who came on board questioned my parents about Walter, who was wearing glasses and hence did not quite match his visa photograph. "We almost had to go to Ellis Island," I report dramatically, although I may well have been exaggerating. My clearest memory of the incident is that the crowded *Veendam*, now in port, was terribly hot (it was late July and none of us had experienced this kind of heat before) and that there was a tense exchange between Daddy and the immigration officers. But it was over soon and we were free to go:

My second cousins picked us up. They had already been in America for three years. We lived in the country in a furnished apartment, which the Kronsteins, for that was my cousins' name, had sublet for us. We, Hedy and Greta, and my grandfather drove there in a car, and my parents and Uncle Otto and Aunt Stella went on the subway. When we arrived and saw the house, which was very pretty, my grandfather sat down on a little bench and we went in the back garden where there were swings and a sandbox. My cousins' house was not far away. Now my mother had to do the cooking herself. On this first evening, she just made us a cold dinner. No wonder, for she must have been very tired. But after a short time, she could make the most wonderful desserts.

The Kronsteins, whom I came to know very well, were a strange family. Heinrich (Heini) was a lawyer from Frankfurt who was to become a prominent law professor at Georgetown University. Käthe seemed to be the ultimate subservient wife. I never heard her express an opinion that wasn't her husband's. The Kronsteins left Germany in 1935, but a few years after our arrival in New York, they moved on to Washington, where Heini had been offered a position in the Antitrust Division of the Justice Department. In Germany, he had been—exceptionally, even on Daddy's side of the family—a devout Jew; he now became an ardent convert to Catholicism. His sons were transferred to parochial schools and later went to Georgetown University, where Heini was now teaching. The elder, Karl, became a mathematics professor at Notre Dame, the younger, Werner, a lawyer. Both sons suffered from a serious speech impairment—a phenomenon Walter and I always related, rightly or wrongly, to the shock of their forced conversion. At Heinrich's house, where my husband Joe and I were frequently invited when we moved to Washington in 1954, one was likely to meet Jesuit professors and hear much talk about theology. For Heini, in all fairness, the choice of Catholicism was not a social convenience, as it had been for so many of the Viennese Jews, but a matter of dogma, of burning conviction. I think he believed that if Germany had not become a godless secular nation, Nazism would not have taken hold. So successful was the training Karl and Werner received that they too married devout Catholics and became active in Catholic causes.

More telling for my immediate story is that my parents, having just arrived in the heat of a New York July, in what must have been a terrifying new world, had to travel to their new home on Johnson Avenue in Riverdale (which I euphemistically call "the country" in my childhood account) on the subway. Evidently we couldn't afford two taxis. What my parents must have thought on that hour-and-a-half trip from Hoboken, and how Mother then had the stamina to make dinner, cold or otherwise, I have no idea; she, like Grandfather Mintz, who "sat down on a little bench," must have been in a state of shock. But from the point of view of a seven-year-old, our "country" apartment was perfect. For it had a garden with swings and a sandbox that I can still see—the ultimate novelty for a city child from the Hörlgasse. Walter and I were more than satisfied and made sand cakes that prefigured the real ones Mother would soon be baking.

Within the month, we were enrolled in P.S. 7, our district public school, which was unfashionably "down the hill"—on 232nd Street in the Kingsbridge section of the West Bronx. In my autobiography, I explain, in a mixture of German and English:

Aber im September musten [*sic*] wir angemeldet werden. Ich und eben der Hansi [the son of Professor Felix Kaufmann, of Geistkreis fame, and his physician wife, Else] kamen erst in die erste A, mein Bruder in die drite [*sic*] A und meine Cousinen in die vierte B. But my Kronstein cousins went to another school. After three days I and George [as Hansi was now called!] skipped to 2A.

I cite the original so as to exhibit the fault line between my Austrian and American selves. Having crossed the threshold of P.S. 7—and skipping a whole grade three days later—the language barrier was about to be crossed. The sudden shift is prefigured by the spelling mistakes, even as my English was not yet idiomatic ("I and George"), much less correctly spelled (a few pages later I talk about being "very anquious" about something), but clearly I *was* "anquious" to participate fully in American life.

A letter I wrote to my Aunt Hilde in London in early 1939 is revealing in this regard. Now writing in English, I give a long detailed description of the World's Fair at Flushing Meadows, which I absolutely adored. Here is an extract, with nearly every word misspelled:

Then we went to the japanise pavilion, were you could see the silk spinning. There was a japanise lady to selling sings. . . .Then we went to the city of light there is a round room and on one side on the wall is the hole city of New York in front the empirestate building then every thing is lighted and a man talks and then it gets night and everybody turns down the light and you can see the eleveters so nice through the windows. Then it gets much lighter and it is day and you can see the subways very good.

I will never forget the dark General Electric pavilion with its panorama of the gorgeously illuminated silhouette of Manhattan streets and buildings. But it is hard to believe that the little girl who had written, some seven months earlier, the perfectly coherent German letter to her father that I cited in the last chapter could write so badly here. My spelling is mostly phonetic: "to" for "too," "hole" for "whole," "selling sings" for "selling things": *th* in Germanic English regularly becomes *s* when the *th* is voiceless, *z*, when voiced. The grammar is even worse: "you can see the eleveters so nice," "you can see the subways very good," where I use adjectives instead of adverbs, no doubt because in German the base form of the adjective and the adverb is the same. Idioms were also a problem: it seems reasonable to form "it gets night" on the model of "it gets light." But at seven, one assimilates a language quickly, and within a few months I was writing quite correctly. As for the German accent, that vanished almost overnight, although to this day I not infrequently come across proper names I don't know how to pronounce and must call on my American husband for help.

For my parents, it was quite different. In the autumn of 1938, my mother was thirty-four, my father almost forty. They had their share of émigré adventures with language, as when the child next door told Mother she was "waiting for Good Humor"—a remark my mother, who had never heard of ice-cream trucks, took to be charmingly quaint. Such misunderstandings are the staple of refugee memoirs, and I don't want to dwell on them here. Rather, let me trace the gradual shift away from Germanic *Kultur*, as it manifests itself in a particular correspondence—the letters my father

wrote, all of them in German, to the famous political
philosopher Eric Voegelin, who had been a Geistkreis
friend. The correspondence covers a twenty-year period
from late 1938 to the late '50s, when Voegelin, who had
returned to Europe, was teaching at the Institute for
Political Science at Munich.[2] The letters contain no small
talk, very little news of family and friends, and focus almost
exclusively on my father's commentary and critique of
Voegelin's ongoing work on what was to become the ency-
clopedic *Order and History*, published in two large volumes—*Israel and Revelation* and *The World of the Polis*—in
the later '50s.

Ironically, Voegelin's first published book was called *On
the Form of the American Mind* (1928): he had studied for a
year at Harvard with Alfred North Whitehead and George
Santayana and had become interested in the Pragmatists
and John Dewey. Back in Vienna, he wrote two books about
the race question (a highly pertinent topic at the moment
when the Nazis had just come to power in Germany) and a
third called *The Authoritarian State: An Essay on the Problem
of the Austrian State* (1936). Voegelin was one of the few
"Aryan" Austrian intellectuals to emigrate immediately
after the Anschluss. Following a term each at Harvard and
Bennington, he taught at Louisiana State University in
Baton Rouge for the next decade and a half. Here his clos-
est associations were with such New Critics as Cleanth
Brooks and Robert Heilman; indeed, a number of his essays
first appeared in *The Southern Review*.

My father's first letter to Voegelin dates from
December 21, 1938, shortly after our arrival in America.
Daddy had enrolled at Columbia for a degree in accounting,

since the study of his own field—law—would have taken years and he needed to find employment. He hoped, as he writes Voegelin, to become once again a man who worked with his mind (*"ein gelernter Arbeiter"*). In Vienna, this had been possible; in the United States, the workload for a successful C.P. A., which Daddy turned out to be, was much heavier, free time much scarcer. But he enjoyed being a student at Columbia, improving his English and working on problems that might distract him from the "daily drama of the world going under."[3] "About a year ago," he writes to Voegelin sadly, "I spent a very happy evening in your beautiful Vienna apartment. It is strange now to think about it." And after the usual formalities (he always addresses Voegelin with the formal you—*Sie*—the informal *Du* being reserved for those one had known at school), the letter breaks off.

When Daddy next writes (January 8, 1939), his six-page handwritten letter is a detailed critique of Voegelin's manuscript. The latter evidently took the line that National Socialism was no more than the latest and most dreadful manifestation of Modernism in its "scientist" or technological phase. Such Nietzschean-Georgean thinking, my father objects, plays down the debt Modernism owes to Renaissance Humanism, particularly to Spinoza, whose *Tractatus Theologico-Politicus* points the way, via Kant's *Critique of Practical Reason*, to the idea of freedom represented by the great finale of Beethoven's Ninth Symphony. Nationalism is itself a discredited concept, the enemy, as Schopenhauer and Grillparzer argued, of Humanism. It is a form of racism, the individual claiming his rights on purely ethnic grounds. Then, too, he argues, nationalism is pagan, anti-Christian. As an idea, National Socialism thus

inevitably represents the extreme negation of the
Humanitätsidee rather than an outgrowth of it.

Here again is the conflict between *Kulturnation* and
Volksnation. For Voegelin, the Augustinianism of the
medieval Church was the heir to a Platonist tradition lost in
the centuries that followed in their march toward a godless
modernity. For my father, the medieval Church itself treated "man as object," and it is the Renaissance and
Reformation that carried on the Classical tradition. What
makes this and later epistolary debates so remarkable is less
the intellectual debate in question, which could be endless-
ly refined and qualified, than that such debate took place at
all. My father had been in the United States for all of five
months, and at forty, he was once again a university student,
his days taken up with the study of finance, taxes, and economics. He must have had countless practical worries, and
his career future was nothing if not uncertain. Then, too, he
had lost his extensive personal library—his Plato, Aristotle,
Kant, Schelling, Schopenhauer—which had to be abandoned when we left Vienna. Thus Daddy was writing from
memory, a situation making the zeal with which he tried to
convince Voegelin of this or that aspect of Plato's theory of
the polis or of Stoic doctrine all the more poignant.

But surely the absorption in complex philosophical
ideas was also a form of escape from what could only have
been a trying environment. 3204 Oxford Avenue, where we
moved when our summer lease was up, was home from
1938 until I went to Oberlin College in the fall of 1949. It
was a red brick house containing four apartments on two
floors, separated from the street by a low hedge and small
front garden. Photographed in front of the house, my par-

ents still wear their best Vienna clothes, but Walter and I, in pictures taken a few months later, look, in our woolies, like the perfect little immigrants [Figures 1-3]. The steps in these pictures lead to the front door that opens directly into

FIGURES 1-3. Max and Ilse Mintz, Gabriele, and Walter in front of 3204 Oxford Avenue, Riverdale, New York, 1939.

the living room. This room, which was also my parents'
bedroom, was about 9 x 12 feet. Next to it was a small
kitchen and a "dinette," which seated four people comfortably, six with necessity. The two bedrooms in the back were
roughly the same size as the living room: Walter had one, I
the other, and the one bathroom was in between, as was a
large crawl-space closet where all four of us kept our
clothes.

How my parents managed the sleeping arrangements is
still a mystery to me. During the day, the beds were couch-
es—that was easy enough—but where did they keep their
things? And suppose one of them wanted to go to bed at a
different time from the other? There was literally no place
to go. But from my perspective, 3204 Oxford Avenue was
just fine, at least until I entered high school and was embarrassed that I could never have sleepovers or parties. Play was
confined to my room or Walter's and was mostly outdoors
on Johnson Avenue, where we roller-skated for hours every
day those first summers, or in Ewen Park across the street.
Unlike the Rathauspark, with its flower beds, well-kept
paths, and vistas of the lovely buildings on the Ringstrasse,
Ewen Park had an abandoned air. A flight of old stone steps
(on which "bums," as the homeless were then called, slept),
led from the top entrance at 235th Street, past weed-choked
meadows and bumpy paths with wooden fences, down to
Kingsbridge below. To walk to school, I set off, usually by
myself, through Ewen Park, then across busy Riverdale
Avenue and another five blocks or so, past empty lots and
modest little stores and houses, to P.S. 7. In 1939, my walk
was considered perfectly safe. There were, in any case, no
school buses and certainly no car pools because hardly any-

one owned a car. We didn't acquire one until the late '40s, and by then Mother and especially Daddy were too old to learn to drive without much difficulty. Indeed, the only test Daddy ever failed in his life was the driving test. I can still see him in our large, unwieldly Dodge, practicing U-turns and parking routines on Oxford Avenue.

Seated at the small desk by the window or in the lounge chair near the front door, Daddy, formally dressed and still wearing his pince-nez, read Voegelin's manuscript and with his fountain pen made corrections and suggestions (Figure 4). Evaluating his friend's theoretical formulations, his dis-

FIGURE 4.
Max Mintz,
living room,
3204 Oxford
Avenue, 1940.

cussions of Leibniz or Locke, Daddy is full of praise but also makes pointed criticisms. On April 21, 1940, for example, he wonders whether the concept of the Greek *polis* is still relevant at a time when public and private discourses have become so separate. Or on October 13, 1940, he questions the relevance of Pericles or Lorenzo de' Medici to the political ethos of the United States. And a few months before Pearl Harbor, there is a long debate about the meaning of the Preamble to the U.S. Constitution, specifically the clause "that all men are created equal" and its relation to St. Paul's doctrine of original sin.

It is characteristic of the *Kulturdrang* that the focus of the letters is almost always on political theory, rarely on actual politics. No doubt, my father must have regarded such discussion as a partial escape from the daily news bulletins emanating from Europe. To cite, as he does from memory, the gnomic sayings of Nietzsche or Schopenhauer was a way of keeping the spirit of the Geistkreis alive. At the same time, practical politics begins to intrude, at least on Daddy's side of the correspondence. In the spring of 1940, he is very pessimistic, convinced that Hitler will win the war. This was the period of the "phony war": France had been defeated, and there seemed little reason to think the British could defeat Hitler on their own. Roosevelt could muster little overt support for England in the United States: in the autumn of 1941, only 17% of the American population thought that we should go to war with Germany. Pearl Harbor, of course, was to change all that.

In the summer of 1940, Daddy graduated from Columbia with high honors and soon obtained a position at the Wall Street accounting firm of Paterson, Teele &

Dennis, where he was to remain the rest of his working life. The P. T. & D. contract had what Daddy describes to Voegelin as an Aryan clause, a clause, evidently waived in his particular case, stating that the firm did not hire Jews. The existence of such a restrictive covenant seems to have neither shocked nor surprised my father; after all, he was accustomed to anti-Semitism. He might of course have tried to find work with one of the many Jewish accounting firms in Manhattan, but here his Viennese snobbery prevailed: the "gentile" firms were considered superior. In a similar vein, Herbert Schüller reports that his first job in America as a salesman for Silberman Furs was not at all to his liking, because "Most of my colleagues were Jewish and disliked me too, mainly because I could not speak Yiddish. They claimed that I only pretended not to know this language. They also disliked refugees in general as a different species of Jew." When his father, Hugo Schüller, arrived in America, Herbert promptly gave his notice at Silberman Furs. "To my snobbish father, the idea of having a son in a business as low-class as the fur business was intolerable." And so Herbert too went back to school and became a C.P. A.

I can still remember Daddy coming home and announcing he had been hired by P. T. & D. for $27.00 a week. Within three months he was advanced to $50.00. To celebrate, Mother baked a cake. She, who had never cooked before the emigration, became a very efficient housewife, and by 1941, when the whole family was reunited, there was a fixed household routine. Monday was laundry day. In that prewashing-machine age, Mother sat at the washboard at the kitchen sink, scrubbing shirts, while Grandfather Schüller, seated at the dinette table, coached Mother in economics in anticipation of her return to the university, as soon as it was feasible, to work toward a doctorate. Tuesday was ironing day, and the conversation would continue. Then Wednesday—baking day—Grandmama Schüller or Grandmother Rosenthal would come over and keep Mother company. It was all quite *gemütlich*.

Meanwhile, Daddy was beginning to make contact with the strange new world of U.S. business. During his first few weeks at P.T.&D., he was sent to do an audit at a large cosmetic factory in Stamford, Connecticut. "It was," he writes to Voegelin, "just like the American factory in films, ridiculously elegant salesrooms, and in the large workroom 300–400 female workers in gray uniforms with blue trimmings and very coquettish little hats; they were heavily made-up. The machinery is brand new, and all the little bottles move on a conveyor belt—in short, a true Hollywood scene."

Voegelin was too much the single-minded philosopher to interest himself in descriptions of U.S. factories. My father sensed this and kept such descriptions to a minimum. By the late fall of 1942, with the war now going badly for the Germans, he continued to read the chapters Voegelin sent and to make additions and corrections when possible. At a Christmas get-together in 1941, the two men had evidently been discussing theories of nationality and race, and so, in his New Year's letter, Daddy quotes—this time in English—Lord Acton's essay "Nationality," in *The History of Freedom and Other Essays*:

A state which is incompetent to satisfy different races condemns itself, a state which labors to neutralise, to absorb, or to expel them, destroys its own vitality; a state which does not include them is destitute of the chief basis of self-government. The theory of nationality, therefore, is a retrograde step in history. . . . But nationalism does not aim either at liberty or prosperity, both of which it sacrifices to the imperative necessity of making the nation the mould and measure of the state. Its course will be marked with material as well as moral ruin, in order that a new invention may prevail over the works of God and the interests of mankind.

"These remarkable sentences," writes Daddy, "were written in 1862. I think the whole essay will interest you."

Such citation, whether or not it did in fact interest Voegelin, marks a subtle change in my father's thinking. The lover of Schopenhauer and George was now beginning his reeducation in Anglo-Saxon culture. From here on, there are increasing references to Oliver Wendell Holmes and George Santayana, to Henry Adams and Henry James, and to British novelists, especially Dickens and Thackeray. All this was new to a Viennese brought up on Goethe and Schiller, Kant and Nietzsche. Daddy devoured Churchill's memoirs and historical writings and cited them at every opportunity. He increasingly used English to express this or that thought. The letters contain the sense that despite his increasing workload, especially during the tax season, when he literally worked around the clock, and despite the lack of time to immerse himself in difficult philosophical writing, he had accomplished the transition to the New World rather gracefully. He never made many American friends: his colleagues at work, who were largely quite nonintellectual, remained primarily lunch companions, whose interests—especially golf and baseball—were entirely alien to him. But he came to admire the political ethos of Britain and the United States, recognizing that a working democracy, whatever its faults and problems, was a rare marvel.

His feelings toward his adopted country were thus rather different from those of the many refugees who complained, over coffee and pastry at Éclair on 72nd Street or Nasch uptown at 200th, how much better everything had been *bei uns* back home. These *byunskys*, as they came to be called, are nicely lampooned in the following joke, told by Mark Anderson: "Two dachshunds [are] walking down Broadway in New York City. One says to the other: *You know, here I'm just a dachshund, but back home in Germany I was a St. Bernard*."[4] Of course many of the refugees *had* been St. Bernards, prominent professionals, business executives, or artists, now reduced to working at menial jobs. But their pretensions were nevertheless problematic.

This was especially the case with the German Marxist intellectuals—Theodor Adorno is the prime example—who sat out the war in the United States, criticizing all facets of U.S. capitalism, technologism, and media culture, while waiting for the opportunity to go back to Germany. Adorno and Max Horkheimer returned to Frankfurt in the late 1940s and became leaders of the new German higher education. By the '60s, ironically, they had become Establishment figures, their theoretical Marxism much too tame for the New Left revolutionary student body. Meanwhile, the Left intellectuals who remained in the United States tended to castigate their fellow refugees for being insufficiently critical of America. Hannah Arendt, for example, insisted that although "we" had been saved "not by good works but by good fortune," "we" should not indulge in "that insuf-

ferable tone of self-righteousness which frequently and particularly among Jews can turn into the vulgar obverse of
Nazi doctrines."[5]

In my father's view, the German Left's linkage of capitalism with Fascism reflected a persistent Germanic misun-
derstanding of American democracy as well as of Soviet
Communism. As François Furet was to observe a half-cen-
tury later in *The Passing of an Illusion* (1995):

. . . although Europe needed the United States more than ever at
the hour of victory, it retained its old habit of ignoring the
American form of government. Future historians will surely be
surprised at the paucity of reflections and research on American
democracy during the postwar period; it was as if the Europeans'
ignorance about the American history experience, which dated
from the era when the United States was still a faraway nation,
were becoming even more entrenched at a time when the power
of the United States was recognized everywhere. Even World War
I had not altered Old Europe's condescending attitude toward the
Americans. Here they were again, in 1945, illustrious victors,
bearing the American Constitution in the basket of liberty.
Nevertheless, Communism rather than democracy was the order
of the day. . . . American democracy was a social *condition*, whereas democracy in Europe was a subversive force constantly at work
in the fabric of history.[6]

"To the Europeans," Furet explains, "American democracy remained too capitalist not to arouse constant suspi-
cions that it was concealing the domination of money under
a discourse of freedom" (FF, 429). Certainly this was the
view of the Frankfurt School and, with some variations, of
the *Partisan Review* circle. But for my father, the affirmation

of individual rights, as guaranteed in the American Constitution, and the separation of powers were the central facts of political life, whereas Communism had to be understood (as it has been increasingly, thanks to the opening of the Soviet archives) as the totalitarian twin of Fascism. Hence, although Daddy was an intellectual snob, although he criticized specific government policies from morning till night and pronounced this or that American politician as hopelessly "stupid" or an "idiot," he came to admire British parliamentary democracy and the U.S. constitutional system as the very best hope, in a fallen world, for freedom. Accordingly, he stayed aloof from the Leftist émigrés who now became hostile to the political system that had, after all, made their new professional lives possible.

Daddy's increasing appreciation of the literature and culture of Anglo-America was to have a decisive influence on my own thinking. I remain suspicious of critical theorists and philosophers, whether on the Right like Paul de Man or on the Left like Adorno, who sought asylum in the United States and, as in de Man's case, remained here all their lives and taught at our leading universities, all the while expressing virtually no interest in American literature, culture, or political theory. Adorno despised what he called our Consciousness Industries, and de Man seems to have known few American icons except for Archie Bunker. Indeed, when Adorno asks whether one can write poetry after Auschwitz, he is really asking whether the European—specifically the German—can write poetry after Auschwitz. He seems to have known nothing of Whitman and William Carlos Williams, Eliot and Stevens, much less the poets of Latin America or the Caribbean. It was as if excessive contact with

American culture might contaminate one's post-Kantian purity. And one recalls Ernst Gombrich's insistence that *"Ich bin kein Engländer,"* his sense of being a citizen nowhere but rather a member of an intellectual community that knew no national borders.

My parents were rather more receptive to Americana, and besides, their careers were more practical. Immersion was a necessity. Mother had renewed her studies in economics and was working toward a doctorate at Columbia under the tutelage of Arthur Burns. She passed her orals with high honors in 1945, the year the war ended. She too was becoming Americanized and made friends with a number of her fellow students. Later, she combined teaching at Columbia with a position at the National Bureau of Economic Research, where she worked with such soon to be famous economists as Martin Feldstein and Milton Friedman. Economics was then still almost entirely a man's field, but she coped and could rely on various mentors from the Austrian School of Economics (Gottfried von Haberler, Fritz Machlup, Herbert Fürth) now in the United States. We knew that Mother was busy with her studies when Paul Samuelson's popular textbook *Introduction to Economics* appeared as a doorstop in the kitchen—a book literally to be kicked around. Her schedule was incredibly busy, because the household took up a great deal of time. Grocery shopping, for example, could only be accomplished "down the hill," which meant pulling a heavy shopping cart up the paths and steps of Ewen Park. Frozen foods did not yet exist, and our "icebox, " as we called the refrigerator, was quite small. Meal preparation was thus much more laborious than it was to be even a decade later.

For my parents, assimilation was obviously difficult—the way of life was so utterly different—but not because Americans weren't friendly and forthcoming. Mother and Aunt Stella received frequent calls and invitations from a refugee help group sponsored by well-off gentile matrons in the New York suburbs—Hastings, Tarrytown, Hudson. These ladies—I remember one appropriately named Louise Trueblood—organized teas and gave tips on shopping and childcare. As for me, I was initially treated at P. S. 7 with the curiosity devoted to the exotic other: I was asked why I didn't wear the wooden shoes that German and Dutch children wore in picture books, even though I did have braids. I was exposed to the wonders of peanut butter (good) and bubble gum (bad). I couldn't stand the smell of the latter and hated the habit my classmates had of pulling it out of their mouths and stretching it so as to make pink bubble-gum bracelets or little balls!

Meanwhile, Art with a capital *A* continued to exert as great a pull as ever on my father's consciousness. In January of 1950, when I was a student at Oberlin, Daddy wrote Voegelin, now back in Europe and a professor at the University of Munich, the following letter:

I went down to Washington to see the Vienna paintings [on loan exhibit at the National Gallery]. They will come here [to the Metropolitan Museum] too, but by then I'll be swallowed up by the tax season. The reunion after nearly twelve years took my breath away. I know, of course, that I cannot look at these paintings quite objectively, since almost every one of them has for me an aura of countless memories and shocks, and I was even concerned that seeing them again would be not only exciting but perhaps disappointing, as it happens sometimes with the loves of one's youth. But fortunately this comparison doesn't hold—the old favorites are as radiant as ever. I only regretted those that weren't there.

It is a poignant moment. By 1950 many of the refugees had made the pilgrimage back to Vienna out of curiosity. My parents refused to do so because they felt it would be too painful: they had loved Vienna too much. And so the encounter with the great paintings of the Kunsthistorisches Museum—the Titians, Tintorettos, Breughels, Rubenses, Velázquezes—was an event to be feared as much as longed for, given the *Aura unzähliger Erinnerungen und Erschütterungen* ("aura of countless memories and shocks") these paintings held for Daddy.

I have frequently taught Walter Benjamin's essays and find that students today are puzzled by the concept of *aura*. For them, being subject to aura seems just a bit unseemly, a bit "much." There is no distinction, so they have been trained to believe, between High and Low, art and the everyday. Besides, taste is relative and contingent, so that "art" is best looked at as a cultural symptom, an index to political or social formations. But for my parents and grandparents, art had a spiritual dimension. Their tastes were narrow but intense: "Art" meant Greek and Roman architecture and sculpture and Western painting and sculpture from the early Renaissance to the end of the nineteenth century. It was the Burckhardtian world picture: Byzantine mosaic and Tang pottery, Spanish Gothic or Islamic tile work—these were regarded as strictly secondary to representational *paintings* like Tintoretto's *Susanna and the Elders* at the Kunsthistorisches Museum.

The concept of aura was thus one I internalized as a child. Perhaps this is why I could never take seriously the defensiveness about "the aesthetic" that haunts the contemporary academy. I attended a recent American Studies conference on the subject where my colleagues were busy trying to convince one another that it was proper for this or that novel or book of photographs to have an "aesthetic" dimension, as if the aesthetic were some sort of additive one put into one's coffee. For me, the question was falsely posed. As Wittgenstein put it in his *Lectures on Aesthetics*, "One might think Aesthetics is a science that tells us what's beautiful—it's almost too ridiculous for words." And again, "Am I to make the inane statement, 'It [the musical theme] just sounds more beautiful when it is repeated'? (There you can see by the way what a silly role the word 'beautiful' plays in aesthetics.) And yet there *is* just no paradigm other than the theme itself."[7]

The less confidence people have in the value of particular artworks, it seems, the more effort they expend in defining what *beauty* is. In the Vienna of Wittgenstein, as of the Geistkreis, the power of the art canon was still so great that questions of *beauty* could readily be subordinated to questions like, "Is Mahler's Third Symphony great, or is it just, as Wittgenstein thought, a pretentious simulation of 'true' music like Beethoven's or Brahms's? And if the symphony *is* great, how and why?" Raising such issues: this, in my parents' refugee circle in New York, is what made for *interesting* discussion.

Meanwhile, the everyday exacted its price. Daddy had no time to see the Vienna pictures during the tax season, which became longer and more complicated year by year, and the letters to Voegelin begin to exhibit a certain strain: one senses that Daddy's literary and philosophical critique was no longer in the same demand now that Voegelin was famous and Daddy had settled into the middle-class existence of the successful C.P.A. Former Geistkreis members living in New York, moreover, were not faring so well. The philosopher Alfred Schütz, whose writings on phenomenology are now held in high esteem, worked at his day job in a bank and then did his "real" work in the wee hours: he died of a sudden heart attack in his mid-forties, as did the psychonanalyst/art historian Ernst Kris. The role of *gelerntner Arbeiter*, it seems, became increasingly an oxymoron.

As children during the war years, Walter and I knew little of these tensions. Indeed, choices in these years were so limited that life was really quite simple for children, even when rationing meant that Mother was constantly serving brains or lungs, both of which I despised, for dinner. Riverdale, in the early '40s, was a small town, made up of two- or four-family brick houses punctuated by still-empty lots that the developers began to pounce on in the '50s. Crime was not an issue, and we roamed the neighborhood quite freely and roller-skated down its streets. We did not own bikes—still a luxury item in those days. The only commercial street was Riverdale Avenue, and when a new delicatessen or even drugstore opened there, it was a major event. Riverdale was considered a step up from Washington Heights (181st Street), jokingly known as the Fourth Reich because so many German and Austrian refugees lived there. Along the Hudson on Palisades Avenue, a fifteen-minute walk from our house, there was an enclave of elegant estates. Daddy soon knew who lived where and provided designations (e.g., Toscanini) when we took walks there on Sunday. On the other side of the Henry Hudson Parkway at 242nd Street, was Fieldston, then an entirely restricted and expensive neighborhood adjoining the Fieldston School, where I would soon be a student, the irony being that the school was about 90% Jewish.

P. S. 7 "down the hill" was a lower middle-class, highly diversified public school with an ugly building and dingy schoolyard where we played hopscotch and rope, the school having no athletic facilities of the sort taken for granted today [see Figure 5]. The most popular girl in my fifth grade class was Lucille Del Pra, whose father owned the

FIGURE 5. P.S. 7, the Bronx, 1944.

local candy store. For a special after-school treat, we went there and ordered ice-cream sodas. There were one or two "juvenile delinquents" like William Sinnett, who was regularly pursued by the truant officer, and a few bullies like Kenny Moynahan and Joseph Pugni, who occasionally chased me home from school, shouting "dirty Jew" or four-letter words that I hadn't yet learned. One of the ironies of my refugee situation was that I knew no dirty words in German—I still don't know many—because I was too young when I left Vienna to have acquired them, but I was not yet familiar with the English ones either. But when one of the teachers, a Miss Waters, who taught the "retarded" students in what was then known as the "Junior Industrial," once made an anti-Semitic remark to me on the playground, I did understand and told my parents. Daddy immediately composed a carefully worded letter of complaint, and it never happened again. I myself did not get upset about it, perhaps because—and I can't stress this enough—I instinctively knew that Miss Waters's behavior was an aberration in what was by and large an atmosphere of great tolerance and generosity. No one, I knew, was going to arrest or jail me, or even single me out as unworthy. And although I was the only girl who wore her hair in braids and my mother thought it was a waste of money to buy the optional school uniform—a white middy-blouse and navy-blue skirt, I soon had scads of girl friends [Figure 6]. In 1942, moreover, I had the leading role in the sixth grade play, *The Birds' Christmas Carol*, which meant that my hair was worn in an "upsweep" and powdered white and that I wore a long dress and apron [Figure 7]. Kate Douglas Wiggin's sentimental tale on which this play was based was

FIGURE 6.
Gabriele and
friends, Miss
Reilly's class,
5B3, in front
of P.S. 7,
June 1941

FIGURE 7.
Gabriele in *The
Birds' Christmas
Carol* costume,
1942.

a far cry from my favorite German childrens' book, *Die lustigen Neun*, despite the comparable Christmas themes. The Birds, so the story goes, already have three strong healthy boys when their first and only girl is born on Christmas and appropriately named Carol. Mrs. Bird's little girl unfortunately turns out to be a very sickly child, and, alas, on the Christmas Day that is Carol's ninth birthday, just when she had prevailed on Mrs. Bird to invite the destitute Ruggles family—poor neighbors down the street—for dinner, "God takes Carol back to heaven." I imagine Mother and Grandmama, who dutifully came to see the production, raised their eyebrows at this bit of treacle, but I thought the play—and my role in it—was wonderful.

The great Saturday adventure of these war years was to go department store shopping with Mother—an outing that involved a long subway ride from 231st to 34th Street, the escalators at Macy's and Gimbel's and—best of all—lunch at Horn & Hardart's, otherwise known as "the Automat." I was usually given $1.25 in quarters which meant that I could choose from the tantalizing windows along the wall the little brown pot of baked beans (25¢), two other vegetables, and a particular white cake with chocolate icing that looked like a squat little tower. To put the quarter into the slot and get *the* thing one wanted instantly: this undoubtedly prepared me for the pleasures of Frank O'Hara's *Lunch Poems*:

> If I rest for a moment near The Equestrian
> Pausing for a liver sausage sandwich in the Mayflower Shoppe,
> That angel seems to be leading the horse into Bergdorf's. . .
> I have in my hands only 35¢, it's so meaningless to eat!
>
> ("Music")

Or
> Neon in daylight is a
> great pleasure, as Edwin Denby would
> write, as are light bulbs in daylight.
> I stop for a cheeseburger at JULIET's
> CORNER.
>
> ("A Step Away from Them")[8]

Imagine making poetry out of the Mayflower Shoppe, across from Bergdorf Goodman's on Fifth Avenue, out of Juliet's Corner on Times Square! Flexibility and attentiveness, these poems tell us, are the qualities needed to enjoy such city pleasures as "Neon in daylight." It was a matter, as O'Hara put it, of "Grace to be born and live as variously as possible." But in 1941 I could not yet articulate this notion, and although I carefully studied each item in the Horn & Hardart windows, I always chose the same three or four things.

ÉMIGRÉ REINVENTION

One refugee who did display the kind of grace I speak of was Grandfather Schüller. Once he recognized that he had no choice but to accept the demise of the old Austria, the seventy-year-old statesman quickly adapted to the New World. The story of his arrival in New York is itself remarkable. While Grandmama Schüller and her mother had to wait for their visas in Oxford, Grandfather obtained his professor's visa because he had been invited by Alvin Johnson to join the University in Exile at the New School. In July 1940, he sailed on a Dutch ship carrying 900 children, bound for Canada. There he was supposed to remain in custody until his papers were processed, but he got leave to go to the barber, boarded the first train, showed his visa at the border, and, before he knew it, had arrived at Grand Central:

In New York, I left my luggage at Grand Central, asked for a [subway] train to Riverdale, where I got off at about 11.30 at night. Not a soul anywhere, no taxi. Saw a light on in a house, knocked at the door, and asked whether I could call for a taxi, which quickly brought me to Ilse. They were very surprised. Bliss of the reunion after two years. (UV, 185)

Grandfather was soon living with his sister-in-law Ida and her daughter Lotte, a psychiatrist, in the upstairs apartment across the hall from us. He began teaching at the New School—an entirely new experience for him—and supplementing his tiny income by helping the banker Max Warburg write his memoirs as well as acting as consultant for a company called Amertrade. When Grandmother and Great-grandmother arrived a year and a half later, the Schüller-Rosenthal family, now without Lotte, moved around the corner to Cambridge Avenue, where their modest little apartment was reached by a steep flight of outside steps that froze over in the winter. Again, Grandfather made the best of it; he had soon befriended the old German who lived in the basement apartment downstairs—Richard Hoeningswald, a philosophy professor from Munich—and embarked on the serious study, first of classical philosophy, and then the mathematical logic of Frege and the phenomenology of Husserl. On their morning walks, they went over philosophical problems, even as my father did in his letters to Voegelin. Occasionally, they would pass Johnson Avenue, where my friend Eileen Moore and I were roller-skating, and Grandfather would stop to chat for a moment and give me tips derived from his years of figure-skating at the beautiful skating rink near the Ballhausplatz. In making a circle, for instance, the inside shoulder and ankle had to be lowered for balance! And Grandfather would give a little demonstation, much to my embarrassment.

Grandmama was less satisfied with New York. She pronounced the buildings ugly and objected to the dirt, snow, ice, and the cumbersome subway ride downtown. The shabby old apartment and lack of household help were a trial to her. When, at the dinner table, Grandmama, Great-grandmother, and Aunt Ida would engage in their frequent "byunsky" rounds of complaint about New York, Grandfather, who was usually very quiet during meals, would finally lose his temper and say, "*Also jetzt Ruhe!*" Enough! And despite all her caveats, Grandmama soon found the right refugee dressmaker near Central Park, took the subway to museums and concerts, played bridge, and read prodigiously. When I was home with a cold or sore throat (which happened frequently!), she would come over and read to me, as did Great-grandmother. What this meant is that my German literary education was, for many years, way ahead of my English one. By the time I was ten, I knew Schiller's *Wilhelm Tell*, *Wallenstein*, *Die Jungfrau von Orleans*, and *Maria Stuart*, as well as Goethe's *Götz von Berlichingen* pretty much by heart. Indeed, I recall that one evening when my father came home from work, I greeted him, much to the amusement of Mother, with the words

"Betrogener törichter Junge!" ("Betrayed, foolish boy!"). These words come from Act V of *Götz*, when the demonic beauty Adelheid von Walldorf persuades the young steward Franz, who is madly in love with her, to poison her husband, who is also Franz's master. *"Es soll sein!* ("It will be!"), declares Franz in this most dramatic of scenes.

What I loved in *Götz von Berlichingen*, as in the Schiller historical dramas, was the realistic psychodrama at the core of their Romantic plots. In *Götz*, for example, the noble Weislingen, himself a betrayer, is betrayed in turn by his own man, Franz, who has fallen under the spell of Adelheid. And in *Die Jungfrau von Orleans*, the warrior saint Joan of Arc loses her nerve in battle when she looks into the eyes of the enemy—the young Englishman Lionel—and refuses to kill him. How dramatic this turning point, especially when Joan's peasant father then declares that his daughter is a witch! Or consider the scene in *Maria Stuart*, when Elizabeth learns that "her" Leicester has also been the lover of her hated rival, Maria. There is no English equivalent to these Romantic dramas, with their medieval and rustic trappings, their insoluble conflicts, their dissection of passion, folly, and betrayal, and their sexual undertones. Moreover, the women, unlike the women in, say, Sir Walter Scott's novels, are strong and complex characters, taking charge of their destinies, often despite historical and social odds. In Goethe and Schiller, women are rarely victims: Gretchen in *Faust* is the exception, and even she has the power of insight not found in comparable English innocents.

Turning from these classics to literature in English, I seemed to regress. My library selections ranged from the Lois Lenski books and the famed twin series (e.g., *The*

Dutch Twins) to biographies of interesting young girls like *Drina* (the young Victoria) and Edna Ferber's big novels like *So Big* and *Giant*. I thus had the oddly skewed notion that Culture was a German commodity. At home, we were always told to speak German, especially when the Grandparents were present, though Mother also employed me, during dishwashing time, to teach her English idioms and correct her mistakes.

In public, having to speak German and be addressed as Gabriele was a regular humiliation. I wanted desperately to "fit in," and hence I hated to accompany Grandmama on the subway, where she immediately spoke German in a loud voice. When I was twelve, Grandmama took me to my first opera at the Met—*Lohengrin*. Wagner was not the ideal choice for a twelve-year-old, and I remember being extremely bored, except during the swan scene. Indeed, although I loved German novels and plays, I never did develop a proper taste for opera, perhaps because every Saturday Walter and I had to tiptoe around the house and be quiet while the opera was on the radio. Forced to listen to *The Marriage of Figaro* and *The Barber of Seville*, we rebelled. At night, I would secretly listen to the *Hit Parade*—at least until Walter, who shared the radio with me, came barging into my room, disconnected the plug, and took the radio into his room so that he could listen to *The Shadow*, *The Great Gildersleeve*, or *Gangbusters*.

On the whole, however, I accepted the dual culture in which I now functioned without much stress. Speaking German, I was good little Gabriele, who spoke in complete sentences, knew no off-color words, and was interested in "good" books. Speaking English, I was slangier, less polite, more inclined toward popular culture. On occasion, the two modes collided, as when my parents were having a *Jause*—that Austrian cross between a cocktail party and high tea. Mother and Grandmama would work all morning making *Brötchen*—the open-faced sandwiches *de rigueur* on such an occasion—a slice of ham with an asparagus stalk on top, or salmon decorated with hard-boiled egg slices and gherkins. There were also two or three cakes or patisserie. Promptly at four the guests—in those early days, all refugee friends—would arrive and immediately there was very loud German conversation and much laughter. First wine or champagne was served with the *Brötchen* and then immediately tea and cakes. By seven p.m. or so it was all over: the noise stopped as abruptly as it had begun.

Walter and I played a particular role during these "ref parties," as we sarcastically called them. We had to dress up, make a brief appearance, and shake hands with the guests, pausing briefly to eat a *Brötchen* or two. Then we were given the high sign, which meant that we should exit as quickly as we had entered and could now play in our rooms without further disturbance. Although as soon as we were out of the room we joked about some of the guests, it did not seem the least bit strange to us that each and every one of them was a German-speaking refugee.

Indeed, the fact that a large proportion of my parents' Vienna social circle, Geistkreis included, was now living in New York made assimilation into American life that much harder. Refugees who settled in Chicago or San Francisco had to fit in; refugees in New York did not and tried to keep up the old ways, although their names were largely Americanized, so that Redlichs became Redleys, Gärtners

Gardeners, and Geiringers Graingers. Later, when I found out that Alfred ("Fredl") Schütz (whose daughter Eva, now Evelyn, I found very boring) was a famous philosopher, whose works some of my colleagues venerated, or that Uncle Max Schur (my father's first cousin) had been Freud's personal physician and was now a leading psychoanalyst, I couldn't quite relate their evident accomplishments to the familiar figures I had seen at Mother's tea parties. And it was also true that, with rare exceptions, only the men did interesting things, whereas the wives, cultured and hence highly opinionated as they were, held entirely subordinate positions. Ilse Schütz, for example, who was a very close friend of Mother's, seemed entirely absorbed in her two children and household. And although there were occasional bachelors like Dr. Winternitz at our parties, I never recall any single women. Indeed, widows like Aunt Gerti, now living at an apartment hotel nearby, or Aunt Ida were invited only by themselves, not to parties. This continued to be the protocol.

In 1942, when I was almost eleven, I was sent, for the first time, to camp. Ironically, Self-Help, the charitable organization that sponsored camp for us Jewish refugee children, sent us to a Y.W.C.A. camp—Camp Owaissa—on Lake Ariel in the Poconos, near Scranton, Pennsylvania. The cost, I remember, was $11.00 per week, and I went for six weeks, three summers in a row. It was one of the happiest times of my young life. I still remember getting on the Greyhound Bus for my very first summer away from home! I sat next to a girl named Ruth Walker (née Wakler), who was to become my best friend. But on that first day I was so excited I became sick repeatedly: the bus had to stop three times so I could get out and vomit. The first morning at camp, we had to eat

Shredded Wheat, which I had never seen before, and I vom-
ited again. After that, everything was perfect.

The morning began with flag-raising followed by
Morning Worship—a half-hour of prayer and hymn
singing. Here, and again at Evening Worship, we learned
such hymns as:

> In Christ there is no East or West.
> In Him no South or North:
> But one great fellowship of love
> Throughout the whole wide earth.
>
> In Him shall true hearts everywhere
> Their high communion find;
> His service is the golden cord,
> Close binding humankind. . . .

And:

> Be Thou my vision O Lord of my heart;
> Naught be all else to me, save that Thou art
> Thou my best Thought, by day or by night,
> Waking or sleeping, Thy presence my light.
>
> Be Thou my Wisdom, and Thou my true Word;
> I ever with Thee and Thou with me, Lord;
> Thou my great Father, I Thy true son;
> Thou in me dwelling, and I with thee one.

No one, least of all I, found it at all odd that a group of
Jewish refugee girls should be participating in this Christian
hymn-singing ritual. The Y.W.C.A., after all, had been kind

enough to reach out to us. Besides, what was Goethe's
"Kennst du das Land wo die Zitronen blühn?" compared to "Be
Thou My Vision," sung in the circle of campers by the fire?
I was a convert, not to Christianity, but to the sounds and
rhythms of these soon-familiar hymns. Many years later,
when I read D. H. Lawrence's great essay "Hymns in a Man's
Life," with its account of the childhood wonder produced by
the "banal Noncomformist hymns that penetrated through
and through my childhood," I knew exactly what he meant.
Ruthie and another refugee girl named Eve Spitz were
somewhat more critical: they reminded me that we were not
supposed to sing songs or say prayers to Christ. But I felt the
way Lawrence did about "Galilee, Sweet Galilee":

To me the word Galilee has a wonderful sound. The Lake of
Galilee! I don't want to know where it is. I never want to go to
Palestine. Galilee is one of those lovely, glamorous worlds, not
places, that exist in the golden haze of a child's half-formed imagination. And in my man's imagination it is just the same. It has
been left untouched.[9]

Then, too, the daily song ritual included more than hymns.
At night, there was the thrilling bugle call of Taps:

> Day is done, gone the sun,
> From the hills, from the lake,
> From the skies.
> All is well, safely rest,
> God is nigh.

I only learned much later that Taps was a military song and
that it originated in 1862 during the Civil War. Of our own

war, the war raging in Japan and Europe in the summer of
'42, we did not speak. While we were making momentous
decisions as to whether to choose boating or archery for the
nine-to-ten a.m. slot or nature study or arts and crafts from
three-to-four p.m., the first Battle of Guadalcanal was
underway in the Pacific and the German siege of Stalingrad
had begun. I don't remember anyone, whether camper,
counselor, or our director, Elsie Borden (known to us as
Elsie the Borden Cow), so much as mentioning the war.
And indeed at camp, the military bugle call of Taps was followed by a second very unmilitary song, which went like
this:

> Now run along home
> And jump into bed,
> Say your prayers
> And cover your head.
> The very same thing
> I say unto you,
> You dream of me,
> And I'll dream of you!

No mention of God this time around, only friendship and
good feeling. Interestingly, however, I don't remember a
single camp friend who was not part of the refugee nexus. I
believe I *had* other friends—girls who came from
Philadelphia or even Scranton nearby—but I can't now
place them. Yet I could give a complete account of the summer's highpoint: learning how to dive. At the beginning of
July, I could swim the breast stroke I had learned at Ostia in
1938, but nothing else. Now—so as to become a Green
Cap—I learned the crawl, the sidestroke, the elementary

backstroke, and back crawl, and then the "spring-dive," performed as gracefully as possible. And having passed the Green Cap test, we swam across the lake with boats beside us for safety. Our happiness was complete.

There was only one major mishap that first summer. In the late afternoon, we were allowed to take out the rowboats for an hour, and one Sunday, Ruthie, Eve, and I went out beyond the island and the boat got caught in the reeds. It took a while to get unstuck, and by the time we approached the Camp Owaissa dock, Evening Worship, which was held down by the lake on Sundays, was in full swing. The whole camp was lined up along the shore, singing "Be Thou My Vision" and other favorites. As we rowed into the dock as quietly as possible, the campers started to giggle and point, and we knew we were in the doghouse. Mrs. Borden was furious, and we were docked for a whole week. To make matters worse, our counselor told us that Mrs. Borden felt the Jewish refugee children had not been sufficiently respectful of the Y.W.C.A. camp's Christian mission. And subconsciously this may well have been true.

It was also true that by seventh grade, P. S. 7 no longer seemed so attractive. These were years when the New York Board of Education was constantly lurching from one pedagogical experiment to another, and when I was in seventh grade, tracking, which had guided all my teaching thus far, was suddenly eliminated. This meant that for the first time we were all in one math or English class and there were students in my class who couldn't multiple nine by five or spell the word *receive*. Some, like Grace Terribile, who was fourteen in seventh grade, had been left back a number of times and were just marking time until they could leave school and get jobs. Many already had boyfriends and paid no attention in class. Our seventh grade teacher, Miss Coyne, who had previously taught in a reform school, always wore dresses with long sleeves because—so rumor had it—she had a huge scar on her right arm where a boy had knifed her. Miss Coyne was a terror, as was the eighth grade teacher, Mrs. Cahill, who had tight white curls and pursed lips and never spoke above a whisper.

My parents had, in the meantime, decided to send me to a private school—the Fieldston School in Riverdale. I received a full scholarship with the proviso that I repeat the eighth grade, because I was a year ahead of myself, having skipped twice at P.S. 7. I didn't like the idea at all: for a thirteen-year-old it is highly humiliating to be put back a grade. I had visited Fieldston for an interview and found it almost too luxurious: it looked more like a country club than a school, and its athletic fields were bigger than all of P.S. 7. But there were two things that happened that changed my mind. The first was the debacle of my graduation dress. In those war years, each girl made her own dress. Mother and I bought five yards of organdy—aqua blue with little white flowers, together with some pink ribbon and a dress pattern. For a while, my sewing efforts (we learned sewing in sixth grade) went quite well, but then I became reckless and made too wide a cut for the square neckline. It was now much too big, and I had to take tucks in it. When I tried it on in sewing class, Mrs. Engel went into a fury. She made me stand up on a chair as an example and announced, much to my humiliation, that Gabriele's dress was the visible emblem of what *not* to do.

The second incident had to do with my eighth-grade

penicillin report. Penicillin was a new drug in those days, and I had researched its origins and manufacture as carefully as I could. Then I made the cover for the report with a stencil, the word "penicillin" appearing in yellow at a diagonal against the blue paper background, with the name Gabriele Mintz in the lower right. But, as was my wont, I spilled some glue on the cover, so that there were some faint spots I couldn't quite eliminate. On the last day of school, Mrs. Cahill called me to the front of the room and informed me that I wouldn't graduate unless I made a new cover because of the glue stains on this one. I had the presence of mind to say, "No, Mrs. Cahill. I won't. It doesn't matter, because I am going to a new school." And suddenly I knew I was happy to begin a new life.

All this happened about a week after D-Day, June 6, 1944. I did, in fact, graduate with my class and wear the unfortunate aqua-blue organdy dress. But given the "march of events," my parents paid little attention to this particular nonmilestone. They were glued to the radio every evening, and already their conversation was full of worries that "we" (Britain and the United States) were allowing the Soviets to make too many gains. In December of '44, during the calamitous Nazi-Soviet clash over Budapest, Daddy wrote to Voegelin:

I fear that Churchill, whom for many reasons, but especially for his prose, I revere, is also responsible for the entirely unnecessary land invasion of Italy. If the Allies had begun the Normandy invasion a year earlier, it would have been an advantage, although it would have helped the Russians too. The Russians, for their part, have succeeded, with their six-month sit-down strike, in dragging out the war, thus helping the Germans hold on to Budapest. . . . Well, the world is ruled with little wisdom, and the prospect that the war may drag on another two or three years and that, in the end, Walter will be sent to Asia, is a source of anxiety.

As it turned out, Daddy was too pessimistic: within five months, the European war was over. I suppose that the calamity of having so grossly misread the Austrian situation a decade earlier made both my parents always expect the worst. On the other hand, Daddy's supposition that the Japanese war might drag on for years and that Walter might have to fight in it was by no means unreasonable in those prenuclear days. Then, too, with victory in May 1945 came the first onsite reports from the concentration camps, guaranteed to strike terror into the hearts of the refugees, who knew that, but for the grace of God, they would have shared the fates of those others, some of whom were their own relatives and friends. One such relative (although I only learned this much later) was Otto Strauss's mother, who could have left with us on the train for Zurich on March 12, 1938, but evidently didn't want to leave her precious jewelry behind. She died at Auschwitz.

For a thirteen-year-old like myself, however, neither the war's end in Europe nor the cataclysm of Hiroshima three months later seemed very real. At Camp Owaissa that summer, the big event was that an "older girl" named Ruth Oppenheimer finally enlightened the whole cabin about sex. We were incredulous! Was *that* really what men and women did? Surely not our parents! By the time I came home with my newly acquired knowledge, it was time to begin a whole new life at the Fieldston School. Almost the first thing I did was to change my name to Marjorie.

CHAPTER FOUR

Kultur, Kitsch, and Ethical Culture

WE BELIEVE

that the supreme aim of human life is working to create a more humane society

that ethics is the central factor in human relationships

that community is not possible without a sense of the individual, and the individual is incomplete without a sense of community

that diversity of thought, rather than belief in prescribed metaphysical or philosophical ideas, is one of our chief strengths

that a democratic process, with its shared responsibility and authority, is essential to a humane social order

that deed is more important than creed

—From "What is Ethical Culture?"
Statement of the New York Society for Ethical Culture[1]

6.42   Propositions cannot express anything higher.
6.421   It is clear that ethics cannot be expressed.
         Ethics is transcendental.
         (Ethics and aesthetics are one.)
6.422   The first thought in setting up an ethical law of the
         form "thou shalt . . ." is: And what if I do not do it?
         But it is clear that ethics has nothing to do with
         punishment and reward in the ordinary sense.
              This question as to the *consequences* of an action
         must therefore be irrelevant. At least these

163

consequences will not be events. For there must be some
sort of ethical reward and ethical punishment, but this must
lie in the action itself.
                    —Wittgenstein, *Tractatus Logico-Philosophicus*[2]

                    Fierce as a lion!
                    Strong as a vulture!
                    Rah rah rah
                    For Ethical Culture.
                              —Football cheer, Fieldston School

THE FIELDSTON SCHOOL, WHOSE EIGHTH GRADE I ENTERED
in the fall of 1945, was sponsored by the New York Ethical
Culture Society (E.C.S.), which had been founded in 1876
by Felix Adler, a champion of social justice and labor
reform. The Society's mission statement declared as its
object "the mutual improvement in religious opinion,
which shall be in part accomplished by a system of weekly
lectures, in which the principles of ethics shall be developed, propagated, and advanced among adults, and in part
by the establishment of a school or schools wherein a course
of moral instruction shall be supplied for the young." One
of the first projects of the Society was the founding of a free
kindergarten for the children of the working people; by
1895, this "Workingman's School" was renamed the Ethical
Culture School. The primary branch, known quite simply
as Ethical, was located on lower Central Park West in
Manhattan, where it remains to this day; the secondary
school (Fieldston), with its large wooded collegiate campus
in Riverdale-on-Hudson, was added in 1928. Along the way,
the E.C.S. helped found the Hudson Guild Settlement
House and its summer camp for inner-city children, Camp

Felicia, and members of its board were among the founders of the N.A.A.C.P. and the A.C.L.U. The Society leader in the '40s, when I was attending Fieldston, was Algernon D. Black, who, among other things, chaired the Civilian Police Review Board in New York City and participated in the Committee for a Sane Nuclear Policy. And in more recent years, Ethical Culture has spearheaded programs for multi-cultural education and affirmative action.

My parents probably knew little, if anything, about Ethical Culture. They chose Fieldston because it was in walking distance from our house on Oxford Avenue—an irony, since the large majority of students lived in Manhattan and were thus known as the "subway crowd"—and because it had a fine academic reputation, somewhat stronger than that of the rival school, the Riverdale Country School for Girls. Fieldston was said to have excellent Latin and French programs and even offered Greek! It had an outstanding library. And best of all, the school awarded me a full scholarship.

But my first year at Fieldston was probably much more of an adjustment than my first year at P.S. 7 had been. Partly, this was just a matter of age: at thirteen, change is surely more difficult than at seven. But it was also a question of class and mores. P.S.7 was largely a working-class school with no pretenses. It taught the basics in a no-frills setting and did a perfectly good job educating its particular constituency. Fieldston, dedicated to lofty principles of "Ethical Culture" and social justice, had, at least in 1945, a student body that was about 90% Jewish and wealthy. Today, from what I read in the alumni magazine, things are different: in 2001, students of color made up 26% of newly enrolled students, and 23% of all students received some financial aid. But in the late war years, scholarship money was scarce and minority recruitment not yet at issue. Then, too, Fieldston was competing with the great New England prep schools, like Andover and Exeter, and in New York itself, there were Horace Mann, Brearley, Dalton, and Lincoln, as well as any number of church-related schools. So the Fieldston I entered was essentially a secularized Jewish, upper-class school. Such non-Jewish whites as attended Fieldston were mainly there because their parents were teachers or staff members: Elinor Bayes, for example, whose mother was the fifth form English teacher; Bart Saunders, whose father was the football coach; and Patsy Barrett, whose mother ran the bookshop and with whom I walked to school every day. There was also a small contingent of African-American students—in our class, the girls were Willie Churchill and Jeanne Allen—who almost invariably went on to have distinguished careers in fields like government or medicine.

To make things even more confusing, the dominant Jewish group consisted neither of practicing Jews nor assimilated and/or baptized ones, as had been the case in Vienna. Rather, Fieldston students were openly Jewish and, given the size and prosperity of the New York Jewish community, traveled in what were almost entirely Jewish social circles. A few boys made their bar mitzvah, but most of the students either belonged to Reform temples, where they were "confirmed" at age sixteen, or to no temple at all. No one seemed to be ashamed of being Jewish, no one tried to pass, but being Jewish was a sociocultural premise (or precondition) rather than a religion or even a fixed ethnicity.

Money, in these immediate postwar years, was the engine that drove everyday school life. Girls wore sweaters and skirts to school, but the sweaters were often cashmere, and for Saturday lunches at Stark's on 91st and Broadway, which was the in-place to go, they wore their sheared beaver coats, high heels, and never the same wool dress or suit twice. The popular students went to Viola Wolf's dancing classes once a week, to expensive Maine summer camps like Kennebunkport (for boys) and Racquet Lake (for girls), later to Bucks Rock or Shaker Village work camps (which were just as expensive), and then on to costly hostel or biking trips around Europe. Their teenage birthday parties were often held at night clubs like the Copacabana or at one of the Jewish beach clubs in the Hamptons. They lived in palatial apartments in the area above Central Park South and below 96th Street between Riverside Drive and Park Avenue; many families also had weekend houses in the so-called country (Scarsdale, Rye, Westport). Some of the Central Park West luxury buildings—the Majestic (number 115, at 72nd Street), the Beresford (numer 211 at 81st), the Eldorado (number 300 at 90th)—were the homes of more than one classmate. I don't recall a single Fieldstonite who lived below 59th Street or east of Park Avenue (the avenues further east were not yet fashionable in the '40s), and the only students who lived north of 96th were African-American or those few of us who lived in Riverdale or Westchester.

The décor of Fieldstonite apartments was curiously consistent and reflected the upward mobility of the head of the household, more often than not a man born on the Lower East Side who had made good in the garment indus-

try or in real estate. There was a large entrance hall, usually partially mirrored, with a hard upholstered bench or
chairs along one wall. The very formal and darkish living
room often had an ornamental grand piano and brand new
"antique" mahogany furniture, upholstered in soft colors—
golds and dark greens. The built-in bookshelves were primarily places to display china vases or knickknacks. The
equally dark and large formal dining room adjoined a rather
sterile kitchen and pantry, where the family maid, invariably
"colored," as she would then have been called, officiated.
(The maid's room adjoined the kitchen somewhere on its far
end.) The kitchen had none of the "gourmet" décor of later
years—the copper pots and French enamel casseroles, elegant wood and steel gadgets—since the lady of the house
rarely set foot in these precincts. The jack-of-all-trades
maid-cook served steak or lamb chops and baked potatoes
or, when the parents were out—which was much of the
time—hamburgers and bacon-lettuce-and-tomato sandwiches (B.L.T.s). Dessert meant Jell-O or chocolate pud-
ding, usually with Oreos or ginger snaps.

The childrens' bedrooms usually faced an inner court-
yard or alley, but they were all large enough to have two
beds, so that sleepovers were routine. Since I could never
have anyone sleep over in our tiny Riverdale apartment—
indeed, could never have anyone over in the evening at all,
because my parents slept in the living room—these teenage
bedrooms, with their ruffled bedspreads and matching cur-
tains, their shag rugs and large closets, impressed me enormously. By the ninth grade, when I had made many friends,
I "slept over" almost every weekend—at Betsy Asher's or
Ann Zabin's or Sally Lewis's.

But I anticipate. A month or so before my first day at Fieldston, I received a "big sister" letter from a Margie Leff, who was, I was soon to learn, the most popular girl in the class. Not only did I want to copy her curvy handwriting; I wanted, at some level, to *become* Margie, and so when it was time, a few months later, to take out citizenship papers, I changed my name officially to Marjorie. To be Margie one had to be Marjorie, a name I didn't much like even then, but it was a small price to pay, so I thought, for having a golden Manhattan name rather than the "foreign" Gabrielle. The real Margie Leff, however, played little role in my life; for one thing, she was not in my section, which had only eight girls and twelve boys, and here my "big sister" was one Bobbie Kasper, who lived in the Eldorado, and to whom I could never think of anything to say.

During the first week of school, whenever Mr. Bassett, our teacher, called on me, I jumped out of my seat as I had done at P.S. 7, much to everyone's amusement. "You may sit down, Gabrielle," Mr. Bassett said kindly. "Here we don't stand up when we speak." He was very understanding, as was Mrs. Bland who taught art. On the first day of art class, when I made a perfectly dreadful clay figure, supposedly a woman in a long dress and apron, holding a large sack, Mrs. Bland smiled encouragingly and said, "What an interesting sculpture!" This was certainly a far cry from P.S. 7, but I'm not sure I didn't prefer the honesty of Mrs. Engel, who told me I had ruined my graduation dress, to Mrs. Bland's blandishments. For the more the teachers smiled at me and treated me "kindly," the more "different" I felt.

My greatest trial at Fieldston, given my refugee background and my previous years at P. S. 7, where the asphalt schoolyard was primarily the site of hopscotch games and jump rope, was the daily gym period. In Vienna, schools located right in the city did not have sports facilities of any sort: one did one's academic work and went home for a late midday dinner—the big meal of the day—and stayed home. Sports were for Sundays and the very long winter and summer holidays, when one skied, swam, and went mountain climbing. But at Fieldston, every day at midmorning we had to put on our yellow gym suits, get out on the hatefully beautiful playing fields, and begin by running the mile around the track. The order was to warm up by climbing up a steep ramp and jumping down, then going over the thirty-foot Jacob's Ladder, maneuvering the horizontal monkey bars, and finally racing round the track itself. Climbing up the rungs of the Jacob's Ladder, I thought I would never have the courage to lift one of my legs so as to cross over the top rung. Suppose you slipped? One false move and you'd be dead! I was terrified. Every day I somehow did it, but it was just as scary the next day. The monkey bars were easier to handle, but I fell off once and sprained my arm, which was in a sling for weeks—blissful weeks, when I didn't have to climb the Jacob's Ladder at all. And when the track warm-up was over, we had to play field hockey, which was less scary but equally distasteful to me. I was a good swimmer, canoeist, and ice-skater, but hockey? Soccer? Weren't these team sports, as my grandmother declared, inferior to the individual display of skill on the ice-skating rink or ski slope? I asked to be fullback so that I could be in the rear of the field where the ball came only rarely. One could stand there and daydream for five minutes at a time, while the center forwards and wings worked themselves into a sweat.

So the beautiful Fieldston facilities—the collegiate graystone quadrangle [Figure 1], the elegant playing fields, art studios, woodworking shop, library, and dining room— were oppressive to me. The academic subjects were more congenial: we read and performed *Macbeth* in the eighth grade, confronting each other during recess with lines like, "Is this a dagger that I see before me?" or "If it were done when 'tis done, then 'twere well / It were done quickly." I loved English class as well as French, a subject that I had

FIGURE 1. Entrance, Fieldston School in winter, Ethical Culture Society brochure.

already studied with Grandmama, but I was easily distract-
ed by the social buzz that dominated the scene. Right outside our classroom in the hall were the mailboxes where
party invitations and similar notes were distributed. For
months I saw the other girls tear open little envelopes, gasp,
nudge each other, and whisper that someone was having a
party. During my first term, I was never invited, and at the
weekly tea dances sponsored by the school itself, I was
rarely asked to dance. So my main memory of eighth grade
is my first party invitation. On Valentine's Day, Bobby
Rosenbloom, a pretty blonde girl whom I had somewhat
befriended, had a party. The week before, I saw the others
reading their valentine-shaped invitations. Then one day
after much whispering between Bobby and Betty
Kronsky—a Larchmont girl who was the cohostess, since
her own house was too far away to serve as a party base—
the two came up to me during recess and gave me an invitation. It seems someone else couldn't come, and there was
an extra spot.

I was paralyzed with fear and anticipation. Parties,
eighth-grade style, were held between six and eight p.m.,
with the parents officiating. The "clique"—about fifteen
boys and as many girls—constituted less than half the class,
for the greater half was made up of assorted undesirables:
overly studious nerds, like Henry Feldman; unsophisticated
WASPS from Westchester, like Gail MacMahon; "colored
girls" (although colored boys like Cliff Alexander and
Walter White were very popular); and especially those
devoid of what was then called Personality. Personality was
a mysterious thing: even some of the richest Jewish Central
Park West girls and boys were judged to be without it.

Personality had little to do with brains or intellect or even looks: Patsy Kook, whose father owned Century Lighting Company, which provided the lighting for the leading Broadway shows, had bad skin and frizzy black hair but was immensely popular. On the other hand, without money, the right clothes, and social activities, personality was not easy to acquire.

Clutching my invitation, in any case, I went home and announced to my mother that I would need a "party dress," since I had none. It was decided that Grandmama would take me shopping that Saturday, and indeed I came home (from a small boutique on Madison Avenue) with a plaid taffeta sleeveless dress that cost $8.95. It was a very nice dress, but I then had no choice but to wear it to any and every party to which I was subsequently invited: we could not afford a second one. Whenever I came home from a party and sleepover, Mother and Grandmama wanted to know *everything*. Who was there? What was the hostess's last name? What did her father do? Was hers what was called in Vienna *eine gute Familie*? I would describe the buffet table as best I could but managed not to say that the party game played ubiquitously was "Scotch, Gin, and Rye." When the father chaperone in question called "Scotch!" you stood still. "Gin!" meant change partners. And "Rye!" meant kiss. That was tremendously exciting, even if I never got to "Rye!" at the same time as the boy I had a crush on, Archer Scherl.

Meanwhile, at school, where Latin and French were being taught quite rigorously enough to please my parents, I was also initiated into the subject of ethics. Once a week, we had an hour of ethics, taught that first year by Henry

Herman, one of the leaders of the Ethical Culture Society. Ethics, it seemed, had no content—no books to read or lessons to learn: it was conducted largely as a rap session, and although I took ethics for five years, one class a week, I cannot now remember anything except that we discussed the meaning of words like "jealousy," and that in my senior year, we were finally privileged to have the head of the Society, Algernon Black, as our teacher. One "lesson" had to do with assessing the "value" our culture placed on certain jobs. On the board was a list including such jobs as taxi driver, banker, lawyer, factory worker, and teacher. "Arthur," Mr. Black asked Arthur Sarnoff, whose uncle, David Sarnoff, was the president of R.C.A., "how would you rate a taxi driver?" "Well," said Arthur, "if I needed a cab, I suppose I would rate him pretty high." Everyone burst out laughing. And this is the extent of my recollection of "ethics," as taught at E.C.S.

Instinctively, I knew that whatever ethics might be, the casual discussions we had in our weekly ethics class had little to do with it. But then, even when, later at Oberlin, I took ethics, reading my way from Aristotle's *Nicomachean Ethics* through Kant and Nietzsche to G.E. Moore's eloquent arguments in his *Principia Ethica* for an ethical intuitionism ("good" is a simple, non-natural, indefinable quality in things that we recognize intuitively), I found all attempts to define the essential nature of Good and Evil curiously unsatisfying. It was not until many years later, when I read in Wittgenstein's *Tractatus* (6.41), "The sense of the world must lie outside the world," and so "there can be no ethical *propositions*" (my emphasis) that ethics began to interest me. For as Wittgenstein put it in his "Lecture on Ethics" (1929):

My whole tendency and I believe the tendency of all men who ever tried to write or talk Ethics or Religion was to run against the boundaries of language. This running against the walls of our cage is perfectly, absolutely hopeless. Ethics so far as it springs from the desire to say something about the ultimate meaning of life, the absolute good, the absolutely valuable, can be no science. What it says does not add to our knowledge in any sense. But it is a document of a tendency in the human mind which I personally cannot help respecting deeply and I would not for my life ridicule it.[3]

The notion of limits, the refusal to express the inexpressible seemed to me even then central to any discussion of the ethical. Wittgenstein, quite rightly I think, cautions us to respect rather than ridicule the "tendency in the human mind" to make ethical pronouncements, but my Viennese upbringing, with its emphasis on individual talent and intellectual achievement, made it difficult to swallow such Ethical Culture articles of faith as "the supreme aim of human life is working to create a more humane society" (what was that anyway?), or that "diversity of thought, rather than belief in prescribed metaphysical or philosophical ideas, is one of our chief strengths." On the contrary, I had been taught that some philosophical ideas were inherently better than others, that indeed some ideas were "great," whereas "diversity of thought" was just a polite term for blandness and lack of resolve. And so I whispered and giggled in class and was sent out of the room on numerous occasions. By spring, my parents received a note from the principal reporting that I was one of only six students (out of ninety) who was sent out of class twice and was asked "to report to Miss Murphy for admonition and correction." Mother and Daddy merely shrugged it off. What mattered were my grades (which were good, but should be, they felt, even better!); never mind this nonsense about ethics class.

In retrospect, I am not proud of this attitude. What now strikes me as even worse than the simplistic Ethical Culture creed was the contempt many of the European intellectuals had for it, opposed as they were to "naïve" forms of American ameliorism—the attempt to "get involved" and build a "better" society. Fieldston students were expected as a matter of course to be counselors at summer camps for ghetto children, to work for settlement houses, and to send C.A.R.E. packages to the men and women in the armed forces. Meanwhile, the Frankfurt School intellectuals, now residing in New York, remained on the sidelines, producing a relentless critique of American technologism and consumer society.

Take the case of Adorno's *Minima Moralia*, written primarily during 1944–45, when the critic found himself in exile in New York. Born Theodor Wiesengrund in Frankfurt to a Jewish father and Catholic mother (whose name he took when he came to the United States), Adorno arrived in New York in 1938, having been invited by the sociologist Paul Lazarsfeld to join the Institute for Social Research. Abhorring the positivism of American sociology, with its scientist faith in induction and deduction, Adorno remained a confirmed outsider, whether in New York or later in California. In 1949, he returned to Frankfurt to officiate at the reconstituted Institute there. His American exile had lasted little over a decade.

I have frequently taught *Minima Moralia* in critical theory courses, because its subtle and arresting fragments, meditating on what Adorno calls "damaged life," provide an excellent introduction to the central theoretical arguments developed at greater length elsewhere in Adorno's writing. The book's extreme pessimism, coupled with a belief that only High Art can provide true *resistance* to the horrors of capitalist culture, has produced a powerful *frisson* in what is currently a deeply disaffected American academy. Then, too, *Minima Moralia* is an interesting example of hybridity: part fiction, part theory, even part poetry, its complex vocal structure is intriguing. But to reread Adorno's text against the backdrop of the refugee experience is to experience this text rather differently. Consider the following:

Every intellectual in emigration is, without exception, mutilated, and does well to acknowledge it to himself, if he wishes to avoid being cruelly apprised of it behind the tightly-closed doors of his self-esteem. He lives in an environment that must remain incomprehensible to him, however flawless his knowledge of trade-union organizations or the automobile industry may be; he is always astray. Between the reproduction of his own existence under the monopoly of mass culture and impartial responsible work yawns an irreconcilable breach. His language has been expropriated and the historical dimension that nourished his knowledge sapped.[7]

Such expressions of alienation were to strike a resonant chord in the post-Vietnam era, when it was *de rigueur* to vilify the "monopoly of mass culture" Adorno speaks of. But in 1944, when Adorno wrote these words, there were surely issues more pressing than the state of American consumer culture. Indeed, however wide the "irreconcilable breach" that made "responsible work" so difficult for Adorno, along with the "expropriation" of language that he complains of, the fact is that, unlike the less fortunate (and less affluent) German Jews of his time, he, at least, was *alive*—alive in a nation that, whatever its deficiencies, was not a Nazi dictatorship that practiced genocide—indeed, was willing, not only to take in Jewish refugees like Adorno and help them find work but, at the same time, was sending its own young men to risk their lives in order to destroy the regime that would have sent him to the gas chambers.

What precisely, moreover, is that "historical dimension that nourished [Adorno's] knowledge" and which, he remarks so mournfully, has been "sapped"? Throughout *Minima Moralia*, it is described in terms like the following:

Do not knock.—Technology is making gestures precise and brutal, and with them men. It expels from movements all hesitation, deliberation, civility. It subjects them to the implacable, as it were ahistorical demands of objects. Thus the ability is lost, for example, to close a door quietly and discreetly, yet firmly. Those of cars and refrigerators have to be slammed, others have the tendency to snap shut by themselves. . . . what does it mean for the subject that there are no more casement windows to open, but only sliding frames to shove, no gentle latches but turnable handles, no forecourt, no doorstep before the street, no wall around the garden? . . . . the movements machines demand of their users already have the violent, hard-hitting, unresting jerkiness of Fascist maltreatment. (MM, 40)

From a literary perspective, the notion that something as trivial as the slamming of a door or the shape of a window latch is not just a random gesture or object, that, on the contrary, it is infused with political significance, is both persuasive and appealing. But read in historical context, as I think it must be, the passage takes on highly problematic overtones. No more doors that close "quietly and discreetly," "no more casement windows to open" with "gentle latches," "no forecourt, no doorstep before the street," "no wall around the garden." These words certainly applied to our little apartment at 3204 Oxford Avenue, where the front door led directly into the small living room and the windows had precisely those "sliding frames to shove" that Adorno refers to with such contempt. But who, in that lost world Adorno mourns, had familiarity with those casements and gentle latches, those walled gardens that are "no more"? Or again, (this time the reference is #77, "Auction") who was it that enjoyed "the faded splendour" and "voluptuousness of travel" of the old railroad trains, with their "goodbye-waving through the open window, the solicitude of amiable accepters of tips, the ceremonial of mealtimes, the constant feeling of receiving favours that take nothing from anyone else" (MM, 119)?

Adorno's "no more," here and throughout the book, takes as its norm the material existence of the upper class to which he belonged. In Vienna, where he spent the years 1925–27 studying music, first with Alban Berg and then with Schoenberg and his circle, working-class housing was so substandard that 70% of all dwelling units still lacked private toilets and sometimes running water. Given these circumstances, and given the special symbolism of window glass associated with the *Kristallnacht* of November 1938, the nostalgia for "real" windows that have casements with "gentle latches" rather than those sliding frames to push up and down, manufactured in America, now strikes me as almost incomprehensible. As for the suggestion that there is

something "Fascist" about the "hard-hitting unresting jerkiness" of mechanized objects, it is an irony of history that the
same capitalist industry that had produced those noisy
refrigerators would soon find ways to make them supersi-
lent, just as the invention of the computer would wholly
undercut the "hard-hitting unresting jerkiness" and ugly
sounds of the typewriter. Advanced technology, it seems,
can no more be equated with Fascism than with any other
political system.

Given these aporias of émigré intellectual ethos, perhaps it was just as well, for a Viennee refugee child like
myself, to encounter the naïve but upbeat progressivism of
Ethical Culture, especially as it was tempered, at Fieldston,
by a perfectly straightforward curriculum in math and science, English and foreign languages. True, the curriculum
lacked the rigor and the depth of the Viennese gymnasium—Mother and Daddy were "shocked" that we studied so
little European history—but the school's emphasis on tolerance, community, and service made up, at least in part, for
some of these intellectual deficiencies. And herein lie some
further paradoxes.

INTELLIGENCE/INTELLECT/SUCCESS

"I do not think," writes Alexis de Tocqueville near the
beginning of *Democracy in America*, "that there is a country
in the world where, in proportion to population, so few
ignorant and fewer learned men are found than in America.
Primary instruction there is within reach of each; higher
instruction is within reach of almost no one." And to unrav-
el this paradox, Tocqueville explains:

In America most of the rich have begun by being poor; almost all the idle were, in their youth, employed; the result is that when one could have the taste for study, one does not have the time to engage in it; and when one has acquired the time to engage in it, one no longer has the taste for it.

There does not exist in America, therefore, any class in which the penchant for intellectual pleasures is transmitted with comfort and inherited leisure, and which holds the works of the intellect in honor. . . .

One therefore encounters an immense multitude of individuals who have nearly the same number of notions in matters of religion, of history, of science, of political economy, of legislation, of government.

Intellectual inequality comes directly from God, and man cannot prevent it from existing always.

But it happens, at least from what we have just said, that intelligence, while remaining unequal as the Creator wished, finds equal means at its disposition.[5]

This was published in 1835 and hence might seem less than applicable to the situation at Fieldston in the 1940s, much less in the next century. Most of us do not believe that "Intellectual inequality comes directly from God"; rather, it depends in large measure on early childhood training, social class, family background, and educational opportunity. But what Tocqueville says about work remains true to this day: Americans, even the richest ones (and the percentage is much higher today than in the 1830s), feel that it is incumbent upon them to *work* at some sort of gainful employment, and that therefore "success," however we define it, takes precedence over something called the intellectual life.

In recent years, much fuss has been made about the

decline of the so-called public intellectual. From Russell Jacoby's *The Last Intellectuals* (1987) to Richard A. Posner's *Public Intellectuals: A Study of Decline* (2001), the theme has been that the "public intellectuals" of the '40s and '50s (the New York or *Partisan Review* crowd) are in decline. By "public intellectual," Posner means someone who applies general ideas and principles to contemporary issues so as to educate the public on key issues. In this scheme of things— and it is typically American—literature and the humanities in general are given short shrift, and it is not surprising that Henry Kissinger is #1 on Posner's list of leading intellectuals, even as Jean-Paul Sartre is only #64, Marshall MacLuhan #82, and Margaret Mead #94. The Supreme Court Justice Antonin Scalia weighs in at #4, ahead of George Bernard Shaw (#17), and so forth.

This sort of list-making is of course nonsensical. But however meaningless Posner's list may be, it suggests that, in our culture, even intellectuals are primarily judged by utilitarian standards. The contemplative life is considered a suspect luxury, as is the scholarly life in pursuit of abstruse knowledge. In the Schlosser seminar at the University of Vienna, let's recall, Otto Kurz and Ernst Gombrich might engage in studies of Dürer's reception in Portugal or the origins of the Islamic clock. If asked what such studies were for, these fledgling art historians would have replied that knowledge is a good in itself. In the United States, as Tocqueville understood, this notion never quite caught on, the liberal arts being generally understood, in our universities and public forums, as designed to improve people, to make them more sensitive and "caring," and especially to produce "better" citizens.

In practice, whether at Fieldston in the '40s or at liberal arts colleges across the country, what this really means is that in a democratic society, all complex theoretical constructs or ideologies are suspect, their abstract formulations being likely to clash with the basic American faith in progress and equal opportunity. Accordingly, Kantian and Hegelian idealism, so valued in the Austrian educational system in which my parents were raised, is subordinated in America to a flexible pragmatism with a Deweyite cast. Aesthetic experience, in this scheme of things, is not intrinsically different from experience in general, and the process of art-making is best understood as a heightened form of all creative human activity. Indeed, the premise that anyone can make "art" is what animates the expensive and beautifully outfitted painting, photography, mosaic, and sculpture studios one finds in such retirement communities as Leisure World. If one has never learned to ski, one is not likely to attempt the sport at age sixty. But painting? Modeling in clay? Of course!

But since our "free" and "creative" social order is also characterized by its emphasis on competition, "doing well" at school was and remains of the utmost importance. The Fieldston ethos was thus notable for an emphasis on a measurable "intelligence" (I.Q.) that had no necessary relation to "intellect." Fieldston boys wanted to do "well" and get into the "right" college so that, when the time came, they would be successful lawyers, doctors, businessmen, executives, and so on; the girls, in those days, wanted to do well so that they could marry the right lawyers, doctors, and businessmen. This means that all students read their assignments, wrote their essays, and took their tests seriously, even as schoolwork was rarely talked about unless a particular difficulty came up. In the fifth form (junior year), we finally read some serious literary texts: Sophocles' *Antigone* and *Electra* (which was read against Eugene O'Neill's *Mourning Becomes Electra)*, Dostoevsky's *Crime and Punishment*, and the poems of Robert Frost. In the sixth form, in the advanced English seminar (entrance by invitation only based on earlier performance) taught by Elbert Lenrow of the New School, we did a Great Books survey from Plato and Aristotle, the King James Bible and Lucretius, down to Thomas Hardy's *The Return of the Native* and André Malraux's *Man's Fate*. In the seminar, discussions of Dante or Montaigne, Descartes or Locke, were extremely lively, but again they rarely continued outside the classroom. School was school, and in one's free time, one talked about things that really mattered, like friendship, sports, and sex. No ideas but in things! Or rather, no ideas but in everyday material life.

When Adorno was fifteen, Martin Jay tells us, "he was introduced to German classical philosophy by a friend of the family, Siegfried Kracauer [later the great film theorist], fourteen years his senior, with whom he began a weekly habit of reading Kant's first *Critique*."[6] My parents and grandparents hardly expected this sort of thing from us— indeed, it was totally exceptional even in the Frankfurt or Vienna of the 1920s—but I think they were disappointed that neither Walter nor I devoted much time to intellectual pursuits. The passion for philosophical rigor, for the poetry of Goethe and Schiller, for the Greek and Roman classics— these were supposed to be the domain of the gymnasium education. Ideas *mattered*, even though it was not quite clear how theory might actually determine *praxis*. It was, in any case, my parents' fond hope that I would read "serious" novels and classical drama and that I would stay away from kitsch or false art, the very enemy of the *Kulturdrang* that had animated their lives in Vienna.

Kitsch, writes Matei Calinescu in an elaborate study of the term, "is a recent phenomenon." The word, which enters the vocabulary in the 1860s and '70s in the jargon of painters and art dealers in Munich, "appears at the moment in history when beauty in its various forms is socially distributed like any other commodity subject to the essential market law of supply and demand." And he talks of the "ubiquity of spurious beauty in today's world, in which even nature (as exploited and commercialized by the tourist industry) has ended up resembling cheap art."[7] Kitsch, explains Adorno in *Aesthetic Theory*, is the "false aesthetic consciousness" inherent in mass culture, a "parody of catharsis."[8] But whereas Adorno and his Frankfurt School colleagues studied kitsch as the inevitable product of the commodification of capitalism and the culture industry, my parents' circle was more interested in its reception. The discrimination of the aesthetic as opposed to its kitschy simulacrum was the sign, so it was held, of *Bildung*: those with genuine education and culture could sniff out the kitsch, could tell that it was not the "real" thing. Kitsch, in this parlance, refers not to popular culture—say, pop music or the soap operas, for these were obviously of a lower order; kitsch, on the contrary, referred to work that has aesthetic pretensions and is therefore all the more reprehensible. Theodore Fontane's *Effi Briest* was "art," whereas Herman Wouk's *Marjorie Morningstar* was kitsch. James Gould Cozzens's *SS San Pedro* was a kitsch version of Melville's

Billy Budd. Arthur Miller's *Death of a Salesman*, while not without merit, reduced the role of the Greek chorus to Mrs. Loman's kitschy speech, pleading that "attention must be paid" to the "tragic" plight of traveling salesmen like her husband, Willy. Factory-made "antiques" were, of course, kitsch, but even furniture that was verifiably "old" might be kitsch if it was pretentious, as in the case of Tiffany lamps with their state-of-the-art light bulbs.

As a teenager, I was always hearing conversations culminating in the phrase, *Dass ist doch nur Kitsch!* (This is merely kitsch!) Once the judgment had been made, the object(s) in question brooked no further discussion. How "art" might be kitschified in capitalist culture, why certain material goods were beloved by the bourgeois public, and what function they might serve in their lives were never at issue. Kitsch was kitsch, and it was our obligation to call it that and display our ability to discriminate.

At Fieldston, I thus had to walk a fine line between my friends' tastes and my family's. Everybody loved *Oklahoma!*, but I wasn't taken to see it, partly because tickets were too expensive, but also because my grandmother suspected it was likely to be kitsch. When Rodgers and Hammerstein's next production, *Carousel*, opened on Broadway, I begged to go see it and, since at least this musical was based on the play *Liliom* by the Hungarian Ferenc Molnar, I was allowed to take a few friends to see it on my birthday. Of course when I expressed my enthusiasm for *Carousel*, my mother and grandmother gave each other a look, as if to say, "Poor child, she doesn't yet *understand*."

I wish I could say that I wholly rebelled against these elitist notions of art, but the fact is that I thoroughly internalized them. Throughout college and graduate school, I found myself wanting to dismiss this or that work that most people seemed to admire—Peter Shaffer's psychodrama *Equus* or Lawrence Durrell's *Alexandria Quartet*—because to my mind it displayed the ersatz profundity of kitsch. A more recent example would be the film version of *Schindler's List*, a film I found it impossible to sit through. I couldn't bear the presentation of Oskar Schindler, the "good" Nazi who becomes the savior of more than a thousand Jews, or indeed the images of those Jewish victims, all of them "sensitive" and resourceful—and fine violinists to boot! And I was offended by Steven Spielberg's pretense to deal with an unspeakable human tragedy, all the while presenting as many lurid sex scenes as possible for the sake of box-office appeal. Such kitsch, I continue to believe, is painful to encounter because of its dishonesty. But it takes a particular commitment to experience this particular dishonesty as some sort of personal violation—a commitment, I suppose, to the religion of Art.

As a teenager, however, I suppressed such thoughts and resented my parents' superior smiles and dismissive remarks. Indeed, I wanted nothing so much as to be exactly like Patsy Kook or Bobby Litt, who went to see *South Pacific* at least two or three times, pronounced Ayn Rand's *The Fountainhead* the best novel ever written, and Maxwell Anderson's *Winterset* the best play. I wished that my mother could be more like *other* mothers—ladies who lunched, shopped, or played cards and who knew the songs featured on the *Hit Parade*, whereas *my* mother didn't even know who Frank Sinatra was. Why couldn't one "keep up" with the fashions? Why couldn't one just have *fun* without being so intellectual?

The only girl in my class whose cultural milieu resembled my own was Anna Kris, the daughter of Marianne and Ernst Kris, both émigré psychoanalysts from Vienna. Unlike my parents, they were affluent, because analysts made a great deal of money in the postwar years. But the life style of the Drs. Kris (Ernst Kris was an art historian/analyst who had worked closely with Ernst Gombrich and my uncle Otto Kurz) was not quite my ideal either. One always had to enter their large apartment at 135 Central Park West by the service elevator and kitchen door so as not to disturb the patients seated in the waiting room near the front door. The large and airy rooms facing the park were consultation rooms, Anna and her brother Tony occupying the darkish back rooms. Marianne Kris (who was to become Marilyn Monroe's analyst!) never had a moment: between patients, she hurriedly popped into Anna's room, to see what her daughter might need. She was plainly dressed and, for my taste, not sufficiently well coiffed or made up. And Ernst Kris presided over Anna's *Bildung* with an iron hand: she had special afterschool tutorials in Latin and other subjects and was taken to museums for serious lessons in art history. I was happy that no such burdens were placed on me.

Indeed at home, despite all the distinctions drawn between art and kitsch in everyday conversation, I was given a large measure of freedom. My mother was busy with her studies at Columbia and was often not at home in the afternoons, so that I could gossip on the phone for hours with Patsy or Betsy. Then too, my parents couldn't afford private lessons; on the contrary, it was my mother's firm belief that my brother and I should learn the value of money by doing odd jobs like washing windows, for which the pay was twenty-five cents per window. We were taught to itemize all expenses, and on weekends I took up baby-sitting. This was a wonderful way to escape the confines of our small apartment, read romance novels or trashy magazines in someone else's living room, and smoke on the sly. In those days, parents gave no instructions whatsoever: I would baby-sit across the street for a rather careless mother, who never told me what to do if the baby cried. When her little boy did cry, as frequently happened, I would pat him on the back and say "Shh," since I knew nothing about bottles or wet diapers. Sooner or later, the baby went back to sleep. "Was everything all right?" asked the father when the parents returned at midnight or so. "Fine," I said, taking the money and running. And my mother, who had no idea about baby-sitting customs in America, never asked me any questions the next day.

WHICH SIDE ARE YOU ON?

If the Ethical Culture creed played a fairly minor role during the school year, when we were all busy conjugating Latin verbs or working in the chemistry lab, it did have a direct impact on those of us who chose to attend the school-sponsored or affiliated settlement work camps in the summer. In 1946, I went to the University Settlement Work Camp near Beacon, a poor industrial town about sixty miles north of New York in the Hudson Valley, recently made famous by the appearance of the new Dia Beacon, a stunning museum of art from the 1960s to the present. The camp itself was on a rather nondescript wooden site nearby. Approximately sixteen of us, mostly from Fieldston and affiliated private schools, like Walden and Dalton, paid a small tuition so as to work four hours a day at tasks like painting buildings, collecting trash, or raking leaves. We also washed our own bed linens, aired out the blankets, and scrubbed the cabins [Figure 2]. One got through these boring chores as best one could, ready for the rest of the day and evening spent having endless gossip sessions with and about one another and about our camp leader, Albert Cook, known as Cookie, who was given to asking embarrassing personal questions and holding forth on politics. But the real politics at Beacon was sexual: it was everyone's first

FIGURE 2. Margie Mintz, University Settlement Camp, Beacon, New York, summer 1946.

intense coed experience away from home, and we were all in a constant state of erotic—mostly unfulfilled—desire, since this was still the period where "nice girls" were virgins.

What made this camp experience special for me is that here at last I was on neutral turf. It didn't matter that I lived in a shabby little apartment, couldn't afford dance lessons at Viola Wolf, belonged to no temple, and possessed no elegant clothes. At camp, we all wore the same shorts and T-shirts and had to do the same chores. It was even more satisfying the next summer, when Ann Zabin, Sally Lewis, and I went to Madison House Work Camp in nearby Peekskill. By this time, we were sixteen and the other work campers (our private school classmates) were not nearly as appealing as the counselors, college students in the C.U.N.Y. system, mostly from the Lower East Side. At Madison, the facilities were makeshift and messy—we had a cesspool right in front of our cabin— and the camp director, Joe Jacobs, never figured out what the "work" was that we were in fact paying to do. Since the sports facilities were very limited, we spent the first few weeks complaining, hanging out, and wishing we could go home.

But gradually, we were caught up in the life of the campers and their counselors. We listened to Joe Jacobs harangue the campers ("How many of you have hot meals to go home to?") and learned by heart the great union songs of the '30s, for example, Woody Guthrie's "Union Maid," made famous by Pete Seeger:

> There once was a union maid,
> She never was afraid
> Of goons and ginks and company finks
> And the deputy sheriffs who made the raid.

She went to the union hall when a meeting it was called,
And when the Legion boys come 'round
She always stood her ground.

CHORUS:
Oh, you can't scare me, I'm sticking to the union,
I'm sticking to the union, I'm sticking to the union.
Oh, you can't scare me, I'm sticking to the union,
I'm sticking to the union 'til the day I die.

Or the Guthrie-Seeger-Jim Garland ballad:

Oh I don't want your millions, mister.
And I don't want your diamond ring.
All I want is the right to live, mister.
Give me back my job again.

Or Florence Reese's memorable song celebrating the coal miners' strikes in the early thirties:

My daddy was a miner,
And I'm a miner's son,
And I'll stick with the union
'Til every battle's won.

CHORUS :
Which side are you on?
Which side are you on?
Which side are you on?
Which side are you on?

No one was too interested in what these songs actually signified, but we thrilled to their sound, their explosive language, and their tone of rebellion. Before long, we had teamed up with the "settlement boys," as the counselors were called, and I had a boyfriend from the Lower East Side named Iggy Stein, who gave me a ring [Figure 3], seemed very worldly, and held forth to me on American injustice.

FIGURE 3. Iggy Stein and Margie Mintz, Madison House Work Camp, Peekskill, summer 1947.

But the great romance of the summer was Sally Lewis's—for hers was with a black man named Harrison Marion Cox Lightfoot, known as Foot, who was twenty-four years old (ancient by our standards) and taught sociology at Howard University. None of these affairs withstood the return to the city at summer's end, but in the meantime I felt

I was being initiated into a world that could be described as "intellectual," with respect to its concern for social and political issues, even though it was hardly "cultured" in Geistkreis terms. In the fall of 1948, Henry Wallace ran for president on the Progressive Party ticket. His pro-Soviet platform attacking the Marshall Plan and his call for disarmament were popular among the Fieldston left, spearheaded by students like Staughton Lynd, whose parents, Robert and Helen Lynd, were the authors of *Middletown*, the seminal study of the effects of class in Middle America, and Roger Baldwin, Jr., whose father was the founder of the A.C.L.U.

My parents, who now feared the Soviets as much as they had despised the Nazis, listened to my reports about Fieldston political rallies with open disapproval. I myself was not "political," but one of my good friends was Debby Willen (now Deborah Meier, a noted educator and MacArthur Fellow), whose beautiful apartment in The Normandy on 86th Street and Riverside Drive was very different from most Fieldston apartments. At the far end of the large entrance hall there was a giant mural of Lenin, Trotsky, and their compatriots, and there were books and pamphlets everywhere. Mr. Willen was a fundraiser for the United Jewish Appeal, Mrs. Willen (one of the few mothers who worked) was a director of the League of Women Voters. The Willens were rarely home on the evenings when I slept over—the maid served us dinner—but in the morning there were often strange little men at the breakfast table, discussing in low voices what seemed to be burning issues. I was very taken by the Willen ambiance until, a few summers later when I was at Oberlin (where Debby's brother Paul organized political rallies at Arch 7 on Tappan

Square), Mrs. Willen asked about my summer plans, and when I said that I was going to be a counselor at University Settlement Camp, she said pityingly, "Oh, doesn't your family have a country place?"

The hypocrisy of limousine liberalism was an aspect of Ethical Culture I have never quite forgiven or forgotten. At the tenth-year Fieldston reunion (the first and last I attended), a questionnaire was sent out that typically posed such questions as, "Do you think criminals should be treated with punitive or rehabilitative methods?" The "right" answer was so obvious that I naughtily wrote in "punitive." The questionnaire was anonymous, but at the reunion I was immediately asked why I had become so cynical. The organizers had easily spotted my questionnaire, because it was postmarked Washington, D.C., and I was the only member of our class who lived there—indeed, one of the few Fieldstonites to have ventured west of the Hudson.

But that was later. In those early postwar years, when I was eager to belong at all costs, I wanted nothing so much as to spend my free time at the Henry Street Settlement House, reading to a bevy of grateful girls and teaching them how to make necklaces and lanyards. Taking the Van Cortlandt Park train home from the Lower East Side on a Thursday evening, I felt as far removed as possible from my childhood world of dirndls, lederhosen, and raspberry juice (*Himbeersaft*), of *Die lustigen Neun* and *Die Jungfrau von Orleans*. My family had become, at that moment, remote figures from the Old World, figures who couldn't understand how thrilling it was to have rap sessions about race, religion, and social issues with the Henry Street program director, Sol Ashkenazi, and his equally thrilling (and sexy) staff. Arriving at 3204 Oxford Avenue, after a long day, and seeing Mother and Daddy reading or working quietly in the little living room, was thus curiously deflating. No doubt, mine was in large part a standard teenage reaction, but it was surely aggravated by my outsider status in a country where family bonds are not nearly as strong as they had been in Vienna. Tocqueville makes an apropos comment in his chapter on individualism:

> In democratic centuries . . . when the duties of each individual toward the species are much clearer, devotion toward one man becomes rarer: the bond of human affections is extended and loosened.
>
> In democratic peoples, new families constantly issue from nothing, others constantly fall into it, and all those who stay on change face; the fabric of time is torn at every moment and the trace of generations is effaced. You easily forget those who have preceded you, and have no idea of those who will follow. Only those nearest have interest. (DIA, 483)

In the tight social fabric of assimilated Jewish Vienna in the '20s and '30s, family and social ties remained powerful. When my mother and her sisters attended balls, everyone knew they were the daughters of Sektionschef Dr. Richard Schüller, and a love affair gone sour, like Susi's with Konrad Zweig, was as commonly known as was Natasha's elopement with Anatole in the high society circles of *War and Peace*. Even later, scattered around the United States, the Viennese kept tabs on family members and kept up not only with the lives of their friends but of their friends' children. And not a day went by in New York that Mother didn't see or at least speak to her mother and grandmother, and often to her sister-in-law Stella as well.

For me, such cultural cohesion, coupled with the frequent reprimand to speak German, seemed in 1948 nothing if not claustrophobic. With Walter away at Reed College in Portland, Oregon, all the way across the continent, I tried as much as possible to avoid *die Familie*. Indeed, so absorbed was I in my daily personal and social round that I paid little attention to developments that now strike me as remarkable. Immediately after the war had ended, Grandfather received a letter from Karl Renner, the chancellor of the Second Republic, enlisting his help in getting the new government on its feet (UV, 69). Renner, a leading Marxist theorist and Social Democrat in the immediate post–World War I years, had been the first elected chancellor of the First Republic, so the wheel had come full circle. Grandfather knew Renner well and admired his intellect: they had worked together over the years on various treaties and diplomatic missions. But in 1938, Renner had made a surprising turnabout. In a newspaper interview shortly before the plebiscite ordered by Schuschnigg, he suddenly called for an affirmative vote for "our Führer Adolf Hitler." According to George Berkley, "He even sought permission from the Nazi authorities to issue an outright appeal to his old comrades to vote for the annexation." "Systems change," he later explained, "but states endure" (GBE, 304; cf. UV, 69). Hitler must have been aware of this support from the left, for Renner spent the war years in comfortable seclusion in the country.

Such was the man selected in 1945 to be chancellor of the new provisional government set up by the occupying powers. This time he owed his post, which he held until 1950, to the Soviets, who were the first to reach Vienna at the war's end. Renner was evidently hand-picked for his new post by Stalin, who was looking for a respected figure who might one day lead a left-wing front for him in Vienna.[9] Born the same year (1870) as Grandfather, Renner was evidently willing in his old age to play off one side against the other in his zeal to serve the Austrian nation. Grandfather seemed pleased to hear from him, as he was by a letter from his old colleague Heinrich Wildner, who informed Grandfather that he had redecorated the *Sektionschef*'s former office in the hope that he might come back to Vienna and take up his former post in the ministry. And Viktor Kienboch, the former finance minister and president of the Austrian National Bank, wrote that he was awaiting his old friend Schüller with open arms.

Grandfather was now seventy-six, and there was no possibility of a return to Vienna, but had he been even ten years younger, it is conceivable that he might have seriously considered it. The whole family, in any case, was proud that Grandfather was once again receiving homage from his former Viennese colleagues and that in 1950, when he celebrated his eightieth birthday, still a professor at the New School, he received so many testimonials from Vienna. It was as if, despite everything that had happened, Grandfather felt that his real home was still the Ballhausplatz. But he was also greatly beloved in the United States. For his birthday, the textile manufacter Bernhard Altmann, whom Grandfather advised from time to time, gave him a vicuna coat that he now sported on his walks around Riverdale, and Leopold Pilzer, who owned the Thonet furniture company, named the eighty-year-old Richard Schüller a director with a salary of $2,000 per year, for which Grandfather did precious little (UV, 188). Thonet plywood chairs, not exactly designed by Otto Wagner or Alfred Loos but reasonably attractive and highly practical, graced both my grandparents' living room and ours.

Now that the war was over, family relations could once more be renewed, both with Aunts Hilde and Susi, who hadn't seen their parents or sister in seven years, as well as with the South American contingent (Aunt Hedi and her sons). In the winter of 1948, Grandmama made her first postwar trip to Rome to visit the Pirolis, and the next year Hilde and Erica came to New York to visit us. For my parents, whose financial situation was now much improved, the late '40s were a time of personal fulfillment. They even found, along with their refugee friends, the ideal summer vacation spot: Mount Desert Island in Maine, whose natural beauty (both ocean and lakes!) had the virtue of *not* reminding them of the Austrian Alps. But Mother and Daddy were deeply pessimistic about the news from Europe, especially after Churchill's Iron Curtain speech in 1946, followed in 1948 by the Soviet blockade of Berlin. The term *Cold War*, which to younger Americans today signifies McCarthyism, surveillance, the loss of civil liberties, and aggressive U.S. militarism, meant something rather different to my parents, who regarded Western Europe, still their mental and spiritual home, as once again in danger of destruction. Out of the Nazi Fascist frying pan and into the Soviet Communist fire.

Grandfather Schüller was perhaps too old to concern himself with the new political and military struggles of the period. Although he was the least introspective of men, he had been persuaded to write his memoirs, and so he had to reconsider the terrible Dollfuss and Schuschnigg years in the '30s. "My greatest failure," he observes, "was that I lacked the perspicacity to understand the weaknesses of others." Accordingly, "I had too little insight into the future and took all sorts of dangerous risks. My colleagues (Wildner etc.) remarked that I was always on the edge of a precipice" (UV, 191). On the other hand, says Grandfather, he compensated for this failure by keeping his distance from others, by remaining as independent as possible. It was this equanimity I witnessed as a young girl, when, on weekly visits to Cambridge Avenue, Grandfather told me his stories about Brest Litovsk or about the role he played in the Hague Conference of 1930, so central to Austria's financial future [Figure 4]. The pessimism of my parents, who, after

FIGURE 4.   Right to left: Richard Schüller, Chancellor Johannes Schober, and two unidentified diplomats, Hague Conference, 1930.

the trauma of the emigration, always seemed to expect the worst, was offset by Grandfather's robust optimism—his sense, perhaps a shade callous but nevertheless comforting, that *things would work out*. As a teenager, I didn't really take his words in, for in those days I was eager to cut the visit short and focus on my own life.

Some twenty years later, however, when I experienced what I took to be a major crisis (I was turned down for tenure by my department at Catholic University), I went to see Grandfather, then a hundred, for advice. Much to my irritation, he did not seem to share my outrage at the iniquities of my colleagues. "One way or another," he said, "the situation will resolve itself favorably. Don't dwell on minutiae you can't change." What he meant—and I have thought of it often—is that you can't always control a specific outcome, but your attitude and behavior will effect the larger picture. He turned out to be quite right. The department reversed its decision, but by this time I no longer wanted to be part of it. And so the "crisis" gave me the push to look elsewhere.

Perhaps, I decided, Grandfather's kind of brinkmanship wasn't so bad after all. As Lyn Hejinian puts it in her long poem *Happily*, "Context is the chance that time takes." And "happiness," in that case, is perhaps "the name for our (involuntary) complicity with chance."[10]

CHAPTER FIVE

"To Turn into a Different Person"

What the borders meant could of course be determined by the context. For whoever accepts the rules and enters the game won't throw the ball out of the playing field. The playing field is language, and its borders are the borders of the world—a world gazed on without question, nakedly and precisely imagined, experienced in pain, and in happiness celebrated and praised.

—Ingeborg Bachmann, "What Good are Poems?"[1]

A small square with tram lines in several directions, bounded on one side by a church. Attempts at recollection succeed soonest with corresponding sepia. I myself cannot discover any "oceanic" feeling within me. Adding up dark cobble stones against more unguessable events.

—Rosmarie Waldrop, *Split Infinites*[2]

IN APRIL 1955, WHEN I RETURNED TO VIENNA FOR THE first time after the war, it was as a tourist. My husband Joseph and I were living in London for the year because he had a Fulbright to the National Heart Hospital on Wimpole Street. Whenever we could, we traveled, first within England, then to Holland and Paris, and finally in the spring we took a six-week driving tour through France, Italy, and Switzerland. Vienna was outside that particular circle, but we decided to take a night train from Venice to Vienna and back so as not to miss the place of my birth on this, my first return to Europe.

The four-power occupation of Vienna was in its final stages: it was to end in October 1955. We still had to have visas to travel from Venice to Vienna, and I recall being awakened in the middle of the night, when, in what was a faint echo of that traumatic 1938 train trip, we came to the border and had to go through immigration control. We arrived at dawn in a Vienna that still looked like the set for *The Third Man*—grungy, poor, and still visibly under military (especially Soviet) occupation. The streets were largely empty, especially at night, and such people as were walking about or sitting in the few open cafés were elderly and badly dressed. We stayed in a modest hotel near the Stadtpark, ate fairly meagerly at places like the Rathauskeller, and dutifully toured the Belvedere, Schönbrunn, and the Kunsthistorisches Museum. By this time, I had taken quite a few art history courses at Oberlin, and in London we had spent much of our spare time reading up on the different architectural styles from Romanesque to Bauhaus that we were about to encounter. Our Baedeker listed lots of smaller *palais* and town houses designed by the two great Austrian baroque architects, Fischer von Erlach and Lukas von Hildebrandt, but when we located these addresses, more often than not the building in question was closed for repairs or had been destroyed by bombs.

I tried to find Hörlgasse 6, where I had lived, but somehow got things mixed up and took a photograph of the wrong house. We did get a good shot of the neo-Gothic Votifkirche [Figure 1], the most prominent building in the Ninth District, but neither the church, completed in 1879 on the site of an unsuccessful assassination attempt on the

FIGURE 1. Votifkirche, Vienna, 1955.

young Kaiser Franz Joseph in 1853, nor the monumental façade of the University nearby [Figure 2] looked familiar to me. The balustraded steps where the Nazis used to attack those they took to be Jews were now empty.

FIGURE 2.
Heinrich
Ferstel,
façade,
University
of Vienna,
1873–84.

I was too young to be nostalgic for a past I had happily escaped. Rather, as the not untypical liberal arts graduate I took myself to be, I equated Vienna with its great museums and Baroque palaces like the Belvedere. At the Albertina Gallery (the great Viennese collection of drawings and prints), we admired the Dürers and Holbeins and even bought some excellent facsimiles. All in all, the ambience seemed quite remote: an old peoples' city, drab and gray, that made one eager to go back to beautiful and colorful Venice, whence we continued, in our little Austin, on to

Verona, Como, and, via the Brenner Pass, north to Montreux in the Swiss Alps.

I knew very little of Austrian postwar politics. I had no idea, for instance, that in a series of public-opinion polls conducted in the late '40s, when the Austrians were asked whether National Socialism, as viewed in retrospect, had been a bad idea or a good one just not carried out properly, almost 40% chose the second alternative. One of the key objectives of Nazism, after all, had been achieved: for all practical purposes, the Jews had been eliminated. Those that remained now constituted less than 1% of the population. Indeed, the majority of Austrians came to resent the ten-year Allied Occupation much more than the seven years (*sieben Jahren*) of Nazi rule that preceded it.[3] Thus, when a strenuous rebuilding program began in the '50s, its drive was to restore the Imperial Vienna of Kaiser Franz Joseph, even as the prominent role that Jews had played in the *Kaiserzeit* was systematically wiped out. The great monuments—the Hofburg and Belvedere, Opera House and Heldenplatz—were soon rebuilt, whereas the architectural treasures—office buildings, villas, and town houses—of the early 20th century, many of which had belonged to Jews, were considered expendable. Joseph Hoffmann's famous villa on the Hasenauerstrasse (Eighteenth District), for example, designed for the poet Richard Beer-Hoffmann in 1906, and clumsily "Aryanized" in 1939 for the manufacturer Kuno Grohmann, was demolished in 1970.[4] Only the original garden wall remains intact, surrounding what is now an empty lot [Figure 3].

From my vantage point in 1955, none of this seemed very real. The United States had, after all, won the war; the

FIGURE 3. Garden Fence, former villa by Joseph Hoffman, Hasenauerstrasse 59, 18. Bezirk, Vienna, 1906. Demolished 1970.

Marshall Plan and all that it entailed represented our largesse vis-à-vis what were now just second- or third-rate powers. As a twenty-four-year-old American-in-Vienna, I felt perfectly self-assured and confident. That blindness was still operative when, in 1967, we returned to a newly prosperous Austria for a summer vacation in the Salzkammergut with our daughters Nancy and Carey, aged ten and eight. My parents took a very dim view of this trip: why, they wanted to know, did we want to take our children to St. Gilgen on the Wolfgangsee (a resort reached from Munich via Berchtesgaden), where the hoteliers and other guests would hardly be well-disposed toward us? Mother and

Daddy turned out to be quite right: every time we entered the dining room of our hotel, we were greeted by nasty stares and rude service, but we thought this was just a question of custom and enjoyed the stunning mountain landscape and the architecture and music of Salzburg, where, like all the other American tourists, we bought the girls dirndls [Figure 4].

FIGURE 4. Carey and Nancy Perloff, Volksgarten, Vienna, 1967.

It would be years later before I understood the actual Austrian situation. But then my formal education had done little to prepare me. At Oberlin College, liberalism was certainly the reigning credo (as it had been at Fieldston), and civil rights issues were now very much in the air, especially since Oberlin had always been in the vanguard of the struggle to improve race relations. But as an English major in the heyday of the New Criticism, I was quite ignorant of the postwar European situation. True, I took a two-semester course in Modern European History, but we had barely gotten through the nineteenth century when the semester was over. Even in a course on the French novel, where we read Sartre's *Le Sursis* (*The Reprieve*), the issue of the actual postwar situation of France or Germany never came up. And in English, the challenge was to read the chosen texts carefully enough so as to answer tricky questions on quizzes and exams. Who was "the Man in the Macintosh at Paddy Dignam's funeral in *Ulysses*?" What Jamesian character said, "We have lived too long in Geneva," and what is the import of that observation? What is the significance of the line, "And never lifted up a single stone" in Wordsworth's "Michael"? What is the import of Melville's Bartleby saying, "I prefer not to"? Why does Frost refer to the water as "shattered" in the opening line of "Once by the Pacific" ("The shattered water made a misty din")? And so on.

I do not mean to make fun of these puzzles: it is at Oberlin that I learned how to read critically. And it may also be the case that in the early 1950s, the war was still so close that postwar politics was not what students wanted to discuss. Everyone was eager to learn about the past and especially those great monuments to culture that no one had been able to visit for years. My own education, in any case, was somewhat erratic, for in the summer before my senior year, I suddenly decided to transfer to Barnard College in New York. I felt I could not face another year of small-town dorm life in bleak and rainy Ohio, and I was eager to meet older men.

At Oberlin, I had used my electives to take such intriguing courses as Augusto Centeno's "The Four Theatres" or John Lapp's "Stendhal, Zola, Sartre." But my English curriculum was full of holes: I had taken a year-long course in "Shakespeare and Elizabethan Drama" and another in "Romantic Poets," but I had never had a course in Chaucer, Milton, or "Eighteenth-Century Literature." The Barnard English advisors were not pleased, and so, as a senior, I had to make up these courses, along with an extra year of calculus and of physical education. Had I known I would be playing miniature golf in front of Gildersleeve Hall or bowling in the basement of the Riverside Church, I might have stayed at Oberlin, which was, at least in my experience, decidedly the better school, even though Barnard girls, many of them sophisticated New Yorkers, tended to have much more successful careers later on.

My parents were delighted to have me back at home. By this time, they had finally moved from the two-family house on Oxford Avenue to a fourteen-story apartment house on the nearby Henry Hudson Parkway—a building with an elevator and even a doorman! Their apartment on the tenth floor had three bedrooms, a living room and dining area, and a balcony with a sweeping view, although it overlooked the noisy parkway. The bedrooms were small, but Daddy felt he and Mother had finally *arrived*. They owned a car, lived in a respectable modern building, acquired some new furniture, and, all in all, no longer felt they had to compare everything to its counterpart in Vienna. New York was now home, and since Mother went down to Columbia three days a week and, the other two days, to the National Bureau of Economic Affairs on Madison Avenue and 38th Street, we often took the train into town together.

Walter was now a graduate student in economics at Columbia, following—or so it seemed—in Mother's footsteps. After graduation from Reed College, he had tried law school at Columbia, but it didn't appeal to him, and he switched to economics. He was living at home, since he certainly didn't have the funds to move out. But within a few years, he began, first part-time, then very much full-time, an alternate career, writing financial articles for *Barron's*. He was so successful that the idea of an academic career began to pall, and soon he was working as a security analyst for Shearson Hammill. By the late '50s, he had his own apartment in the Village and was well on his way to becoming a great financier—specifically, the founding partner of the investment firm Cumberland Associates. If my own interests derived from the family *Kulturdrang*, Walter represents their other great family drive, which was just as powerful: the theory and practice of economics and finance, as disseminated by the Austrian School of Economics and its successors. Grandfather, after all, had begun his career by studying customs regulations and tariff policies, and Mother's numerous studies for the National Bureau of Economic Research dealt with the relation of foreign loans to business cycles.

In high school, Walter and I had gone our separate ways, especially since he went to a large public school, DeWitt Clinton, whose ambience was very different from that of Fieldston. In the ninth grade, Walter had refused a scholarship to Fieldston, declaring that private schools were for "sissies." But now that we could share stories about Oberlin and Reed, we became good buddies and even dated each other's friends. Walter's favorite novel at the time was Hemingway's *The Sun Also Rises*, which was invariably lying on top of the bathroom hamper, its pages damp and stuck together. We debated the merits of this novel frequently, since to my mind, Hemingway was excessively *macho*, although that word was not yet part of the vocabulary. Walter and I were both still smokers, and in the evening, when our parents had retired for the night, we would quickly go through a pack and then ransack the wastebaskets for cigarette butts. It was a concession to addiction that both of us would soon reject.

Meanwhile, my social life was picking up considerably: I had broken up with my refugee boyfriend Rudi Boschwitz (who was to become a Republican senator from Minnesota!) and met a young physician from New Orleans named Joseph Perloff, who was to become my husband. But intellectually my senior year was little more than a boring obstacle course, in which I fulfilled this or that requirement. In "Chaucer," W. Cabell Greet rambled on about the White Cliffs of Dover or made lewd jokes about the Wife of Bath. "Milton" was no better: Professor Rosalie Colie began the class by diagramming the cosmology of *Paradise Lost* on the blackboard. "Heaven," she pointed, "is here, Hell is there," and so on. But since I had not yet read any of Milton's poems, this elaborate map meant nothing to me. And the 18th-century course (the second half of the century), taught by the eminent James Clifford at Columbia, was the nadir— a list of names, dates, and labels like "Topographical Poem" or "Bluestockings" that never came to life except for that brief moment when Clifford described how, in the late '20s, Colonel Isham discovered the Boswell Papers at Malahide Castle in Ireland—a discovery whose details made Professor Clifford almost speechless with excitement.

I dutifully memorized the necessary materials and got

A's in most of these courses, but by the time I graduated magna cum laude, I had decided that although I had been accepted by the Columbia Ph.D. program, I did not want to go to graduate school, at least not in English. Like so many girls in the '50s, I got married the summer after I graduated, in 1953, and since Joe was still a medical resident, earning almost nothing, I decided it would be much better for me to get a job! My parents did not try to influence me in these matters. The important thing to them was that I was getting married—and to a man they wholly approved of, indeed adored. Joe was handsome, had wonderful Southern manners, very good earning prospects (as a physician training at Mt. Sinai Hospital), and although from a Russian-Polish immigrant Jewish family that was obviously not up to "our" standard, had, so they felt, transcended his background to become a very cultivated young man. He had been to Europe (I hadn't yet) and to China (at the end of the war), where he had learned a little German from a priest named Father Aulicky. Indeed, Grandmama paid Joe the ultimate compliment by saying he looked like a handsome Italian! The question of graduate school versus this or that job was thus fairly immaterial, for surely I would soon have children, which, even to my mother who was now a professor at Columbia, was the primary goal.

My job year in New York, in any case, proved to be a full-scale initiation into American popular culture. After literally pounding the pavements trying this or that advertising agency or publishing house, I landed a job at the Bettmann Archive on East 57th Street. The reassuringly intellectual Dr. Otto Bettmann, himself a German refugee, tried to convince me that here I would be doing the Higher

Research. But in fact, the job mostly involved answering the phone and combing the files for prints of such items as *The Old Woman Who Lived in a Shoe*, which Gucci or whatever shoe company might be able to use in an ad. After six weeks of this routine, I decided that there must be something more interesting I might do and found a job with Loews, Inc. (the home of Metro-Goldwyn-Mayer) at 46th Street and Broadway.

The position in question, that of title writer trainee at $60.00 per week, was advertised as requiring membership in Phi Beta Kappa as well as knowledge of at least two foreign languages. I qualified, but then came a test I almost failed. I was sent to the Thalia theater on 95th Street to see a film called *Ride, Vaquero!* (starring Robert Taylor and Ava Gardner) and write a précis of it. My problem was that I didn't then—and still don't—understand the plots of Westerns. They somehow pass right over my head; I cannot describe what it is that is happening. And so my précis of *Ride, Vaquero!* was less than elegantly written or even accurate, and my soon-to-be boss, Bernard Doret, had to red-pencil many things and correct my grammar and spelling. Surprisingly, however, I did get the job and so began a "career" that was to send me right back to graduate school.

Title writers at M-G-M did not, nor do they now, write subtitles in a specific foreign language: that would have been much too expensive. The translators didn't have to see the movie at all; they simply worked from the English scripts we title writers provided. Our job was to condense the actors' speeches, since it takes longer to read a title than to hear a given set of utterances. More important, I had to learn to write ALTs—"alternative" lines to replace puns or other verbal/syntactic ambiguities not readily transferable to other languages. Thus when, in *The Long, Long Trailer* Lucille Ball tells Desi Arnaz, "You turn left right here," and he swerves the car to the right, an ALT must be produced so as to make sense of the swerve, Lucy's consternation, and the shouting match with Desi that follows. Or again, for *Kiss Me, Kate*, I had to find an ALT for the punning lines, "If my wife has a bag of gold / Do I care if the bag be old?" Finding ALTs was especially hard in the shorts I was given to work on—mostly "Pete Smith Specials," those slapstick little films with names like *Acro-Batty* and *Mealtime Magic*, in which the lead character bumped into doors and dropped boxes of eggs on the rug, with the narrator making such telling remarks as, "Come, come, chum!"

One day, when I had viewed four Pete Smiths in a row, I began to cry. My boss, Bernie Doret, who had become a good friend, was dumbfounded. I couldn't explain why I was so upset; it just seemed that none of it mattered. Suppose no one ever saw another "Pete Smith Special"? Or another Lucille Ball–Desi Arnaz comedy? Suppose the wrong title appeared under Petruchio's "Where is the life that late I led?" And not only were the titles pointless, the movies were mostly *terrible!* Why couldn't M-G-M do better? I was, it seems, beginning to adopt the Frankfurt School's view of the iniquities of the Culture Industries, even though I had not read a word of Adorno or Horkheimer. Bernie Doret, on the other hand, maintained that the studio did no more than to give the masses precisely the pictures that *they* wanted. M-G-M accommodated the audience, not vice versa. Over lunch at the Astor Grill or Horn & Hardart's, next door to the penny arcades and bars where the prostitutes and pimps were beginning to gear up for the evening ahead, we hammered out these issues. What was the *point* of making these mass movies? If they were "better," would they still be popular? And so on, the irony being that Bernie was extremely bright and, far from distrusting High Art, knew Joyce's *Ulysses* by heart and read it regularly on the long subway ride to his home in Brooklyn. He could quote Leopold Bloom's words and even knew who the Man in the Macintosh was. But the M-G-M world didn't offend him. His was a job, he shrugged, like any other, and one did the best one could. So he assured me that I was getting more proficient; indeed, that my ALTs were getting more creative all the time.

I was too immature to understand the comic potential of the material I was dealing with—the droll contradictions that a Frank O'Hara might record as he too crossed 46th and Broadway on his lunch hour:

> It's my lunch hour, so I go
> for a walk among the hum-colored
> cabs. First, down the sidewalk
> where laborers feed their dirty
> glistening torsos sandwiches
> and coca-cola, with yellow helmets
> on. They protect them from falling
> bricks, I guess.[5]

I could not yet appreciate this campy humor, no doubt because my childhood conditioning was coming to the fore. Why, I told Bernie, should one spend one's life reading and looking at kitsch? Surely there must be a loftier mission in life. Surely I wasn't going to be like my in-laws in New

Orleans, who watched the Jack Benny and Sid Caesar shows
on their giant TV, night after night. And in any case, I knew
(though my boss didn't) that within six months Joe and I
were going to Europe, probably for a whole year—to the
Europe of Art and Culture where one didn't have to write
summaries of *Ride, Vaquero!*, eat at Juliet's Corner, or conceive of ALTs for those rhymes in "Indian Love Call," that
featured song in the 1954 remake of Nelson Eddy's *Rose
Marie*. When we left for London a few months later, I did
take along the trapper's raccoon hat I had received as a gift
for my work on *Rose Marie* [Figure 5]. It was a reminder of
what I had left behind now that we had embarked on our
new cultural life.

FIGURE 5. Marjorie Perloff, in Austin, in front of 30A Acacia
Road, London, fall 1954.

In London, we immediately made contact with my Aunt Hilde and Uncle Otto Kurz, who were, of course, card-carrying intellectuals. Their daughter Erica was only fourteen at the time but was an ardent ballet (pronounced *bállay*) student and also claimed expertise in questions of art history. I recall that shortly after we had arrived, we went to the National Gallery and especially admired Leonardo's *Madonna of the Rocks*. The next evening at the Kurzes, we declared our enthusiasm for this Leonardo, only to have Otto and Hilde raise their eyebrows and exchange amused glances. "It's not *really* a Leonardo," announced Erica condescendingly. "It's only a Luini!" So much for the knowledge of young Americans, who were the source of much amusement at Hilde's dinner parties, where art historians like Hans and Erika Tietze-Konrat and, of course, Ernst (not yet Sir) and Ilse Gombrich came together. Seated in a circle in their little Bayswater flat in Ralph Court, the hosts and guests played School for Scandal. One made fun of almost all British art historians—especially Kenneth Clark and Anthony Blunt—who were said to *know nothing*. One despised Bernard Berenson, who was dismissed as a greedy art collector, merely dabbling in scholarship. But the greatest contempt in this almost exclusively émigré circle was for American graduate students, who obviously lacked the languages and historical knowledge to do the work required at the Warburg Institute or at Oxford. And no wonder, since the attributions in American museums were mostly wrong, so Otto told us, and he, after all, should know, since he had written the definitive book on Fakes.

All this hard-core *Wissenschaft* must have proved too much for Erica, who later married a fellow student at

London University named Raymond Barrett. After graduation, he went straight into business (for a long time he sold
hot-water heaters), Erica taught kindergarten, and their son
Philip, now in a media-related business in Texas, never
attended university at all. "Imagine," said Aunt Susi to me
one day, "Otto Kurz's grandson never having set foot in the
British Museum!" In Newcastle, where Philip and his sister
Caroline grew up, he was a choir boy at the cathedral; when
I visited one time and we went to hear him sing, Erica, to
my surprise, knelt in her pew, crossed herself, and closed
her eyes in prayer. Perhaps Anglicanism was her way of
dealing with the difficult role in which she had been cast
since childhood: she had never been allowed to be like the
other English girls.

Such are the aporias of diaspora. Settled in a charming
sublet flat, part of a large private house owned by a Dr. Janet
Aitken in St. John's Wood [see Figure 5], Joe and I found
the Kurz circle somewhat oppressive, but Hilde and Otto
did give us a lot of help in planning itineraries and locating
specific churches, cathedrals, and museums we hoped to see
on our upcoming *Italienische Reise*. Meanwhile, we used our
weekends to visit Canterbury and St. Albans, Winchester
and Salisbury, Hampton Court and Windsor, Apsley House
and the Wallace Collection. When in London, I can still
identify every Watteau in the latter and, of course, Titian's
Bacchus and Ariadne, Crivelli's *Annunciation*, or Van Eyck's
Arnolfini and His Wife in the National Gallery.

Since I was not working in London, I made out an elaborate study plan for myself and took weekly trips to the
Senate House at the University of London, where I could
borrow books. I began with Roman literature, especially

Horace, Catullus, and Propertius, and then moved on to French fiction from Balzac to Proust. By the spring I had read my way through the entire *A la recherche du temps perdu* and was moving on to German literature: Goethe, Hölderlin, Heine. And although I read dozens of art books, I had already made up my mind to go to graduate school, upon my return to America, in comparative literature. For although I found London fascinating and loved the English countryside, I really wasn't *that* captivated by English literature. Given the choice of reading Dickens or Balzac, I would always choose the latter, and there are many 19th-century British novelists—Walter Scott, Elizabeth Gaskell, George Gissing—that I have barely read at all. I was very fond of the Romantic poets, but I followed Grandmama Schüller in believing that Wordsworth's *Prelude* or even Keats's odes could never quite measure up to Goethe's *Harzreise im Winter* and the *West-Oestlicher Divan* or Hölderlin's *Brot und Wein*. Baudelaire's *Fleurs du mal* was a thrilling book of poems, unmatched, I felt, in the England of Tennyson and Browning. Accordingly, when I was leafing through the Harvard catalogue and found a course called "Proust, Joyce, and Mann," taught by Harry Levin, I decided that was my kind of course.

"A NETWORK OF EASILY ACCESSIBLE WRONG TURNINGS"

But at this juncture, and many times later, my career did not quite turn out as planned on the living room sofa at 30A Acacia Road. In the fall of 1955, we moved to Washington. Joe felt he couldn't practice medicine in as crowded and frantic place as New York; I knew I could never live in the

222

THE VIENNA PARADOX

provincial New Orleans of his loving but overpowering Jewish family. So we *chose* Washington the way most people choose schools. I wasn't sure what my career plans were going to be, and Joe, who did not yet know he would later go into academic medicine, specifically cardiology, found a good third-year residency at Georgetown University Medical School. Washington had the National Gallery, the Phillips Collection, the Freer Gallery, and Dumbarton Oaks; it had the Library of Congress and some good little theaters, and there were lovely (and inexpensive) apartment houses right in the Northwest, minutes from downtown. Our families were not too far away, and Joe had a close school friend in town named Billy Kohlmann. Billy, having taken a degree in history at Yale, had gone to Paris on a State Department assignment, where he was suddenly stricken with polio. Flown back to New York, he spent months in an iron lung—a time he evidently used to study languages. When he was well enough to walk with a cane, he got a job with the C.I.A., although of course he was nominally still working for the State Department. We met him during what I call his Hungarian phase: he was mastering this difficult Asiatic language so as to accept a position in Budapest, when the abortive Hungarian revolution occurred in 1956, putting a stop to those particular plans. Later, he was posted to Vietnam.

Today, when the C.I.A. is uniformly lampooned or reviled, it is hard to comprehend how respectable it was in the late '50s. Humanities graduates with an M.A., some with a Ph.D., often chose to work for it or for related government agencies like the A.I.D. (Association for International Development), the U.S.I.A. (United States

Information Agency), and the State Department itself. Working for one of these agencies gave one the life of what my father had called *ein gelernter Arbeiter*: it was interesting work but not all-consuming, so that one could read books, go to concerts, and so on. It was also, at that time, highly idealistic work. One A.I.D. friend, Bill McIntyre, was sent to India to set up a birth control program; another, Ted Curran, married to my Oberlin friend Marcia Mattson, spent two years trying to create infrastructure in Yemen; and so on. The scene was intellectual and artistic without being academic. And soon I had a circle of friends, much more congenial than at Oberlin or Barnard: Carey Westervelt, a Southern belle turned painter/poet, who could recite Donne's "Canonization" in its entirety over lunch at Martin's in Georgetown; the British Meryle Secrest, who was to become a very successful biographer; and a Viennese refugee named Alice Mavrogordato, some ten years older than I, who had worked for years as a maid in England before getting a visa to the United States. An Abstract Expressionist painter, Alice later sold a number of her paintings to the Austrian embassy.

The universities in Washington, on the other hand, were a problem. The town seemed to be full of them— American, George Washington, Georgetown, Maryland, Howard, Catholic—but only Catholic University, the National Pontifical University, had Ph.D. programs in the various humanities. Maryland had temporarily lost its accreditation due to some football scandal, and the others were primarily undergraduate schools. Of course there was Johns Hopkins in Baltimore—a great Comparative Literature department where émigré scholars like Leo

Spitzer had flourished—but the city seemed much too far away, and besides, an old Barnard friend told me horror stories about the sexism of Hopkins English professors like Earl Wasserman and Don Cameron Allen, who were rumored to say right in class that women were intellectually inferior to men.

My favorite Oberlin professor F.X. (Francis Xavier) Roellinger, whose course in essay writing had been the highlight of my junior year, told me he had two good friends at the Catholic University—J. Craig LaDrière and Giovanni Giovannini—who would be fine mentors. Before I knew it, I was enrolled for the fall term as a full-time graduate student in English; the Comparative Literature department did not offer enough courses I found appealing. There were no fellowships or teaching assistantships in those days; one paid a few hundred dollars a year in tuition, and that was it.

My first class at Catholic U. was in English Renaissance poetry. There were some twenty Christian Brothers and assorted priests in the class and only a handful of lay people like myself. Father Jordan, who sat next to me, began by telling me how much he liked my blue sweater. I didn't know quite how to react to this compliment, but it was not as bizarre as Kirby Neill's first lecture, which argued that the Renaissance (a word with happy connotations at Oberlin, Barnard, and Fieldston!) was a bad thing, because it went hand in hand with the Reformation, which destroyed true Christian Humanism. We were assigned Hiram Haydn's *Counter-Renaissance* and C.S. Lewis's *English Literature in the Sixteenth Century*, both of which made the case against Protestantism forcefully. Here was a new wrinkle indeed, and I could hardly think what to make of it.

But "Renaissance Poetry" was nothing compared to J. Craig LaDrière's "Introduction to Literary Theory," which was a required two-semester course. LaDrière was rumored to have been called Jimmy Ladreer back in Missouri, where he attended St. Louis University. But when I knew him, he was a charismatic figure—a man of *aura*. He always arrived in class ten or fifteen minutes late, reciting the Hail Mary (yes, this is how classes began at Catholic U.) in French and crossing himself. It was high drama. And when, in the course of a Thomist disquisition on *theoria* versus *praxis*, Professor LaDrière observed that the highest form of knowledge was the *Vis Cogitativa*, which is the faculty that the angels have, I was half incredulous, half intrigued by a notion so alien to everything I knew.

"Introduction to Theory" turned out to be a great challenge. LaDrière had written little—an essay in *Modern Philology* on "The Problem of Plato's *Ion*," an English Institute essay on "Sound and Poetry" (his specialty), and many entries in the *Encyclopedia of Poetry and Poetics* on such topics as "Prosody," "Prose and Verse," "*Ut pictura poesis*," and so on. As his students, we felt duty bound to read every word of these strenuous exercises, and there was much talk of rhythmic "centroids" and the difference between *mimesis* and *diegesis*. The reading list included the Russian Formalists, especially Roman Jakobson, rhetoricians like Kenneth Burke, linguists like Thomas Sebeok, and semioticians like Charles Morris, who had written *Signs, Language, and Behavior*. When my husband was a student at the University of Chicago before entering medical school, he had taken a course from Morris.

In 1955, the emphasis on theory was very unusual. The

New Criticism was in its heyday, but Drs. LaDrière and Giovannini scorned Cleanth Brooks and Robert Penn Warren as mere explicators, and they were especially exercised over W. K. Wimsatt, a properly Catholic and classically trained critic, who was a renegade in that he had chosen to teach not at a Catholic university, but at Yale. I am always amused when students now refer to the New Criticism as "close reading" or "formalism," for we were taught that, on the contrary, Wimsatt and Brooks could not get beyond thematics (e.g., the paradox in Donne's "Canonization" that lovers are like saints), whereas *we* studied problems of form, structure, and language—the very ontology of poetry. *Explication de texte* was frowned upon, as was the "survey" of this or that poetic movement or set of novels.

In a curious way, we were thus way ahead of the game as it was then played at most universities. Short as I was of knowledge of periods and authors, I was well versed in poetics and the theory of narrative. Then too, Drs. LaDrière and Giovannini (the latter very thin, unsmiling, with a beautiful shock of white hair, like one of Pound's own *I Vecchi*) were close friends of Ezra Pound's, who had been incarcerated at St. Elizabeths since 1946. When Pound was discharged from "St. E's" in 1958, he evidently stayed for a few weeks at LaDrière's apartment. In her memoir, *Discretions* (1971), Pound's daughter, Mary de Rachewiltz, singled out LaDrière and Giovannini as the "only saving element" in the circus that Pound's daily round at St. E's had become. "They were," she wrote, "men with an education and manners—*éducation du coeur*. But out on the lawn or behind the windscreen in the corridor these gentlemen were outnumbered by the 'disciples' who, as often as not, would tease them about their political and racial non-commitment."[6]

And what disciples! There was, for example, the young John Kasper, a white supremacist, Ku Klux Klan member, and self-declared Nazi who tried to prevent school integration in the South and ended up with a long jail sentence. Pound wrote to him frequently and apologized for his behavior. Another disciple was Eustace Mullins, who called himself Director of the Aryan League of America and had a letterhead printed with the slogan "Jews are betraying us." Mullins later wrote a biography called *This Difficult Individual Ezra Pound* (1961).[7] And there were many such others, even though most of the significant poets, from Eliot and Williams to Robert Lowell and John Berryman, Marianne Moore and Elizabeth Bishop, Charles Olson and Allen Ginsberg, were making the pilgrimage to visit the Great Poet. When my friend Elizabeth Hartley once joined this pilgrimage, she came away wholly disillusioned. It seems that the Great Poet was lolling in a deck chair in Bermuda shorts, gossiping with his acolytes, especially his then mistress Sheri Martinelli, and reading aloud favorable comments about himself in the Italian newspapers. He had not a word to say about poetry or art. Elizabeth felt rather like Proust's Marcel meeting La Berma or Bergotte for the first time.

Indeed, on the face of it, the Pound cult was much more problematic than, say, the Stefan George cult in which my father participated as a young man. At the same time, I never heard Drs. LaDrière or Giovannini make a single remark in class or office hours that could be construed as anti-Semitic or racist. In Giovannini's "Modern Poetry" seminar, which I took in 1956, Pound's poetry was central, but political and economic issues never came up. We studied Imagism and Vorticism, the adaptation of Fenollosa's *Chinese Written Character* and the "pidgin" Latin of "Propertius," all the while studying how the "live tradition" of these poems came out of Dante and Dante Gabriel Rossetti, out of Byron and Flaubert, Pater and Yeats. We analyzed closely the lineation and visual layout of such poems as "The Coming of War: Actæon." And the *Literary Essays*, *Gaudier-Brzeska* and *ABC of Reading* were mined for definitive aphorisms about poetry, such as "Poetry is news that *stays* news."

No doubt, this aestheticism represented a particular bias, although I'm not sure that the opposite take on Pound was any better. In 1946, Bennett Cerf, the president of Random House, refused to include any of Pound's verse in the new edition of their *Anthology of Famous English and American Poetry*, and in 1949, the awarding of the Bollingen Prize to *The Pisan Cantos* set off a firestorm. Those who voted for Pound (including a reluctant W. H. Auden) argued that *The Pisan Cantos* was by far the finest book of poems published the previous year, regardless of its author's politics or prejudices. Those against, like Karl Shapiro, suggested that "the poet's political and moral philosophy ultimately vitiates his poetry."[8]

I take both Auden and Shapiro to be right. History has shown that no doubt *The Pisan Cantos was* the "best book of poems" of 1948, and Random House soon realized that its readers did want Pound to be included in its future anthologies. On the other hand, the 1949 Bollingen jury can be accused of insensitivity: it *was* much too soon after the war

to foreground the work of a poet who had Pound's views—
views that cannot in any sense be divorced from the poetry
itself. But the important thing, so far as my own Viennese
Odyssey is concerned, is that in the United States, Pound's
anti-Semitism could be—and was—openly discussed, and
that one major publisher could—and did—refuse to publish
Pound, even as another, James Laughlin at New Directions,
became Pound's champion. Despite the Cold War ethos of
these years, the cultural field was marked by a real diversity
of opinion and a singular openness—an openness, I like to
think, that persists in the university classroom today, despite
the overt lip service to political correctness.

Despite the interest in Pound at Catholic University, I
myself kept aloof from the case: I wanted nothing to do with
Nazi sympathizers of any stripe. My M.A. dissertation,
directed by a young professor named James Hafley, who
had written an excellent book on Virginia Woolf called *The
Glass Roof*, was called "Privileged Moments in Marcel
Proust and Virginia Woolf." Today, I don't think much of
this exercise in Bergsonian thought, with its focus on the
nature of the epiphany and its function in modern fiction.
Indeed, the application of these concepts harked back to my
Barnard days, when I wrote an honors thesis on the nature
of stream of consciousness. Still, it was manageable, and I
had to finish my M.A. within the year, because I was going
to have a baby in September. By the time I returned for my
Ph.D. in 1961, now the mother of five-year-old Nancy and
three-year-old Carey, I had shifted allegiances from fiction
to poetry and poetics, minoring in American Literature and
in Structural Linguistics, which was taught by a
Smithsonian anthropologist named Wallace Chafe. In tan-

dem with the theory courses I was taking, linguistics became the backdrop of my dissertation, "Rhyme and Meaning in the Poetry of Yeats." This statistical monster was full of tables, cataloguing the kinds of rhyme the poet used and their function in a given stanza. The numerical analysis could no doubt now be accomplished by the computer, but I also studied the theory of rhyme under the larger rubric of repetition and invented categories of semantic rhymes: those involving symbolism, those using metonymy or metaphor, and so on. Dr. LaDrière was away at Harvard during my writing year and didn't read the thesis till the next fall, when I had begun to teach. At that point, Dr. Giovannini called me in and informed me that I would have to rewrite the whole thesis, using as a principle of organization a new chapter outline that LaDrière had come up with. When I became tearful, Giovannini said, "Don't worry. This will make a much better man of you, Mrs. Perloff!" That was standard discourse in those prefeminist days.

What did LaDrière find so problematic in my thesis? He liked all the sections on sound and syntax, but when I became more speculative and looked at the way rhyme (sound) and trope (meaning) are interrelated, he demurred. I was now in an area not amenable to empirical evidence and hence in a suspect gray zone. He couldn't understand my striking out on my own, for hadn't I dutifully—and he thought brilliantly—regurgitated what I had been taught at Catholic U. during my orals, showing how thoroughly I had mastered the poetics of Plato and Aristotle, of Longinus and even Dionysius of Halicarnassus? What he couldn't bear, I think, is that my work, technical though it was, showed that I was not a full-fledged disciple. This later proved to be my big problem.[9]

But not yet. For in the spring of 1964, one day when I was standing at the card catalogue looking at Yeats entries, Dr. Neill came up to me and asked me if I'd like to have a job at Catholic U. in the fall. A job? I was not even thinking of jobs yet, for I thought I had better have the dissertation finished and behind me. No one talked about jobs in those days: the important thing was to become a Ph.D. A doctorate had *status*, especially for women: it was *there* for all to know about, whatever one's final career path. But I immediately said yes, and Kirby Neill said, "Well, good, we would really like to have you teach here. I'll send you some papers in the mail." And he patted me on the shoulder and walked off.

When I tell colleagues and graduate students this story today, they are incredulous. Obtaining a first job in academe has become a frightening obstacle course, a professional activity that takes a year or so of minute planning. The letters, the applications, the M.L.A. interview, the fly-back: none of these existed in 1964. I began as an instructor but became an assistant professor after a year. The first year, I was to teach eight courses, four in the fall, four in the spring. Two of the four would be "Freshman Composition," the third was a genre course called "Reading List," and the fourth the "Co-ordinating Seminar" required of all students in the fall of their senior year. In the spring, instead of the "Reading List," I was to teach "Modern Poetry," because Dr. Giovannini was going on sabbatical.

It was customary in those days that graduate students did no teaching so that they could concentrate on their coursework and thesis. I was therefore a total novice, and no one gave me any tips or told me how to teach. But

"Freshman Composition" was easy and, once I had prepared for the "Reading List" by going over medieval,
Elizabethan, and Restoration drama as well as exemplars of
epic, romance, and the novel, and the various phases of
English poetry, that too was quite manageable. For the seminar, I read Father Rooney's essay, which provided pedagogy
for the course. This article, called "The Coordinating
Seminar: The Climax of a Liberal Education," always made
me think that some sort of orgasm was about to take place
in class. But in fact, each of the six or seven seminar students
chose one author from a fairly short list that extended from
Chaucer and Spenser to Yeats and Eliot. In the seminar,
each student wrote three twenty-page papers on his or her
author a semester, and another student served each week as
discussion leader. All I had to do, therefore, was to read the
paper and moderate the discussion. It was great fun, because
it forced me to keep up with writers like Donne or Swift,
outside my field of specialization.

I would have coped quite well, had it not been for the
rewriting of the dissertation. Since I taught four days a
week, that task was relegated to Thursdays. I recall sitting
in the guest room (we had no study then), typing away. In
the digital age, it seems inconceivable that everyone did
this: if one made a single mistake, one had to retype the
page. The job was extremely tedious, but somehow by
spring, it was done and duly accepted. I was a Ph.D. and the
nuns and Christian Brothers now addressed me as "Dr." as
in "Oh, Doctor, could you tell me . . . ."

My Catholic University story does not, however, have a
nice happy ending. I was, after all, an outsider, and once I
was on the other side of the classroom, my non-Catholicism

began to show. In teaching *Ulysses*, I could not always explain points of theology properly; in teaching Eliot's *Ash Wednesday*, I missed some of the liturgical allusions and the Eucharistic symbolism. And in the "Coordinating Seminar," I advised a Christian Brother named René Massé that he might petition to work on D.H. Lawrence (not on the list!), only to incur the anger of Father Rooney, who had a long talk with the Brother and got him to choose Eliot instead. René Massé never looked me in the eye again. Soon thereafter, however, he left the order, so there must have been some kind of disconnect between himself and the authorities.

Meanwhile, I was publishing quite actively and was quickly made an associate professor—although not yet with tenure. Emboldened by my new status, I began to speak out at faculty meetings and try new things in class. When I had finished my dissertation, Dr. Giovannini had suggested that I now apply my particular form of rhyme analysis to the work of another poet: perhaps Byron? The very thought of such narrow specialization made me wince: I had visions of myself performing the sort of service that had distinguished my tenure as a subtitle writer for M-G-M. So, for better or worse, I struck out on my own. I started writing on problems of genre and convention and issues of literary history that blurred boundaries, calling into question the mimesis/diegesis distinction Craig LaDrière had taken to be so central.

More important: I wanted to become a different kind of Modernist: no longer the student of Anglo-American poetics from Yeats to Robert Lowell, but of the larger, early 20th-century world called the Avant-Garde. Joyce certainly played a central role in that world, but the Joyce not of *Portrait of the Artist*, Exhibit A at Catholic U., but of the more experimental sections of *Ulysses* and *Finnegans Wake*. As for Pound, I wanted to teach, not the *Hugh Selwyn Mauberley* Dr. Giovannini spent so much time explicating, but the collage technique of the *Cantos*, especially its connection to the visual arts. Accordingly, when Giovannini and the others kept insisting that the Modernist orals should focus on Imagism, I objected. A whole qualifying exam on Imagism? It seemed patently absurd. The upshot was that the department voted against my tenure, a decision they were forced to reverse by the higher administration because members of neighboring departments came to my rescue. When I went to visit Dr. Giovannini after it was all over and asked him what I had done wrong, he said, "Mrs. Perloff, you have been insubordinate!"

That was it. Although I stayed another year, then being hired away by the University of Maryland, the Era of Good Feeling at Catholic U. was over. I realized, perhaps for the first time, that although I had been a star graduate student, I was after all a freethinking Jewish woman, whose Viennese culture contained a measure of irony, of inherent skepticism as to the nature of absolutes quite at odds with Dr. Giovannini's or Father Rooney's submission to Church authority. It was less a matter of specific religious doctrine or practice than of attitude. After years of playing the role of not-quite-Catholic but sympathetic professor who dutifully goes on the faculty retreat and tries to participate in discussions of ethics and pedagogy, I had to recognize who and what I was.

"But why," as Walter Benn Michaels puts it in his controversial and much discussed *Our America*, "does it matter who we are?"¹⁰ "Why [is it] that *any* past should count as ours?" Surely, according to this line of "antiessentialist" thinking, it is absurd to assume that just because one had some distant ancestor—perhaps a great-great-grandfather who came from a town in Galicia or a village in the Ukraine—one must forever be labeled as a Jew, no matter how complex the making of one's identity and no matter what one really believes or does. America, by this account, is the land of opportunity and performativity, of rebirth and makeover. "Be what you wanna *be*," as the song has it.

The problem inherent in this argument is that Jewish identity can never be merely expunged, for the simple reason that, as the refugees from Hitler were forced to learn the hard way, one is always a Jew in the eyes of the Other. In the past few years, as the Arab-Israeli conflict has steadily worsened, this truth has come home with a vengeance even to those who are only nominally Jewish. Think of the passengers shot on the Fourth of July (2002) by a fanatic at the El Al ticket counter at the Los Angeles County International Airport, for no better reason than that they were assumed to be Jews. Or consider the case of the Jewish boys' soccer team in France—a group of teens that may not have had the slightest relationship to—or even interest in— what is going on Israel. By their own account, the Muslims who attacked this team did so simply because the boys in question were Jewish. Such attacks are now quite frequent in Europe and of course in the Arab world. And whatever the hotly contested role of the "Jewish lobby" in the United States, it is clear that there are no such lobbies in the European nations—countries that no longer have Jewish communities sizable enough to make a difference. Indeed, "anti-Semitism without Jews" has now become a reality, and by no means only in Austria.

Given this state of affairs, one cannot stop being a Jew, whatever one's response to the Jewish *religion* and however strong one's rival affiliations, whether professional, intellectual, national, or familial. It is a reality the upper-class Viennese Jewish refugees were reluctant to face: many remained staunchly in denial even after they came to America. Herbert Schüller, for example, reports that he and his wife Lorle, concerned during the war years that their young son Tom seemed ashamed at school that he was not a "real" American, discussed the problem with Tom's first grade teacher:

She ameliorated the situation considerably by telling the class how many artists, especially musicians, had lived in Vienna. She asked the children who had pictures of Vienna to bring them to school the next day. Tom was the only one in his class to have such pictures. He felt important and was no longer so unhappy to have been born an Austrian.

Nowhere is the "J" word mentioned. One would think that Tom's parents had to leave Austria simply because their country was taken over by a foreign power. But then, why did most Austrians remain in place? At some point it must have been a troubling question for a boy growing up in the 1940s.

Indeed, in the spring of 2003, when the charming, cultured, and indomitable Herbert Schüller died at 97, I witnessed the recycling of the "Austrian" myth. The memorial service was held at Kimball Farms, the elegant Episcopal retirement home near Tanglewood, Massachusetts, where Herbert and his wife Lorle had moved about a decade before. When it was Tom's turn to give his memorial speech, he admitted that he had for years been rather alienated from a father who had ignored his "social needs" in his boyhood, had never taken him to a ballgame, and so on. But lately, Tom (now sixty-seven) remarked, he had come round to appreciating his father's culture and intellect. And he told the story of Herbert's past in "golden Vienna," where Herbert's grandfather had owned a castle with sixteen servants, and where his father had had ample opportunity to indulge his youthful passion for opera and the symphony. Later, his work as a lawyer had taken Herbert to Budapest, where he and Lorle lived an idyllic life and where Tom was born in 1936. There was just one thing wrong. In 1938, when Herbert and his brother George were on a ski trip, the Germans annexed Austria and "my parents felt we had to emigrate."

It is a scenario straight out of *The Sound of Music*, the irony being that Grandmama Schüller would have dismissed this film, with its idyllic Alpine scenery, its brave and beautiful von Trapp family, and its Reverend Mother intoning the song "Climb every mountain!" as so much kitsch. Listening to Tom talk of family castles in Austria to an audience including residents of Kimball Farms, I felt deeply uncomfortable. Yet—and this is my double bind—it is not as if I would have felt at home at a Jewish ceremony either. Raised as I was on Christmas and Easter pageantry, on notions of Christian ethics and the religion of *Kultur*, Jewish observance and ritual remain alien to me. In my case, then, Jewishness was to become an ethnic, cultural, and political complex—an identity (among other identities) that I take quite seriously. And here let me come back to the idea of Viennese Jewish High Culture with which I began: specifically, the oeuvre of Arnold Schoenberg, as that oeuvre was mediated by Schoenberg's famous Los Angeles pupil, John Cage and, at least implicitly, vice versa. The Schoenberg-Cage relationship, I would posit, provides us with a nice paradigm for the complex and contradictory ways that Viennese and American artistic culture have interacted in the 20th century. For although Schoenberg, in his proud Viennese way, paid little attention to his young and irreverent pupil, the implicit dialogue between their respective "forms of life," to use Wittgenstein's phrase, is central to the ways I myself now construe the Vienna paradox.

FROM THE RINGSTRASSE TO KING'S ROAD

John Cage was born in Los Angeles in 1912. His family's roots, as he told an interviewer, "are completely American":

There was a John Cage who helped Washington in the surveying of Virginia. My grandfather was an itinerant Methodist Episcopal minister . . . . He was a man of extraordinary puritanical righteousness and would get very angry with people who didn't agree with him. As a child my father [John Milton Cage] used to run away from home, whenever he got the chance. He was regarded as a black sheep.

My mother [Lucretia Harvey] was married twice before she married my father, but she never told me this until after he died. She couldn't remember her first husband's name.

My father invented a submarine just before the First World

War which had the world's record for staying underwater, and he dramatized this by making an experimental trip on Friday the thirteenth, with a crew of thirteen, staying under water for thirteen hours. But it never entered his mind that the value of staying underneath water lay in being invisible to people above. Because his engine ran on gasoline it left bubbles on the surface of the water. So his sub wasn't used in the war and Dad went bankrupt.[11]

Cage has told this story in various places, always with good-humored detachment. He developed early on the ability not to take himself too seriously. His father, John Milton Cage, invented a number of other things—a hydrophone for submarine detection, an inhaler for treating colds, mixing menthol and thymol in an alcohol suspension—but often his designs failed and the itinerant family was always strapped for money.

I give this background only to make clear that no two artists could be less alike than Cage and Schoenberg. The latter, born into an orthodox Jewish family in the imperial Vienna of 1874, raised in modest circumstances in the Leopoldstadt (his father was a shoe manufacturer), composed his first pieces for two violins before he was nine years old. He left school when he was sixteen and, after a brief stint at the private bank of Werner & Co., took over as conductor for the Mödling Choral Society in 1891. Like so many of his fellow Austrian musicians, Schoenberg converted to Protestantism as a young man (1898), thinking that at least a nominal Christianity was essential for a serious musical career in Vienna. In 1926, he received a call to Berlin to lead a master class at the Akademie der Künste. Here he flourished until the Nazis came to power, and in

1933 Schoenberg, having reconverted to Judaism and spoken out against Nazi abuses, emigrated to the United States.

The composition of music was, of course, the central event of Schoenberg's life: art was taken entirely seriously; it was that which mattered! For Cage, things were much more tentative: at the age when Schoenberg was already composing violin pieces, Cage was biking to school and the beach, attending Boy Scout meetings, and, when he was twelve, conducting a weekly radio program on KNX for the Scouts. He started piano lessons in the fourth grade, but music was only one of his manifold activities. Although he graduated from Los Angeles High School with the highest scholastic average in the history of the school, a year later he dropped out of Pomona College and went off to Paris, ostensibly to study architecture. He returned in the fall of 1931 (the year I was born), drove cross-country from New York in a Model T Ford, and lived with a friend at various residences, the most interesting of which was the Schindler House on King's Road in Hollywood [Figure 6].

Rudolf Schindler had come to Chicago from his native Vienna in 1914 so as to work with Frank Lloyd Wright. He and his wife Pauline (with whom Cage was briefly in love) moved to Los Angeles in 1921, and Schindler built a uniquely Californian Modernist house of concrete, redwood, and glass, cleverly designed for fluid passage between indoors and outdoors as well as maximum privacy. The Schindler House became a kind of commune *avant la lettre* for artists, writers, and composers. Today, the house has been restored as the MAK Center–LA, which is financed by Vienna MAK (Museum der Angewandten Künste), the

FIGURE 6. Schindler House, King's Road, West Hollywood, California, 1921–22. *Photograph by Thomas S. Hines*

Republic of Austria, and a local support group. It sponsors symposia, lectures, workshops, and performances: in the summer of 2002, for example, a lecture on the noted Austrian architect Coop Himmelblau was followed by a concert of Cage's *Credo in Us* and other early pieces.

But the Bohemian life at the King's Road house, where artists were always moving in and out, was hardly Schoenberg's world. The composer, settling in Los Angeles a decade later, lived in what Cage describes as a "dark quasi-Spanish house" in Brentwood, where he could work without distraction and interruption. He soon became a legendary figure. In 1934, Cage, who had been making a living gardening, washing dishes, and giving lectures on modern art to a group of Santa Monica housewives, decided that he wanted to study music with Schoenberg:

> Schoenberg was a magnificent teacher, who always gave the impression that he was putting us in touch with musical principles. I studied counterpoint at his home and attended all his classes at USC and later at UCLA when he moved there. I also took his course in harmony, for which I had no gift. Several times I tried to explain to Schoenberg that I had no feeling for harmony. He told me that without a feeling for harmony I would always encounter an obstacle, a wall through which I wouldn't be able to pass. My reply was that in that case I would devote my life to beating my head against that wall—and maybe that is what I've been doing ever since. In all the time I studied with Schoenberg he never once led me to believe that my work was distinguished in any way. He never praised my compositions, and when I commented on other students' work in class he held my comments up to ridicule. And yet I worshipped him like a god. (Interview with Calvin Tomkins, 1965, CC, 5). [Figure 7.]

Elsewhere Cage remarks that Schoenberg "looked as though he was haunted. As far as I was concerned, he was not an ordinary human being. I literally worshipped him." But he never quite won Schoenberg over:

> Someone asked Schoenberg about his American pupils, whether he'd had any that were interesting, and Schoenberg's first reply was to say there were no interesting pupils, but then he smiled and said, "There was one," and he named me. Then he said, "Of course, he's not a composer, but he's an inventor—of genius." (CC, 6.)

And there we have it. On the one hand, there is Schoenberg, the Ultimate Modernist Composer, solitary, seri-

FIGURE 7. Arnold Schoenberg teaching a class of students in the living room at his Brentwood, California, home, *c.* 1948. Front row: Natalie Limonick, H. Endicott Hansen, and Alfred Carlson.   *Photograph by Richard Fish copyright 1953, renewed 1981*

ous, and dedicated, who becomes, in the eyes of many, the great composer of the 20th century. On the other, there is Cage, who, far from being wedded to the notion of the individual masterpiece, frequently collaborates with composers (e.g., David Tudor), dancers (Merce Cunningham), and artists (Jasper Johns). For Cage, *sound* rather than *music* is the proper frame of reference. Perhaps Schoenberg was right to call Cage "not a composer, but an inventor—of genius." It is inconceivable, in any case, that Schoenberg would have been satisfied with a career as wide-ranging and eclectic as Cage's, even as it is equally inconceivable that Cage could have spent his entire life on musical composition as did Schoenberg.

And yet Cage tells us that, even though Schoenberg paid zero attention to his own compositions, "I worshipped him like a god." No doubt he had never before come across the single-mindedness, devotion, and pure genius that Schoenberg manifested—a devotion to Art, whatever its costs, that became a model to be adapted for use on the very different, highly diversified, decentered, and multiplex American scene. Different because Schoenberg's problems—particularly the anti-Semitism that almost destroyed his life—were hardly Cage's, but then Cage had to work at odd jobs that Schoenberg would have found hopelessly demeaning. Gentlemen in Vienna, after all, did not perform the work of "laborers" or vice versa. Then, too, Cage regarded himself as essentially "free" to do whatever he liked (even if few people seemed to care what that was), provided he could scrape together enough money to get by, whereas Schoenberg could earn a living in Vienna as a composer/teacher but had none of the freedom that Cage took for granted. Schoenberg's musical world—rigid, hierarchical, and opinionated—was a world always *deeply engaged*. Cage's world was fluid and sometimes fortuitous but, in the end, just as engaged, although in the United States it is bad form to make the sort of fuss the Viennese composer was making.

The difference between the two artists is wonderfully pinpointed in a collage essay Cage wrote for the *Kenyon Review*, which had asked him to write a book review of the U.S. edition of the *Arnold Schoenberg Letters*. Cage did not want to write an ordinary review; rather, he selected, by chance operations, phrases and sentences from the letters and embedded these, in italics, along with statements Cage had heard the composer make as well as his own third-person narrative presentation of Schoenberg. The resulting essay, "Mosaic," reprinted in *A Year from Monday*, is an artwork in its own right. Consider the following sequence:

Now seriously . . . I . . . (. . . have only contempt for anyone who finds the slightest fault with anything I publish. One God. The questions he asked his pupils had answers he already knew. Answers his pupils gave didn't tally with his. Schoenberg needed to be sure of himself, so that when leading others, he might be ahead. "You'll devote your life to music?"[12]

By pasting into the narrative decontextualized passages from Schoenberg's rather formal letters as well as statements made in conversation that Cage recalls, a complex portrait of Schoenberg emerges. At once vain and endearing, self-important and yet entirely honest and reliable, the composer emerges as the perfect foil to the much more informal, less judgmental, Zenlike John Cage. The juxtaposition of "Now seriously . . . I have . . . only contempt. . . ." with "One God" implies that Schoenberg not only believes in One God but is himself the "One God"—the very god Cage has worshipped. But Cage could never have said about himself: "*The fact is I am the only composer of any reputation at all whom the Philharmonic have not yet performed*" (YFM, 47).

Emigration had left Schoenberg curiously vulnerable. His letters reveal a persistent fear of "*opponents*" (whoever they are), public quarrels with colleagues ("*I disagree with almost everything"*), and a combative streak: *"For . . . all I want is to compose. Even the fact that I write so many letters is a very harmful deviation from this principle. And though any one who means well by me should certainly write to me as often as possible (for I am always glad of that), it should be in such a way that I don't have to answer!"* (YFM, 45). This comment doesn't exactly testify to the high opinion in which the composer held a given letter's recipient! But Schoenberg is just being honest: he takes himself to be a great man and must act accordingly! Here again the contrast with Cage is instructive. Asked by Richard Kostelanetz why he keeps his name in the phone book, thus allowing for constant interruptions of his work, Cage replies: "I consider it a part of twentieth-century ethics. . . . I think that this thing I speak of about fluency is implied by the telephone."[13]

Such easy availability would have been anathema to Schoenberg. Like so many of the refugees from Hitler, he never really tried to understand the American way of life or political system. "Becoming an American citizen didn't remove his *distaste for democracy and that sort of thing.*" Of former times when a prince stood as a protector before an artist, he writes: *"The fairest, alas bygone, days of art."* (YFM, 45–46). It was as if—and this is characteristic of the *Kulturdrang* of Jewish Vienna—the actual government of his country had nothing to do with him, that he did not care to know anything about the public world. Accordingly, when his private world came crashing down, there was no recourse.

Throughout "Mosaic," Cage, who never speaks directly in his own person, pokes gentle fun at Schoenberg's high seriousness (*"A glass of brandy and . . .*

enjoyed it"), but clearly finds the older man wholly endearing. The collage ends on an upbeat note:

We'd all written fugues. He said he was pleased with what we'd done. We couldn't believe our ears, divided up his pleasure between us. First afraid *(each new person might be a Nazi)*, later delighted and grateful: someone was interested in his art (YFM, 49).

However foolish Schoenberg sometimes appears in all his gloom and paranoia, his posturing and vanity, he emerges from Cage's piece as a figure larger than life, a giant in a land of the less ambitious. But this statement too demands qualification, for in his own quiet way, Cage was by no means unambitious: those who knew him agree that he would go to astonishing lengths to get what he wanted. The difference is partly one of style rather than substance. At the same time, it is Cage's concept of a communal art or "circus" ("Here Comes Everybody!") that distinguishes him from the assured individualism of Schoenberg. A work like *Roaratorio* (1979*)*, based as it is on a "writing through" of James Joyce, has a centrifugal thrust quite different from Schoenberg's individual, self-contained compositions. What Cage lacked in depth—he is, of course, not a composer of Schoenberg's stature—he made up in breadth. We think of him today as an astonishing polymath—composer, but also inventor, thinker, poet, and performer.

Grandmama Schüller, born in 1880, six years after Schoenberg, had no interest whatsoever in his difficult music. Richard Strauss and Gustav Mahler were as far as she would go, and she much preferred Mozart and Beethoven to either. She herself played the piano every day, but not the *atonal* music of Schoenberg! Or even the dissonances of Stravinsky! The taste for these composers came after her time: in my parents' generation, it became a sign of cultivation and sophistication. As for Cage, Grandmama would simply have laughed and pronounced the work *Ein Unsinn! (Nonsense!)* How could one call this noise "music"? As for *4'33"*, she would surely have dismissed it as mere trickery. The Emperor's New Clothes! And discussion would have stopped right there.

The *Kulturdrang* of the educated Viennese Jews was thus itself more than a little anachronistic. Even if the Anschluss had never occurred, the concept of *paideia* that guided the gymnasium education of the upper middle classes—a system in which the Jews were so heavily invested—could not have lasted much longer. I smile now when I think of the assurance with which Grandmama would have dismissed both Schoenberg and Cage's "music" as not worth listening to, the former too nonmelodic and hence boring, the latter simply "ridiculous." But it is the enormous *caring* that is so impressive: the devotion to Art, not as a sideline, as it so often is in our society, but as the discourse and discipline that makes living worthwhile. Indeed, the term *art for art's sake* has always struck me as a misnomer: the absorption of the George circle in their poet, the emotional response of my father to the National Gallery exhibition of the Vienna paintings, may more properly be designated as *art for life's sake*.

But the fact is that it didn't serve "life" very well. And

so whenever we mourn the loss of the devotional intensity associated with Schoenberg, we might remind ourselves that our own geography and ecology demand dispersal—a dispersal that makes artistic and cultural activity more differentiated but possibly also more challenging. "A mythology," in Wallace Stevens's words, "reflects its region."

EPILOGUE

> . . . as I ran I reflected that the city through which I was running, dreadful though I had always felt it to be and still felt it to be, was still the best city there was, that Vienna which I found detestable and had always found detestable, was suddenly once again the best city in the world, my own city, my beloved Vienna . . . .
> —Thomas Bernhard, *Holzfällen* (*Woodcutters*)[1]

ON MAY 28, 1970, GRANDFATHER SCHÜLLER CELEBRATED his hundredth birthday at my parents' apartment in Washington. When Daddy retired from Paterson, Teele & Dennis in 1968, Mother and Daddy moved to Washington to be near us and their grandchildren—a move that turned out to be problematic, since they had to adjust yet again to a new city and Mother had given up both Columbia and the National Bureau for an adjunct professorship at Catholic University. Grandmama Schüller died shortly before the move, so Grandfather came alone to Washington and lived with my parents. It wasn't so easy for him anymore—his hearing and sight were largely gone—but I never heard him complain and he still had visitors—now the circle of Austrian School Economists in Washington, like Herbert Fürth and Gottfried von Haberler.

On the birthday itself, celebrated with a Viennese feast culminating in a *Dobostorte*, the Austrian ambassador and his attaché came to see Grandfather and brought him a testimonial from the new Chancellor Bruno Kreisky, a moderate Socialist of Jewish ancestry, who had spent the war years in Sweden. Grandfather had known him slightly in the old days. In the picture below, my father, himself now seventy-one, looks on somewhat ironically as the birthday greeting is read. Perhaps Daddy, who had few illusions about the state of the world, sensed that despite this new Era of Good

FIGURE 1. Left to right, Richard Schüller, Max Mintz, Austrian embassy officials, living room, 4201 Cathedral Avenue, N.W., Washington, D.C, May 28, 1970.

Feelings some things never change. And indeed, two years later, shortly after Grandfather's death at one hundred and two, Kreisky nominated for the post of secretary-general of the United Nations a career diplomat named Kurt Waldheim, who duly won the election. His success was taken as evidence that "neutral Austria" was enjoying a new trust throughout the world (PH, 322). Waldheim served two "successful" five-year terms and was a candidate for the (largely ceremonial) post of president of the Austrian Republic, when news leaked out that he had been an S.S. officer during the war and had probably been involved in war crimes in the Balkan campaign. Despite protests from the Socialists within Austria and from Jewish organizations around the world, Waldheim was elected to the presidency in 1986.

Grandfather would probably have taken this turn of events in his stride, as just another example of the Way of the World. In the United States, where the new president was quickly declared an "undesirable alien" and hence barred from American territory (PH, 327), the affair quickly generated the phrase "Waldheimer's Disease"—forgetting one had ever been a Nazi. The "disease" was common enough: some ten years after the Waldheim affair, with the coming to power of Jörg Haider and his Freedom Party, it sometimes seems as if little has changed.

But I have changed. Gone are the days when I went to Vienna as an innocent tourist, buying dirndls for our little girls and posing them for photographs in front of the Salzburg Cathedral or in the mountains above the Wolfgangsee, with their *Sound of Music* aura. In recent years, I have gone to Vienna only infrequently, and then for

specific occasions. Like Proust's Venice, my imaginary
Vienna is much more appealing than the real thing, just as
one eats better at the Café Sabarsky in the Neue Galerie on
Fifth Avenue than in the actual restaurants of Vienna.

In the Neue Galerie bookshop, I bought Rolf Toman's
gorgeously illustrated *Vienna: Art and Architecture* (1999),
which now graces the coffee table in my study. When I look
at the images of the great Romanesque and Gothic churches like St. Ruprechts and the Michaelerkirche, the Baroque
palaces and fountains, the Adolf Loos and Joseph Hoffman
houses, and Wittgenstein's house for his sister Margarete—
I am transfixed by the sheer beauty of the city, by the rich-
ness of the history of Mitteleuropa. And when I read Musil's
Mann ohne Eigenschaften (*The Man Without Qualities*), or
Schnitzler's *Der Weg ins Freie* (*The Road into the Open*), or,
among more recent works, Ingeborg Bachmann's *Malina*
and Thomas Bernhard's *Holzfällen* (*Woodcutters*), which
gives me my epigraph above, when I hear Mahler's Fourth
Symphony and Schoenberg's *Gurrelieder*, or attend a performance of Richard Strauss's *Der Rosenkavalier*, I am drawn
to my long-ago Gabriele days. Indeed, I have come to feel a
new affinity for Vienna through the writings of Ludwig
Wittgenstein—the philosopher poet who was, in Terry
Eagleton's words, "an arresting combination of monk, mys-
tic, and mechanic; a high European intellectual who
yearned for Tolstoyan *simplicitas*, a philosophical giant with
scant respect for philosophy, an irascible autocrat with a
thirst for holiness."[2]

In 1915, contemplating the Austrian rout by the
Russians in Galicia from his war post on the troopship
Goplana, Wittgenstein wrote in his journal:

I feel the terrible sadness of our—the German race's—situation. The English—the best race in the world—*cannot* lose. We, however, can lose, and will lose, if not this year then the next. The thought that our race will be defeated depresses me tremendously because I am German through and through.[3]

I find these words strangely moving. Here is Wittgenstein, who found his niche as philosopher only in Cambridge, England, where he was to spend the greater part of his life, and yet felt so "German through and through" that he refers to both nations in racial terms—a curious irony given the polyglot, multiracial character of the Austro-Hungarian army in which he was serving. Perhaps, as was so often the case with Austrian upper-class Jews, the very denial of his own Jewish background, soon to be translated into purely racial terms by the Nazis, gave him a greater allegiance than was warranted to a German nationalism reconceived in racial terms—a nationalism that ran counter to his actual belief that the English, whom circumstances had made his overt enemy, were somehow better.

It is a curiously Modernist double bind. In the terms of Yeats's astrological charts in *A Vision*, Wittgenstein was born "out of phase," a man, I would guess, of Phase 16, close to the full moon, but stuck, like Yeats himself, in phase 23, when civilization was running down and dissolving into a new "primary" darkness. Wittgenstein thoroughly disliked Modernism, and yet he was himself the quintessential Modernist, indeed in many ways an avant-gardist, whose understanding of the "limits of language" was so far ahead of its time that we are only now catching up with it.

Thus, when Wittgenstein calls the English "the best

race in the world" as compared to the Germans, he may sound fatuous, but the fact is that, given the historic moment, he was quite right. For the England Wittgenstein knew was, whatever its inequities and shortcomings—its colonialism, imperialism, and class divisions—a parliamentary democracy, which the Austro-Hungarian Empire certainly was not. Had Wittgenstein been pressed, he might well have shared Schoenberg's *"distaste for democracy and that sort of thing."* But perhaps he knew instinctively—and certainly experientially—that democracy was a requisite for the continuity of a culture, even if, especially in a media- and money-driven mass culture like ours, democracy gives fairly low priority to the pursuit of High Culture and the Arts.

The penultimate chapter of my *Eine Reise nach Amerika* is called "The Statue of Liberty":

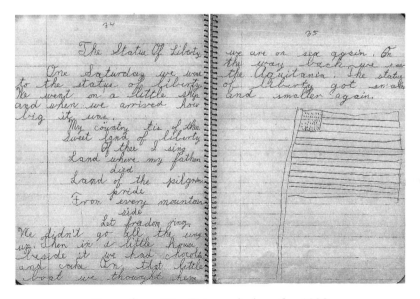

FIGURE 2. Pages from *Eine Reise nach Amerika*, 1938.

The *H.M.S. Aquitania* was the Cunard Line flagship: it had survived two World Wars and was still considered the model ocean liner. Seeing it in New York harbor must have been a strange reminder of our own crossing on the Veendam the previous July: "On that little boat we thought here we are on sea again." But it was evidently also nice to see the *Aquitania* from our new position of safety in America, now spelled with a *c*. That afternoon, after all, we were just sightseers like everyone else. And so here I was, a child patriot, writing an ode to the wonderfully "big" Statue of Liberty in the form of "My country tis of thee," and making (badly!) a drawing of the American flag.

It is a feeling I have never quite lost, even if "the Statue of Liberty got smaller and smaller again," even if, unlike my refugee mother, I never so much as took my own children to see it. My little narrative, in any event, pinpoints a particular Viennese trace even here: rather than climbing all the way to the top inside the Statue of Liberty's huge round head, we went to the café next door and had hot chocolate and cake. The *Sachertorte* tasted sweet . . . .

Family Tree

Note for Family Tree

This is a very partial family tree of the Rosenthal-Schüller-Mintz families, detailing only those branches whose members are discussed in some detail in the book. It is designed not to furnish information about my family as a whole, but only to help the reader with otherwise confusing names and relationships. Since this book has a very particular perspective, focusing on my mother's paternal family—the Schüllers—many close relatives are not included. This is in no way meant to be a slight.

THE ROSENTHAL FAMILY

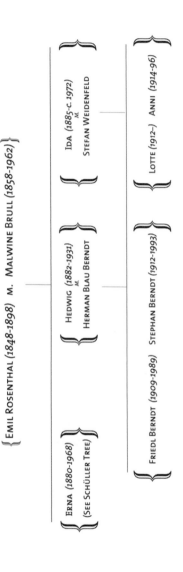

{ Emil Rosenthal (1848-1898) m. Malwine Brull (1858-1962) }

Erna (1880-1968)
(See Schüller Tree)

Hedwig (1882-1931)
m.
Herman Blau Berndt

Ida (1885-c. 1972)
m.
Stefan Weidenfeld

Friedl Berndt (1909-1989)   Stephan Berndt (1912-1993)

Lotte (1912–)   Anni (1914-96)

Herman and Hedwig Berndt divorced 1917;
Herman marries Lili Fanto Schüller 1918(see Schüller Family Tree)

THE SCHÜLLER FAMILY

{ SIGMUND SCHÜLLER (1840–1911) M. EMMA KOHN (1847–1934) }

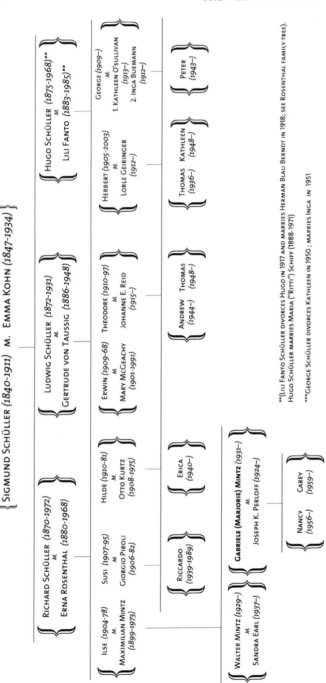

** (LILI FANTO SCHÜLLER DIVORCES HUGO IN 1917 AND MARRIES HERMAN BLAU BERNDT IN 1918; SEE ROSENTHAL FAMILY TREE).
HUGO SCHÜLLER MARRIES MARIA ("RITTI") SCHIFF (1888–1971)

*** GEORGE SCHÜLLER DIVORCES KATHLEEN IN 1950; MARRIES INGA IN 1951

RICHARD SCHÜLLER (1870–1972)
M.
ERNA ROSENTHAL (1880–1968)

LUDWIG SCHÜLLER (1872–1931)
M.
GERTRUDE VON TAUSSIG (1886–1948)

HUGO SCHÜLLER (1875–1968)**
M.
LILI FANTO (1883–1985)**

ILSE (1904–78)
M.
MAXIMILIAN MINTZ (1899–1973)

SUSI (1907–95)
M.
GIORGIO PIROLI (1906–82)

HILDE (1910–81)
M.
OTTO KURTZ (1908–1975)

ERWIN (1909–68)
M.
MARY MCGEACHY (1901–1991)

THEODORE (1910–97)
M.
JOHANNE E. REID (1915–)

GEORGE (1909–)
M.
1. KATHLEEN O'SULLIVAN (1913–)
2. INGA BUEMANN (1912–)

HERBERT (1905–2003)
M.
LORLE GEIRINGER (1912–)

WALTER MINTZ (1929–)
M.
SANDRA EARL (1937–)

GABRIELE (MARJORIE) MINTZ (1931–)
M.
JOSEPH K. PERLOFF (1924–)

RICCARDO (1939–1989)

ERICA (1940–)

ANDREW (1944–)

THOMAS (1948–)

THOMAS (1936–)

KATHLEEN (1948–)

PETER (1943–)

NANCY (1956–)

CAREY (1959–)

THE MINTZ FAMILY

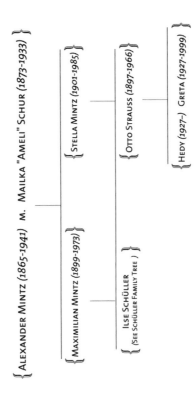

ALEXANDER MINTZ (1865–1941) M. MAILKA "AMELI" SCHUR (1873–1933)

MAXIMILIAN MINTZ (1899–1973)

STELLA MINTZ (1901–1985)

ILSE SCHÜLLER
(SEE SCHÜLLER FAMILY TREE)

OTTO STRAUSS (1897–1966)

HEDY (1927–)   GRETA (1927–1999)

Prologue

1 Robert Musil, *The Man Without Qualities*, vol. 1, trans. Sophie Wilkins, ed. Burton Pike (New York: Alfred A. Knopf, 1995), p. 29.

2 Ingeborg Bachman, Interview with Joseph-Hermann Sauter, 15 September 1965, in *Wir müssen wahre Sätze finden: Gespräche und Interviews* (Munich: Piper, 1991), pp. 63–64. Translation mine.

3 Thomas Bernhard, *Heldenplatz* (Frankfurt am Main: Suhrkampf, 1995), p. 163. Translation mine.

4 For detailed biographical information, see the website of the Arnold Schoenberg Center, <http://www.schoenberg.at/>. The Schoenberg website, like that of the Neue Galerie in New York, is unusually well designed, in keeping with the aestheticism of fin-de-siècle Vienna. I use the spelling *oe* here rather than *ö* because it is the standard practice in all Schoenberg references.

5 See Mark Swed, "Now He's the Pride of Vienna," *Los Angeles Times Calendar Section*, 21 June 1998, pp. 7, 78. Subsequent information about the facts, figures, and terms of the sale of Schoenberg's estate are taken from Swed's article.

6 This story is told by Mark Swed in "Driven to Express Himself," *Los Angeles Times Calendar Section*, 21 October 2001, pp. 7–8, 54–55.

7 Holland Cotter, "Viennese Tales from the Berkshire Woods," *The New York Times*, 19 July 2002, pp. 29, 36.

8 Brigitte Hamann, *Hitler's Vienna: A Dictator's Apprenticeship* (New York: Oxford, 1999).

9   See Ronald S. Lauder, preface to *New Worlds: German and Austrian Art 1890–1940*, ed. Renée Price with Pamela Kort and Leslie Topp (New York: Neue Galerie, 2001), pp. 8–9. The question of provenance has recently come up as part of the larger ongoing dispute about restitution of artworks to their original Jewish owners: see Celestine Bohlen, "Lauder's Mix of Restitution and Collecting," *The New York Times*, 27 February 2003: B1, 10.

10 Janet Forman, "Neue Galerie brings bourgeois Central Europe to Museum Mile," *Toronto Globe and Mail*, 16 February 2002, pp. 6–7.

11 Tina Walzer and Stephan Templ, *Unser Wien: "Ariesierung" auf Oesterreichisch* (Berlin: Aufbau Verlag, 2001). See also Richard Bernstein, "A Cemetery Mirroring the History of a City's Jews," *The New York Times*, 13 March 2003, p. 12, which takes up the controversial issue of the elegant old Jewish cemeteries in Vienna.

12 See Svetlana Boym, *The Future of Nostalgia* (New York: Basic Books, 2001), xiii–xiv.

13 Austrian Cultural Forum website, <http://www.acfny.org/s59asp>.

14 W. H. Auden, *The English Auden. Poems, Essays and Dramatic Writings 1927–1939*, ed. Edward Mendelson (New York: Random House, 1977), p. 245.

15 Charles Bernstein, *My Way: Speeches and Poems* (Chicago: University of Chicago Press, 1999), p. 109.

16 See my *Wittgenstein's Ladder: Poetic Language and the Strangeness of the Ordinary* (Chicago: University of Chicago Press, 1996), and Charles Bernstein, *Content's Dream: Essays 1975–1984* (Los Angeles: Sun & Moon Press, 1986), and *My Way*.

17 Peter Hewitt, director, *Bill & Ted's Bogus Journey* (Orion Pictures, 1991); Stephen Herek, director, *Bill & Ted's Excellent Adventure* (Orion Pictures, 1989).

18 John Ashbery, "'They Dream Only of America,'" *The Tennis Court Oath* (Middletown, CT: Wesleyan University Press, 1962), p. 13.
19 *The Collected Poems of Frank O'Hara*, ed. Donald M. Allen (Berkeley: University of California Press, 1995), pp. 17–18.

Chapter One

1 Gertrude Stein, *History or Messages from History* (1930; Los Angeles: Green Integer, 1997), p. 40.
2 Ludwig Wittgenstein, *Culture and Value*, ed. G. H. von Wright, in collaboration with Heikki Byman; trans. Peter Winch (Chicago: University of Chicago Press, 1980), p. 5e.
3 The word *Aryan*, originally applied to the Indo-European languages in their pure form, was introduced by the Nazi regime in 1932 to designate Germans of "pure" or non-Jewish blood. As such, *Aryan* is of course a racist term that I dislike using. But it was the term used by both Jews and non-Jews at the time to differentiate the two, and so one cannot gloss over it.
4 See Brigitte Hamann, *Hitler's Vienna*, pp. 11, 382–84.
5 Richard Schüller, *Unterhändler des Vertrauens*, ed. Jürgen Nautz (Munich: R. Oldenbourg, 1990), p. 112. This memoir is mostly in German but contains an English section called "Finis Austriae" that repeats some of the most dramatic stories about the post–World War I reconstruction period in Vienna (see pp. 216–72). Subsequently cited as UV.
6 The exhibition at the Carolino Augusteum in Salzburg opened on 26 July 2002. The catalog essay (Salzburg: Pustig Verlag, 2002), sent to me by Andrew Schüller, Teddy's son, who visits Austria quite regularly, contains a

well-documented, illustrated essay by Helga Embacher, which I cite here.

7 Thomas Albrich, *Wir lebten wie Sie: Jüdische Lebensgeschichten aus Tirol und Voralberg* (Innsbruck: Haymon, 1999), pp. 239–70.

8 Egon Schwarz, *Keine Zeit für Eichendorff: Chronik unfreiwilliger Wanderjahre* (Königstein: Atheneum, 1979), pp. 33–35.

9 Doris Ingrisch has since published some very interesting essays on my mother and myself for the reference book *Wissenschaftlerinnen in und aus Oesterreich*, ed. Brigitta Keintzel and Ilse Korotin (Vienna: Bölau, 2003).

10 Elias Canetti, *The Tongue Set Free: Remembrance of a European Childhood*, trans. Joachim Neugroschel (1977; New York: Farrar, Straus & Giroux, 1979), pp. 81–82.

Chapter Two

1 J. W. von Goethe, *Goethe's Werke*, III: *Wilhelm Meister's Lehrjahre* (Wiesbaden: Insel, 1952), p. 234. My translation. For a helpful translation of the novel, see Goethe, *Wilhelm Meister's Apprenticeship*, ed. and trans. Eric A. Blackall (New York: Suhrkamp, 1983).

2 Thomas Bernhard, *Wittgenstein's Nephew: A Friendship*, trans. David McLintock (1982; Chicago: University of Chicago Press, 1988), pp. 29–30. For a discussion of the Wittgensteinian mode of this novel, see my *Wittgenstein's Ladder*, pp. 155–61.

3 E. H. Gombrich, "Otto Kurz 1908–1975," *Proceedings of the British Academy, London*, 65 (1979): 719–35.

4 George E. Berkley, *Vienna and its Jews: The Tragedy of Success, 1880s–1980s* (Cambridge, MA: ABT Books, 1988), pp. 204–5. Subsequently cited as GEB.

5 Denis Scheck, "Ein Interview mit Ernst Gombrich am Anlass seinen 90. Geburtstags," 30 March 1999, Deutschlandfunk, Deutschland Radio Berlin, <http://www.dradio.de/cgi-bin/user/fin1004.es/neu-lit-g/81.html>. My translation.

6 The Jewish Museum opened in 2000, and Daniel Libeskind's design as well as the collection have been widely discussed in the press and in art journals.

7 Paul Mendes-Flohr, *German Jews: A Dual Identity* (New Haven: Yale University Press, 1988), pp. 4–5, 16. Subsequently cited as PMF.

8 *The Correspondence of Walter Benjamin 1910–1940*, ed. Gershom Scholem and Theodor W. Adorno, trans. Manfred R. Jacobson and Evelyn M. Jacobson (Chicago and London: University of Chicago Press, 1994), pp. 18, 117. Subsequently cited as CWB.

9 Cited in Ernst Robert Curtius, *Kritische Essays* (Bern: Francke, 1950), p. 153; my emphasis. "Curtius," writes Mendes-Flohr, "whose sympathies for French literature disqualified him from membership in Stefan George's elitist circle, was nonetheless close to the circle, especially its Jewish members" (PMF, 112).

10 See Robert Wistrich, *Socialism and the Jews* (East Brunswick: Rutgers University Press, 1982), cited in GEB 70; cf. Carl Schorske, *Fin de siècle Vienna* (New York: Vintage, 1981), pp. 7–9.

11 See Brigitte Hamann, *Hitler's Vienna*, pp. 26–29. Subsequently cited as BH.

12 Robert Musil, *The Man Without Qualities*, p. 14. The Theresianum is the school the novel's hero Ulrich, a "man without qualities," attends.

13 See Gordon Brook-Shepherd, *The Austrians: A Thousand-Year Odyssey* (New York: Carroll & Graf, 1997), p. 263. Subsequently cited as BRS.

14 Benito Mussolini (with Giovanni Gentile), "What is Fascism?" (1932), in *Modern History Source Book*, <http://www.fordham.edu/halsall/mod/mussolini-fascism.html>.

15 Walter Benjamin, "Stefan George in Retrospect" (1933), *Selected Writings*, 2, 1927–34 (Cambridge: Harvard University Press, 1999), pp. 706–11. Subsequently cited as WB. "Entführung" is in *Das Jahr der Seele* (1897; Berlin: Georg Bondi, 1929), p. 64.

16 Stefan George, *Der siebente Ring* (1907; Berlin: Georg Bondi, 1922), p. 158. My translation.

17 Theodor Adorno, "Lyric Poetry and Society" (1954), trans. Bruce Mayo in *The Adorno Reader*, ed. Brian O'Connor (Oxford: Blackwell, 2000), pp. 211–29. See pp. 225–26.

18 See Alan Ebenstein, *Friedrich Hayek: A Biography* (Chicago and London: University of Chicago Press, 2003), pp. 37–38. *Geistkreis* translates roughly as intellect or spirit circle, more colloquially, as Ebenstein says, as "soul brothers."

Chapter Three

1 Goethe, *Zahme Xenien*, in Goethe's *Werke, Vollständige Ausgabe letzter Hand* (Stuttgart und Tübingen: Cotta 1827–30), Vol. 4 (1828), p. 132.

2 A courtesy copy of my father's letters to Eric Voegelin were sent to me by Dr. Paul Carangella, a independent research scholar at the Hoover Institution at Stanford University. The Hoover has an extensive Eric Voegelin Archive and regularly publishes volumes of his work. Note that, like Schoenberg's name, Voegelin's is regularly anglicized, so I use the *oe* rather than *ö* form here.

3 All the letters are in German. My translation.

4 Mark D. Anderson, ed., Introduction, *Hitler's Exiles: Personal Stories of the Flight from Nazi Germany to America* (New York: The New Press, 1998), p. 5.

5 Cited in Anthony Heilbut, *Exiled in Paradise: German Refugee Artists and Intellectuals in America from the 1930s to the Present* (Berkeley: University of California Press, 1997), p. 330.

6 François Furet, *The Passing of an Illusion: The Idea of Communism in the Twentieth Century*, trans. Deborah Furet (1995; Chicago: University of Chicago Press, 1999), p. 365. Subsequently cited as FF.

7 Ludwig Wittgenstein, *Lectures and Conversations on Aesthetics*, Compiled from notes taken by Yorick Smythies, et al., ed. Cyril Barrett (Berkeley: University of California Press, 1967), p. 11; *Culture and Value*, ed. G. H. von Wright, trans. Peter Winch (Chicago: University of Chicago Press, 1980), p. 52.

8 *The Collected Poems of Frank O'Hara*, pp. 210, 258.

9 D. H. Lawrence, "Hymns in a Man's Life," *Phoenix II: Uncollected Writings of D. H. Lawrence*, ed. Warren Roberts and Harry T. Moore (New York: Viking, 1970), p. 597.

Chapter Four

1 See "What is Ethical Culture?" on New York Society for Ethical Culture website <www.nysec.org>.

2 Ludwig Wittgenstein, *Tractatus Logico-Philosophicus*, trans. C. K. Ogden, with an Introduction by Bertrand Russell (1922; London and New York: Routledge, 1988).

3 Ludwig Wittgenstein, "Lecture on Ethics," *Philosophical Occasions 1912–51* (Indianapolis: Hackett, 1993), p. 44.

4   Theodor Adorno, *Minima Moralia: Reflections from Damaged Life*, trans. E. F. N. Jephcott (1951; London: Verso, 1989), p. 33. Susbequently cited as MM.

5   Alexis de Tocqueville, *Democracy in America*, trans. and ed. by Harvey C. Mansfield and Delba Winthrop (Chicago: University of Chicago Press, 2000), p. 51. Subsequently cited as DIA.

6   Martin Jay, *Adorno* (Cambridge: Harvard University Press, 1984), p. 25.

7   Matei Calinescu, *Five Faces of Modernity. Modernism, Avant-Garde, Decadence, Kitsch, Postmodernism* (Durham: Duke University Press, 1987), p. 229. Subsequently cited as FFM.

8   Theodor Adorno, *Aesthetische Theorie* (Frankfurt: Suhrkampf, 1970), pp. 225ff.

9   See BRS, pp. 383–84.

10 Lyn Hejinian, *Happily* (Sausalito, CA: Post-Apollo Press, 2000), p. 5.

Chapter Five

1   Ingeborg Bachmann, "What Good are Poems?" (1955), rpt. in Bachmann, *In the Storm of Roses: Selected Poems*, trans. and ed. Mark Anderson (Princeton: Princeton University Press, 1986), p. 204.

2   Rosmarie Waldrop, *Split Infinites* (Philadelphia: Singing Horse Press, 1998), p. 54.

3   See BRS 392–93; Paul Hoffman, *The Viennese* (New York: Doubleday, 1988), pp. 306–7.

4   Tina Walzer and Stephan Templ, *Unser Wien: "Arisierung" auf Oesterreichisch* (Berlin: Aufbau, 2001), pp. 186–87, and Plate XIX. Walzer and Templ give dozens of comparable examples of "selective" reconstruction and

the accompanying failure to make reparations to the former Jewish property owners.

5 "A Step Away from Them," *The Collected Poems of Frank O'Hara*, p. 258.

6 Mary de Rachelwitz, *Discretions: Ezra Pound, Father and Teacher* (New York: New Directions, 1975), pp. 294–95.

7 See Humphrey Carpenter, *A Serious Character: The Life of Ezra Pound* (London: Faber and Faber, 1988), pp. 799–801, 827–31.

8 Cited in Carpenter, p. 791.

9 A few years later, Craig LaDrière was offered a position in the Harvard Comparative Literature department, but he did not flourish there, his formalist studies of prosody being, by the late '60s, wholly outside the mainstream. But ironically, in the summer of 2003 I received notice from a former student of LaDrière's that there is now a Craig LaDrière website called "The Proplyaean Academy" at <www.propylaean.org>. I found it quite moving to see those obscure scholarly articles I had once tried to memorize and understand, on the web!

10 Walter Benn Michaels, *Our America* (Durham: Duke University Press, 1995), p. 128.

11 John Cage, interview with Jeff Goldberg (1976); rpt. under "Autobiography," in Richard Kostelanetz, ed., *Conversing with Cage* (New York: Limelight, 1988), p. 1. Subsequently cited as CC.

12 John Cage, "Mosaic," *A Year from Monday: New Lectures and Writings* (Middletown, CT: Wesleyan University Press, 1967), pp. 43–44. Subsequently cited as YMF.

13 Richard Kostelanetz, "Conversation with John Cage," *John Cage: An Anthology* (New York: Da Capo, 1991), p. 6.

Epilogue

1   Thomas Bernhard, *Woodcutters*, trans. from the German by
    David McLintock (Chicago: University of Chicago Press,
    1987), pp 180–81.
2   Terry Eagleton, "Introduction to Wittgenstein," *Wittgen-
    stein. The Terry Eagleton Script, the Derek Jarman Film*
    (London: BFI, 1996), pp. 7–8.
3   Cited in Ray Monk, *Ludwig Wittgenstein: The Duty of Genius*
    (New York: Free Press, 1990), pp 113–14.

INDEX

(NB: numbers in italics refer to figures)

275